Eating Out: London

Pétrus

Eating Out: London

The best places to dine in London

AA

Please contact
Editorial Department: lifestyleguides@theaa.com

Front cover photograph courtesy of The Capital (SW3)

Printed by Canale, Italy

Restaurant descriptions have been contributed by the following
team of writers: Cathy Fitzgerald, Sarah Gilbert, David Hancock,
Julia Hynard, Denise Laing, Melissa Riley-Jones, Allen Stidwill,
Derryck Strachan, Mark Taylor and Kate Trew.

Published by AA Publishing, a trading name of Automobile
Association Developments Limited, whose registered office is
Fanum House,
Basing View, Basingstoke, Hampshire RG21 4EA.
Registered number 1878835.

A CIP catalogue for this book is available from the
British Library.

ISBN-10: 0-7495-5459-2
ISBN-13: 978-0-7495-5459-0
A03592

Maps prepared by the Mapping Services Department of
The Automobile Association. Maps © Automobile Association
Developments Limited 2007.

Contents

Using the Guide

This comprehensive guide to the best places to eat in London has been compiled to include all the restaurants awarded ratings from one to five Rosettes by the AA team of Inspectors. In London there are many kinds of eateries to choose from, such as a lively one Rosette gastro-pub to a grand five Rosette fine-dining restaurant with a famous chef at the helm. The cuisine type covers cooking from around the world, from traditional British, French, Italian and Mediterranean cooking to Indian, Thai, Chinese and Japanese fare. With easy-to-find map reference supported by street mapping, there will be a London restaurant to suit every occasion, taste and pocket.

The following features will help you to use this guide.

⚙ **The AA Rosette Award:** This guide includes all London restaurants with 1, 2, 3, 4 and 5 AA Rosettes (see also page 7)

🍷 **Notable Wine List symbol:** Denotes a wine list that has been judged to be a high quality, well presented listing, with diversity/coverage across grapes and /or countries and style, and the best individual growers and vintages.

V **Vegetarian symbol:** Denotes the restaurant has a separate vegetarian menu.

Chef and Owner: The names of the chef (s) and owner(s) are as up to date as possible at the time of going to press, but changes in personnel often occur, and may affect the style and quality of the restaurant.

Times: Daily opening and closing times, plus seasonal information, are included. However these times are liable to change without notice. It is wise to telephone in advance to avoid disappointment.

Prices: These are given for fixed dinner and à la carte main course. Prices quoted are a guide only and are subject to change with out notice.

Book Order: The restaurants are listed in London postcode order, then alphabetically by name.

Rosette Awards

The AA's Rosette award scheme was the first nationwide scheme for assessing the quality of food served by restaurants and hotels. The Rosette scheme is an award, not a classification, and although there is necessarily an element of subjectivity when it comes to assessing taste, we aim for a consistent approach throughout the UK. Our awards are made solely on the basis of a meal visit or visits by one or more of our hotel and restaurant Inspectors, who have an unrivalled breadth and depth of experience in assessing quality. They award Rosettes annually on a rising scale of one to five.

So what makes a restaurant worthy of a Rosette Award?

For our Inspectors, the top and bottom line is the food. The taste of a dish is what counts, and whether it successfully delivers to the diner the promise of the menu. A restaurant is only as good as its worst meal. Although presentation and competent service should be appropriate to the style of the restaurant and the quality of the food, they cannot affect the Rosette assessment as such, either up or down. The summaries below indicate what our Inspectors look for, but are intended only as guidelines. The AA is constantly reviewing its award criteria, and competition usually results in an all-round improvement in standards, so it becomes increasingly difficult for restaurants to reach award level. For more detailed Rosette criteria, please visit www.theAA.com.

⚜ One Rosette
- Excellent restaurants that stand out in their local area
- Food prepared with care, understanding and skill
- Good quality ingredients

⚜⚜ Two Rosettes
- The best local restaurants
- Higher standards
- Better consistency
- Greater precision apparent in the cooking
- Obvious attention to the quality and selection of ingredients

⚜⚜⚜ Three Rosettes
- Outstanding restaurants demanding recognition well beyond local area
- Selection and sympathetic treatment of highest quality ingredients
- Timing, seasoning and judgement of flavour combinations consistent
- Excellent intelligent service and a well-chosen wine list

⚜⚜⚜⚜ Four Rosettes
Dishes demonstrate:
- intense ambition
- a passion for excellence
- superb technical skills
- remarkable consistency
- appreciation of culinary traditions combined with desire for exploration and improvement
- Cooking demands national recognition

⚜⚜⚜⚜⚜ Five Rosettes
- Cooking stands comparison with the best in the world
- Highly individual
- Breathtaking culinary skills
- Setting the standards to which others aspire
- Knowledgeable and distinctive wine list

Any restaurant without Rosettes has had a recent change of chef and/or owner and is awaiting an inspection.

East London

Canary Wharf, Docklands

Cafe Spice Namasté

Indian

Authentic Indian café dining

16 Prescot Street, E1 8AZ
Tel: 020 7488 9242
Email: binay@cafespice.co.uk
Website: www.cafespice.co.uk
Chef: Angelo Collaco,
Cyrus Todiwala
Owners: Cafe Spice Ltd

East London eatery occupying a listed building that began life in the 18th century as a magistrate's court. These days it offers an altogether warmer welcome – 'namasté' means 'gracious hello', and you'll certainly be received like an old friend here. The speciality menu changes every fortnight, and this together with an extensive and well-annotated carte provides a choice of unusual dishes from all over Asia, conjured from the very best of British produce. Classic dishes jostle for attention with more modern fare: tuck into Goan lobster curry perhaps, or one of the most intricate of all Indian curries, galinha xacutti, which requires more than 21 different ingredients, each pan-roasted individually.

Times: 12–3/6.15–10.30, Closed Xmas, BHs, Sun, L Sat
Prices: 3 Course Fixed D £30
Main £14.25–£19
Directions: Walking distance from Tower Hill

Canteen

Modern British

All-day eatery in Spitalfields

2 Crispin Place, Spitalfields, E1 6DW
Tel: 0845 686 1122
Email: info@canteen.co.uk
Website: www.canteen.co.uk
Chef: Cass Titcombe,
Patrick Clayton-Malone, Dom Lake
Owners: Patrick Clayton-Malone, Dom Lake

This unpretentious eatery in Spitalfields Market opened in 2006 to rave reviews and has heaved with an eclectic mix of foodies, locals and city types ever since. Glass-walled on three sides, it teams retro booth seating with long shared tables and prides itself on offering high-quality cuisine at reasonable prices. A lengthy all-day menu includes breakfast items and designated 'fast service' dishes, as well as a daily roast, home-made pies and fish options. Expect British classics conjured from the freshest of ingredients – macaroni cheese, for example, or pie, mash, greens and gravy – plus a diet-busting array of delicious homely desserts such as steamed syrup pudding and custard, or orange jelly with ice cream and shortbread.

Times: 8/11, Closed 25–26 Dec
Prices: Main £4.50–£13.50
Directions: Overlooking Spitalfields Market

Lanes Restaurant & Bar

British, European

Modern city brasserie with cooking to match

This modern but relaxed, informal basement restaurant and bar comes conveniently tucked away off Bishopsgate, just a short stroll from Liverpool Street station. Decked out with polished-wood floors, the split-level space is laid out with burgundy leather banquettes and chairs, while mirrors or large contemporary artworks top part-clad walls and pillars. Leather tub chairs and matching bar stools populate the bar area, while service is suitably youthful and attentive. The cooking fits with the contemporary styling, its modern-European brasserie repertoire driven by quality ingredients and a carefully presented, clean-cut, accomplished approach. Expect a fillet of halibut wrapped in pancetta and served with braised fennel and vine tomato, or classic seared rib-eye with chips and herb butter.

109–117 Middlesex Street,
E1 7JF
Tel: 020 7247 5050
Email: info@lanesrestaurant.co.uk
Website:
www.lanesrestaurant.co.uk
Chef: Liam Cooper
Owners: James Robertson &
Hamish Smith

Times: 12–3/5.30–10, Closed BHs,
25 Dec, 1 Jan, Sun, L Sat
Prices: 3 Course Fixed D £21.50
Main £13.50–£24.95

St John Bread & Wine

British

Unpretentious restaurant, bakery and wine shop

Tucked behind the old Spitalfields Market, this no-frills sibling to big brother St John (see entry) is a resolutely British affair. Whitewashed walls, parquet flooring and simple wooden tables and chairs set a wholly unpretentious, utilitarian edge. The British food is flavour-driven and unfussy, using quality produce while delivering some earthy dishes using humble ingredients. Ox faggot and mash, brawn and pickled cucumber, Blackface lamb and fennel or sea bass, ruby chard and green sauce set the style. Service is attentive, friendly and informed, while wines, like the wonderful breads, are on sale to take away.

94–96 Commercial Street,
E1 6LZ
Tel: 020 7251 0848
Email: reservations@
stjohnbreadandwine.com
Website:
www.stjohnbreadandwine.com
Chef: James Lowe
Owners: Trevor Gulliver &
Fergus Henderson

Times: 9/11, Closed 24 Dec–2 Jan,
BHs, D Sun
Prices: Main £11–£15

Les Trois Garçons

Modern French

Quirky ex-pub with authentic French menus

1 Club Row, E1 6JX
Tel: 020 7613 1924
Email: info@lestroisgarcons.com
Website: www.lestroisgarcons.com

The cooking is classically French, though you might wonder at the setting, a cross between an exotic Eastern bazaar and a Victorian antique shop. Colourful objets d'art fill every conceivable space, a surreal background to the serious dining and an amusing conversation piece. There's nothing funny about the set lunch and dinner (Monday to Wednesday pm only) menus or the evening carte, where duck rilettes, carrot velouté and tempura frogs' legs served with asparagus translate into authentic French starters. Seared sweetbread with braised shin, petit artichoke, salsify and sherry jus is a typical main dish, with tarte Tatin a suitably Gallic dessert.

Times: 12–4/7–12, Closed Sun
Directions: 10mins walk from Liverpool Street station, at the end of Brick Ln

---

Wapping Food

Modern International

Inspired cooking meets industrial heritage

Wapping Hydraulic, Power Station, Wapping Wall, E1W 3ST
Tel: 020 7680 2080
Website:
www.thewappingproject.com
Chef: Cameron Emirali
Owners: Womens Playhouse Trust

A hydraulic pumping station in the East End may not sound like a conventional place to dine, but then Wapping Food isn't a conventional eatery. Part restaurant, part art gallery, it teams old machinery, tiles and girders from its industrial days with dangling chandeliers, designer furniture and flickering candles to create a chic urban décor. Expect a menu of inspired international dishes distinguished by high-quality ingredients and imaginative combinations. Smoked eel is a typical starter, served with beetroot, horseradish and mixed herbs, while mains might include roast middle white pork with braised cavolo nero and butternut squash.

Times: 12–3/6.30–11,
Closed 24 Dec–3 Jan, BHs, D Sun
Prices: 3 Course Fixed D £45
Main £12.50–£20
Directions: Turn right from tube, walk east & parallel to the river (approx 4 mins)
Parking: 20

The Thai Garden

Thai **v**

Authentic vegetarian Thai restaurant

249 Globe Road, E2 0JD
Tel: 020 8981 5748
Email: thaigarden@hotmail.com
Website:
www.thethaigarden.co.uk
Chef: Napathorn Duff
Owners: S & J Hufton

The vegetarian and seafood Thai cuisine here is the real deal, despite its unlikely setting in Bethnal Green. The unpretentious shop-front bistro gives way to a small dining room with 20 seats. The cooking is fragrant with some serious chillies, so be prepared – or go for dishes with delicate herb flavours as a gentler option on the palate. The menu is written in Thai and English and presents a wide choice with some unique, flavoursome options. Think water chestnuts fried with dry chilli and vegetables, or perhaps prawns in red curry with coconut cream.

Times: 12–2.30/6–11, Closed BHs, L Sat & Sun
Directions: 2nd left off Roman Rd (one-way street). Near London Buddhist Centre

Wapping Food

13

Curve Restaurant & Bar

Curve Restaurant & Bar

Fish & Seafood v

Relaxed docklands dining with fabulous views

London Marriott West India Quay,
22 Hertsmere Road, Canary Wharf,
E14 4ED
Tel: 020 7517 2808
Email: mhrs.loncw.restaurant.
supervisor@marriotthotels.com
Website: www.marriott.co.uk
Chef: Surjan Singh
Owners: Marriott Hotels

Located in a spectacular skyscraper, this new-build hotel overlooks
West India Quay in the heart of Docklands. The Curve restaurant
is an upmarket choice for a relaxed bite. It takes its name from the
imposing glass sweep of the building's façade, and the full-length
windows afford unrestricted views over the quay. The emphasis
is on fresh fish from nearby Billingsgate, plus a number of grills.
Dishes are modern, fresh and simple in presentation and typical
options include New England clam chowder, lobster tortelloni, and
glazed Alaskan black cod, followed by an interesting Thai crème
brûlée with coconut sago, lime and pandan leaf.

Times: 12–2.30/5–10.30
Prices: 3 Course Fixed D £30–£35
Main £11.50–£22.75
Directions: Telephone for
directions

14

Four Seasons Hotel Canary Wharf

Italian
Simple Italian fare in chic surroundings

Westferry Circus,
Canary Wharf, E14 8RS
Tel: 020 7510 1999
Website:
www.fourseasons.com/canarywharf
Chef: Marco Bax
Owners: Four Seasons Hotels

Expect Italian sophistication at Quadrato, a sleek and chic Thames-side eatery set in this stylishly modern Docklands hotel. With superb views over the London skyline, you can tuck into a versatile range of modern Italian dishes or some classic regional specialities, all prepared with contemporary flair from first-class ingredients in the impressive open-to-view theatre kitchen. Simple, flavoursome combinations might include risotto mantecato with porcini and mascarpone, or perhaps oven-baked herb-crusted rack of lamb served with roasted artichokes and potato tortino. The predominantly Italian staff are friendly, enthusiastic and passionate about food and wine.

Times: 12–3/6–10.30
Prices: 3 Course Fixed D £34–£40
Main £14.50–£29
Directions: Just off Westbury Circus rdbt
Parking: 26

The Gun

British
Smart docklands gastro-pub serving modern food

27 Coldharbour, Docklands,
E14 9NS
Tel: 020 7515 5222
Email: info@thegundocklands.com
Website:
www.thegundocklands.com
Chef: Mickey O'Connor
Owners: Tom & Ed Martin

A fabulous Thames-side location with a stunning terrace affording great views of the Millennium Dome and the river are among the attractions at this beautifully restored 18th-century former dockers' pub. Inside you'll find oak timber floors, Georgian-style fireplaces, crisp linen-clothed tables in smart dining rooms, and an inviting bar. Competent modern British cooking results in versatile menus that include the likes of mussel, fennel and saffron broth, or sirloin steak with garlic butter and fat chips, alongside pan-fried John Dory with shellfish velouté. The Gun is also a great spot for Sunday brunch and summer barbecues.

Times: 12–3/6–10.30, Closed
25–26 Dec
Prices: Main £12–£19
Directions: From South Quay DLR, E down Marsh Wall to mini rdbt, turn left, over bridge then take 1st right

The Narrow

British

Gordon Ramsay's inaugural waterside pub

44 Narrow Street, E14 8DP
Tel: 020 7592 7950
Email:
thenarrow@gordonramsay.com
Website: www.gordonramsay.
com/thenarrow
Chef: John Collin & Mark Sargeant

Gordon Ramsay's first excursion into the pub market saw him open The Narrow on London's Limehouse back in April 2007. Set on the edge of the Thames, this Grade II listed building – formerly the dockmaster's house – commands wonderful river views. The ground floor is divided into a bar area, a relaxed section for eating, and a dining room. Sympathetic renovation has retained bags of character, with half-wall panelling, fireplaces and black-and-white vintage photography and prints. ('The Captain's Table' private dining room is on the first floor.) The food focuses on classic British dishes based around quality seasonal produce; take cock-a-leekie pie and mash, or perhaps braised Gloucestershire pig cheeks with mashed neeps.

Times: 11.30am–10.30pm
Prices: Main £9–£14.50
Parking: 20

Plateau

Modern French

Sophisticated fine-dining in futuristic landscape

Canada Place, Canada Square,
Canary Wharf, E14 5ER
Tel: 020 7715 7100
Email:
plateau@conran-restaurants.co.uk
Website: www.conran.com
Chef: Tim Tolley

This modern glass-and-steel restaurant is the epitome of contemporary style, overlooking Canada Square and its Manhattan-style skyline. A stunning complex with floor-to-ceiling glass frontage and two dining areas divided by a semi-open kitchen, each side with its own outside terrace and bar. The bustling Bar & Grill (offering a simpler menu) is first up, while the restaurant beyond offers a calmer atmosphere. The design mixes classic 1950s with warm, restrained colours and contemporary spin. Think white tulip-style swivelling chairs, marble-topped tables, swirling banquettes and huge floor-standing arching lamps. The menu follows the theme, with highly accomplished, clean-cut modern dishes driven by high-quality ingredients and delivered dress to thrill. Expect dishes like monkfish wrapped in Parma ham with a fennel and tomato terrine. Service is slick and professional.

Times: 12–3/6–10.15, Closed
25–26 Dec, 1 Jan, BHs, Sun, L Sat
Prices: 3 Course Fixed D £27
Directions: Facing Canary Wharf
Tower and Canada Square Park
(The restaurant is accessed via
a lift from shopping mall.)
Parking: 200

Royal China

Traditional Chinese

Accomplished Chinese food with wonderful river views

Canary Wharf Riverside,
30 Westferry Circus, E14 8RR
Tel: 020 7719 0888
Email: info@royalchinagroup.co.uk
Website:
www.royalchinagroup.co.uk
Chef: Man Chau

An impressive glass-fronted building on the river's edge at Canary Wharf is the setting for this popular Chinese restaurant. The interior features lots of black and gold lacquering and crisp white linen. Head outside in summer for fantastic views and savour the wholesome, traditional Cantonese cooking, which makes the most of good ingredients. Dishes range from set meals and gourmet seafood including lobster to dim sum, cold appetisers, plenty of seafood, meat dishes, vegetables and bean curd. There's also a good selection of rice and noodle dishes.

Times: Noon/11, Closed 23–25 Dec
Prices: 3 Course Fixed D £30
Main £6.50–£30

Ubon by Nobu

Japanese, American

Celebrity hangout with impeccable dining experience

34 Westferry Circus,
Canary Wharf, E14 8RR
Tel: 020 7719 7800
Email: ubon@noburestaurants.com
Website:
www.noburestaurants.com
Chef: Nobuyuki Matsuhisa
Owners: Nobuyuki Matsuhisa

One of London's most fashionable restaurants, Ubon continues the exceptional fusion of stylish design, flawless service and innovative food that has made Nobu one of the hottest names in restaurant dining in the world. This chic Docklands restaurant, with an exceptional Thames-side location, has a panoramic view with floor-to-ceiling glass walls on three sides of the dining room. You can sample some truly cutting-edge cuisine that takes classic Japanese and adds a liberal sprinkling of South American tastes and textures with oodles of contemporary panache. Indulge your palate with dishes such as lobster with wasabi pepper sauce, perhaps sea urchin tempura, Chilean sea bass with moro miso, beef toban-yaki or anti-cucho Peruvian-style spicy rib-eye steak.

Times: 12–2/6–10,
Closed BHs, Sun, L Sat
Prices: 3 Course Fixed D £80
Main £12.50–£29
Directions: Follow signs to Canary Wharf, then Canary Riverside. Restaurant behind Four Seasons Hotel

East Central London

St Katherine's, Docklands

Ambassador

European

Relaxed, super-friendly Clerkenwell dining

This unassuming Exmouth Market newcomer to its trendy, bustling street proves a jewel in the Clerkenwell crown, with a focus on the friendliest of service and enjoyable cuisine at reasonable prices. Plainly decorated in magnolia, offset by the odd print or mirror, the long room comes decked out with dark green tables, simple wooden seating and crimson banquettes. A long bar struts its stuff along one wall, while glass doors open out onto the street with the bonus of outside, fair-weather seating. The kitchen's modern approach is assured and accomplished, and suits the surroundings; try chicken breast served with ceps, leeks and macaroni, or a warm chocolate pudding with almond ice cream to finish.

55 Exmouth Market, EC1R 4QL
Tel: 020 7837 0009
Email:
clive@theambassadorcafe.co.uk
Website:
www.theambassadorcafe.co.uk
Chef: Tobias Jilsmark
Owners: Clive & Stella Greenhalgh

Times: 12–3/6.30–12, Closed
1 wk Xmas, D Sun
Prices: Main £5.50–£17
Directions: Take 1st right off
Roseberry Av, heading N from
Farringdon Rd junct. Turn right
into Exmouth Market

The Bleeding Heart

Modern French 🍷 NOTABLE WINE LIST

Discreet and hospitable French restaurant

Behind the unusual name is a gruesome story: the Dickensian building stands on a cobbled courtyard where Lady Elizabeth Hatton was found murdered in the 17th century. The establishment comprises a tavern, bistro and restaurant, exuding atmosphere, with wooden floors and beams. The place buzzes with gallic charm, slick service and modern French cuisine. Outstanding fresh fish impresses in the form of herb-crusted John Dory, served with roasted salsify and watercress sauce, offered alongside classics like pan-fried foie gras with beetroot and herb salad, and Chateaubriand with sauce béarnaise. Desserts take in the likes of brochette of exotic fruit on French rice pudding, or warm chocolate pudding with vanilla ice cream.

Bleeding Heart Yard, off Greville
Street, EC1N 8SJ
Tel: 020 7242 2056
Email:
bookings@bleedingheart.co.uk
Website:
www.bleedingheart.co.uk
Chef: Christophe Fabre
Owners: Robert & Robyn Wilson

Times: 12–3.15/6–11, Closed
Xmas & New Year (10 days),
Sat, Sun
Prices: 3 Course Fixed D £29.50
Main £12.45–£22.95
Directions: Turn right out of
Farringdon Stn onto Cowcross
St, continue down Greville St for
50mtrs. Bleeding Heart Yrd on left.

20

Le Café du Marché

French

Welcoming French brasserie near the markets

Charterhouse Mews, Charterhouse
Square, EC1M 6AH
Tel: 020 7608 1609
Website:
www.cafedumarche.co.uk
Chef: Simon Cottard
Owners: Anna Graham-Wood

Tucked away down a cobbled mews, a short hop from several major markets, is this truly welcoming little brasserie. Friendly French staff add their bit to the authentic atmosphere, which comes undiluted from provincial France. Exposed bricks and beams, and closely packed tables, lend a cosy touch, and though it's usually packed with business people it doesn't feel overcrowded. The pick of the markets finds its way on to the fixed price menus, where the freshest of fish, perhaps pan-fried marlin, and the hottest cuts of meat (rib of veal with morels maybe), are well matched by the day's soups, starters and desserts.

Times: 12–2.30/6–10, Closed
Xmas, New Year, Easter, BHs, Sun,
L Sat
Prices: 3 Course Fixed D £29.95
Directions: Telephone for
directions (or see website)

Clerkenwell Dining Room & Bar

Modern European

Relaxed fine dining in trendy Clerkenwell

69-73 St. John Street, EC1 4AN
Tel: 020 7253 9000
Email:
restaurant@theclerkenwell.com
Website: www.theclerkenwell.com
Chef: Andrew Thompson
Owners: Zak Jones &
Andrew Thompson

Behind a blue and terracotta-red frontage, The Clerkenwell's interior surprises with its clean, warm tones and contemporary lines. White-clothed tables, black leather chairs and cream leather banquettes provide the comforts, while parquet floors, modern artwork and flamboyant flower displays catch the eye, combining with slick and professional service to create an upbeat mood and style. The ambition of the kitchen echoes the surroundings. Its creatively presented, cultured and confident modern approach combined with quality produces lamb saddle served with tagliolini, mint, sweet pea emulsion and pea shoots, or perhaps halibut accompanied by baby squid with lemon and parsley, white coco bean purée and tomato and light curry sauce. (Also see sister restaurant, The Chancery, EC4, page 34.)

Times: 12–3/6–11, Closed Xmas,
BHs, Sun, L Sat
Prices: 3 Course Fixed D £19.50
Main £14.50–£17
Directions: From Farringdon
Stn, continue 60mtrs up
Farringdon Rd, left into Cowcross
St, left into Peters Ln, left into St
John Street

Club Gascon

Modern French

Smithfield stalwart with a huge following

With a location overlooking St Bart's hospital and the main entrance to Smithfield's market, this chic London restaurant is a favourite spot for the fabled 'long lunch' of the City. You can expect to be greeted on arrival by stunning flower arrangements, created by the chef himself, marble-clad walls and old oak flooring in this small bustling dining room. Service from the smart, black-tied waiting staff can be unhurried so leave plenty of time to indulge. The cuisine here has its roots in the French provincial cooking of Gascony and comes with a contemporary twist. All the ingredients are of the best quality, sourced from South West France; so expect the likes of Charolais beef fillet with pickled trompettes, oyster and crosnes, and to finish, perhaps 'Gold Sensation' – sweet foie gras, vanilla, candied chestnuts and gold martini. There is an extensive French wine list.

57 West Smithfield, EC1A 9DS
Tel: 020 7796 0600
Email: info@clubgascon.com
Website: www.clubgascon.com
Chef: Pascal Aussignac
Owners: P Aussignac & V Labeyrie

Times: 12–2/7–10, Closed Xmas, New Year, BHs, Sun, L Sat
Prices: 3 Course Fixed D £35–£60
Main £17–£23
Directions: Telephone for directions

Le Comptoir Gascon

Traditional French

Bistro/deli serving classic French dishes

Part of the Club Gascon collection, this small establishment opposite Smithfield Market comprises a bistro-style restaurant with around a dozen small tables and a deli serving quality takeaway items in the same room. The aim is to provide generous portions of traditional French food inspired by the South West of France in a setting that recreates easy-going country chic in the city. Many items are sourced directly from France. Don't miss the cassoulet, or try the Toulouse sausages and French fries cooked in duck fat. Prunes in Armagnac and nougat might feature at dessert. Booking is highly advisable.

61-63 Charterhouse Street, EC1M 6HJ
Tel: 020 7608 0851
Email: comptoirgascon@btconnect.com
Website: www.comptoirgascon.com
Chef: Laurent Sanchis
Owners: Vincent Labeyrie, Pascal Aussignac

Times: 12–2/7–11, Closed 25 Dec, 1 Jan, Sun, Mon
Prices: Main £9.50–£16
Directions: Telephone for directions, or see website

Moro

Moro

Islamic, Mediterranean

Exotic fare from an open kitchen in the City

34/36 Exmouth Market, EC1R 4QE
Tel: 020 7833 8336
Email: info@moro.co.uk
Website: www.moro.co.uk
Chef: Samuel & Samantha Clark
Owners: Mr & Mrs S Clark &
Mark Sainsbury

High ceilings, round pillars and a simple understated style
– imagine unclothed tables and a polished wooden floor – make
the long zinc bar all the more striking at this expansive Clerkenwell
restaurant, with its open-view kitchen and lively, relaxed
atmosphere. Tapas are served all day at the bar, and the kitchen's
unpretentious approach suits the surroundings, with food cooked
on the charcoal grill or wood-burning oven. Dishes generally
explore something less familiar, with the robust flavours of Spain
and the exotic spices of North Africa and the Middle East. So
expect the likes of charcoal grilled lamb served with tomato bulgar,
grilled peppers, yogurt and allspice, and perhaps Malaga raisin ice
cream with Pedro Ximenez to finish.

Times: 12.30–2.30/7–10.30,
Closed Xmas, New Year, BHs, Sun
Prices: Main £14.50–£17.50
Directions: 5 mins walk from
Sadler's Wells theatre, between
Farringdon Road and Rosebery Ave

Malmaison Charterhouse Square

Modern British, French

Boutique hotel with accessible, easy-going brasserie

18–21 Charterhouse Square,
Clerkenwell, EC1M 6AH
Tel: 020 7012 3700
Email: london@malmaison.com
Website: www.malmaison.com

An attractive red-brick Victorian building, once a nurses' residence for St Bart's, the hotel is set in a cobbled courtyard just off Charterhouse Square and shares the same high production values upheld by the other establishments in the Malmaison chain. In the lively, brasserie-style restaurant tables are set on two levels, some in brick-backed alcoves. The menu offers mainly French cuisine delivered with simplicity, skill and fresh flavours throughout. Dishes such as a warm salad of chicken livers and pancetta, followed by sautéed monkfish cheeks and braised oxtail with herb risotto, and vanilla crème brûlée show the style.

Times: 12–2.30/6–10.30

Rudland & Stubbs

Fish

City-based fish and seafood restaurant

35-37 Green Hill Rants, Cowcross Street, EC1M 6BN
Tel: 020 7253 0148
Email:
reservations@rudlandstubbs.co.uk
Website:
www.rudlandstubbs.co.uk
Chef: Koenrad Ingelrahm
Owners: Raymond De Fazio

Set in a one-time sausage factory a stone's throw from Smithfield Market. After a refit, new owners relaunched this long-established Clerkenwell fish restaurant and bar back in 2006, . Cream tile work, wooden floors and high ceilings are among the original features retained, while marble-topped tables, wooden chairs, retro lighting and friendly, relaxed service add to its appeal as a welcoming neighbourhood eatery. The menu is almost exclusively fish, delivering colourful and well-presented dishes that combine the traditional alongside the more adventurous. Try miso-glazed tuna with bean sprouts, gai lang and pickle, or pan-fried baby turbot, braised oxtail, summer greens and saffron.

Times: 12–3/6–10.30, Closed Xmas 1 week, BHs, Sat, Sun
Prices: Main £9.50–£14.95
Directions: Next to Smithfield Market

Smiths of Smithfield

Modern British

Warehouse conversion in Smithfield Meat Market

Boasting views over the City and St Paul's Cathedral, this Grade
listed four-floor restaurant is situated in London's Smithfield
Meat Market. The building was empty for over 40 years before
conversion by the Smiths team and is now a popular and stylish
dining venue. Original brick walls, reclaimed timber and steel all
add to the ambience, with each floor having its own individual
style. This also extends to the food, which offers something to suit
every pocket and occasion. The menu in the Top Floor restaurant
includes luxury ingredients like Irish rock oysters and caviar, as well
as the best aged steaks. For mains, try venison Wellington with
spinach and juniper sauce.

(Top Floor) 67–77 Charterhouse
Street, EC1M 6HJ
Tel: 020 7251 7950
Email: reservations@
smithsofsmithfield.co.uk
Website:
www.smithsofsmithfield.co.uk

Times: 12–3.30/6.30–12, Closed
25–26 Dec, 1 Jan, L Sat
Directions: Opposite Smithfield
Meat Market

St John

British

The best of British nose-to-tail cooking

Fergus Henderson's stark, utilitarian-styled former smokehouse sits
across the road from Smithfield Market and continues to draw the
crowds. Upstairs, above the bustling bar and bakery, the
high-ceilinged dining room is an equally pared-down affair of
coat-hook-lined white walls, white-painted floorboards, white
paper-clothed tables and wooden café-style chairs, set in serried
ranks that echo the rows of industrial-style lights above. The
kitchen's open to view, staff are knowledgeable, friendly and
relaxed, in tune with the robust, honest, simplistic, bold-flavoured
British food that utilises the whole animal. Menus change twice
daily and there's plenty of humble ingredients; think roast bone
marrow and parsley salad, perhaps tripe and chips or beef and
squash, or bread pudding and butterscotch sauce. (See also
Spitalfields spin-off, St John Bread & Wine, page 11.)

26 St John Street, EC1M 4AY
Tel: 020 7251 0848
Email: reservations@
stjohnrestaurant.com
Website:
www.stjohnrestaurant.com
Chef: Christopher Gillard
Owners: T Gulliver & F Henderson

Times: 12–3/6–11, Closed Xmas,
New Year, Easter BH, Sun, L Sat
Prices: Main £12.80–£28
Directions: 100yds from Smithfield
Market, northside

25

Aurora at Great Eastern Hotel

Aurora at Great Eastern Hotel

Modern European

Modern cooking with flair in a dramatic setting

Set within the chic, designer City hotel adjacent to Liverpool Street station, Aurora is a stunning, palatial Victorian dining room dominated by a majestic stained-glass dome. Ceilings reach lofty cathedral height, enhanced by the billowing voiles and striking chandeliers that keep things contemporary while making the most of the original architecture. The kitchen's modern European approach – underpinned by a classical theme – is delivered via a range of menus that make the best of seasonal produce. Exciting dishes of flair, imagination and flavour fit the fine-dining City bill; take poached pork loin and confit belly with carrot and cumin and roasting juices, and to finish, perhaps a pistachio soufflé with pistachio ice cream and chocolate sauce. A daily lunchtime carving trolley plus a seven-course dégustation option and breakfasts for early-morning business meetings complete the slick package.

Liverpool Street, EC2M 7QN
Tel: 020 7618 7000
Email: aurorareception.longe@
hyattintl.com
Website:
www.aurora-restaurant.com
Chef: Dominic Teague
Owners: Hyatt

Times: 12–2.30/6.45–10, Closed Xmas, New Year, BHs, Sat, Sun
Prices: Main £18–£32
Directions: Telephone for directions

Boisdale of Bishopsgate

Traditional

A great taste of Scotland in the heart of the City

Set down a narrow Dickensian alley off Bishopsgate, Boisdale oozes character. Like its Belgravia sister venture, it comes decked out in patriotic Scottish style with a buzzy, clubby atmosphere. The ground floor is a traditional champagne and oyster bar, while the restaurant and piano bar are in the cellar downstairs. Vibrant red-painted brick walls laden with pictures and mirrors, tartan carpet or dark floorboards, leather banquettes and tartan or leather chairs all create a moody, upbeat atmosphere. The Caledonian menu supports the theme, the kitchen's approach driven by traditional, high-quality north-of-the-border produce. Favourites include Speyside Angus beef steaks, Macsween haggis, Lochcarnan hot-smoked salmon or Shetland Isle scallops.

Swedeland Court,
202 Bishopsgate, EC2M 4NR
Tel: 020 7283 1763
Email: katie@boisdale-city.co.uk
Website: www.boisdale.co.uk
Chef: Neil Churchill
Owners: Ranald Macdonald

Times: 11–3/6–12, Closed Xmas,
31 Dec, BHs, Sat & Sun
Prices: 3 Course Fixed D £29.50–
£37.50 Main £12.15–£26.50
Directions: Opposite Liverpool
St Station

Bonds

Modern French

A grand setting for some slick modern cooking

Built to imperious Victorian specifications, this grand dining room retains many features recognisable from its days as a financial institution. The client base is strictly city business people with generous expense accounts, and the menu is succinctly scripted, studded with luxury produce and shows clear aspiration from a talented kitchen. A good-value lighter lunch is offered, while the carte lifts quality, technique and pricing accordingly. Try ravioli of lobster with Armagnac bisque, or Dorset crab with smoked salmon, crème fraîche and Oscietra caviar, followed by roast duck with caramelised red onion tart Tatin, fondue of gem lettuce and Madeira jus, or roast cod, scallops and octopus daube, confit celeriac and potato purée, with banana and caramel parfait and passionfruit sorbet to finish.

Threadneedles, 5 Threadneedle
Street, EC2R 8AY
Tel: 020 7657 8088
Email: bonds@theetongroup.com
Website:
www.bonds-restaurant.com
Chef: Barry Tonks
Owners: The Eton Collection

Times: 12–2.30/6–10, Closed
2 wks Xmas, 4 days Etr & BHs,
Sat, Sun
Prices: Main £15.50–£23

27

Eyre Brothers

Spanish, Portuguese

Lively Iberian dining in trendy Shoreditch

70 Leonard Street, EC2A 4QX
Tel: 020 7613 5346
Email: eyrebros@btconnect.com
Website: www.eyrebrothers.co.uk
Chef: Dave Eyre, Joao Cleto
Owners: Eyre Bros Restaurants Ltd

Tucked away down a long street of reclaimed Shoreditch loft buildings, this gem is just a short hike from Old Street and Liverpool Street stations. The plate glass windows and smart sign offer a hint of what is inside, but the sharp metropolitan blend of dark wood, cool leather and long trendy bar are still a welcome surprise. It's a place for relaxed business lunches, for groups of friends to spread out and feel at home, and there are quiet spots for more discreet get-togethers. Authentic Portuguese regional cooking and classic Spanish cuisine combine effortlessly to achieve bold rustic dishes with big flavours and lively colours: grilled Mozambique tiger prawn piri-piri with pilaf rice fits the bill nicely. Attentive staff encourage the mood.

Times: 12–3/6.30–11, Closed Xmas–New Year, BHs, Sun, L Sat
Prices: Main £12–£24

Fishmarket

Modern European, Seafood

Enjoyable seafood dining in a city hotel

Great Eastern Hotel, Liverpool Street, EC2M 7QN
Tel: 020 7618 7200
Email: restaurantres.longe@hyattintl.com
Website: london.greateastern.hyatt.com
Chef: Stuart Lyall
Owners: Hyatt

This trendy seafood restaurant is located in an elegant marble-clad corner of the Great Eastern Hotel. A wide selection of fresh and saltwater fish is offered plus an award-winning wine list. The centrepiece is the attractive display of fish and the 'altar' where chefs prepare crustacea in front of diners. The Champagne Bar, dominated by a mosaic-covered horseshoe bar, has an extensive list of Champagnes, including some rare vintages, and serves favourite dishes from the restaurant menu. These might include crab and pickled mackerel spring roll or escabèche of Cornish sardines, followed by black bass with olive mash, aubergine and snakebean cannelloni and sauce vièrge, or crisp fried sea bream with globe artichokes, girolles, truffle and cauliflower purée, and pesto sauce.

Times: 12–2.30/6–10.30, Closed Xmas, New Year, BHs, Sun, L Sat
Prices: Main £12.75–£32
Directions: Please telephone for directions

Great Eastern Dining Room

Pan Asian

High-octane Asian-style eatery

54 Great Eastern Street, EC2A 3QR
Tel: 020 7613 4545
Email:
martyn@thediningrooms.com
Website:
www.greateasterndining.co.uk
Chef: Gerrard Mitchel
Owners: Will Ricker

A trendy bar-restaurant in the vibrant and up-and-coming City extremities. This place gets packed even on mid-week evenings, so don't expect much space at your paper-clad table. Service is relaxed with knowledgeable staff, while darkwood walls and floors, leather seating and funky chandeliers reign alongside high decibels. A well-executed Pan-Asian menu – based on the grazing concept and ideal for sharing – delivers on presentation and flavour. From dim sum to sashimi, curries to barbecues and roasts or house specials; think black cod with sweet miso, perhaps an aubergine and lychee green curry, or coconut and pandon pannacotta dessert.

Times: 12–3/6–10.30, Closed
Xmas & Etr, Sun, L Sat

Mehek

Indian

Stylish Indian dining with innovative dishes

45 London Wall, Moorgate,
EC2M 5TE
Tel: 020 7588 5043
Email: info@mehek.co.uk
Website: www.mehek.co.uk
Chef: A Matlib
Owners: Salim B Rashid

Tardis-like, Mehek opens out from an inconspicuous entrance in a row of shops into several stylish eating areas. A long, glamorous bar draws in the local office crowd after work, while discreet lighting, smartly dressed tables and genuinely interested waiters make it easy to linger over a meal. The food is a modern take on northern Indian traditional dishes, though the creative kitchen team bring in classics from other parts of the subcontinent as well. You'll find biryanis, kormas and pasandas, but also the likes of duck in a coconut and peanut sauce, and lots of novel seafood choices.

Times: 11.30–3/5.30–11, Closed
Xmas, New Year, BHs, Sat, Sun
Prices: 3 Course Fixed D £24.50–
£28.50 Main £6.90–£18.90
Directions: Close to junct of
Moorgate and London Wall

Rhodes Twenty Fou[r]

Rhodes Twenty Four

Modern British

Truly classic Rhodes cuisine overlooking the City

This chic restaurant is set on the 24th floor of the tallest building in the Square Mile and enjoys stunning views over London. The sophisticated operation has its own bar, while the dining room comes dressed in its best white linen armed with stylish appointments, where all tables enjoy the spectacular panoramas. Service is slick, with good attention paid to wine, while the cuisine is Gary's hallmark modern British with a twist, as you'd expect. Impeccable ingredients, crystal-clear flavours, perfect balance and sharp presentation parade on exciting dishes. Clearly defined menus might feature roast beef fillet with red wine onions, oxtail hash and poached egg béarnaise, or perhaps steamed fillet of brill served with crayfish tails and buttered leeks, and to finish, it has to be the bread-and-butter pudding. And do leave time for security check-in at this tower block.

Tower 42, Old Broad Street, EC2N 1HQ
Tel: 020 7877 7703
Website: www.rhodes24.co.uk
Chef: Gary Rhodes & Adam Gray
Owners: Restaurant Associates

Times: 12–2.30/6–9, Closed BHs, Xmas, Sat, Sun
Prices: Main £17.50–£24
Directions: Telephone for directions, see website

Rivington Bar & Grill

British v

Straightforward British classics in a lively setting

28-30 Rivington Street, EC2A 3DZ
Tel: 020 7729 7053
Email:
shoreditch@rivingtongrill.co.uk
Website: www.rivingtongrill.co.uk
Chef: Damian Clisby
Owners: Caprice-Holdings Ltd

A combined restaurant, bar and deli, this buzzy place is tucked away down a narrow side street in fashionable Hoxton. White walls and wooden floors make for a suitably relaxed backdrop to a parade of simple, seasonal, no-frills modern British cooking using top-notch produce. Main courses include roast Lancashire suckling pig with greens and quince sauce, or fish fingers and chips with mushy peas, while comforting desserts might feature Bakewell tart with vanilla ice cream. Nice touches include chips served in little buckets and your own small loaf of bread. (Also sibling establishment in Greenwich, see entry on page 62.)

Times: 12–3/6.30–11, Closed Xmas & New Year, L Sat
Prices: Main £9.25–£25.50
Directions: Telephone for directions

Tatsuso Restaurant

Japanese

Authentic City Oriental

32 Broadgate Circle, EC2M 2QS
Tel: 020 7638 5863

This slick, glass-fronted, atmospheric, two-tier City Japanese – on the lower level of Broadgate Circle – comes brimming with corporate suits, professional service and clean modern lines. Lightwood furniture and screens set the scene with waitresses in traditional Japanese dress. On the ground floor there's the theatre of the teppan-yaki grill to enjoy, where lobster, Dover sole and sirloin with foie gras tempt, while in the basement, a lengthy, authentic carte and sushi menu reign in a more relaxed atmosphere. You will find quality ingredients, plentiful set-menu options and City prices.

Times: 11.45–2.45/6.30–10.15, Closed Xmas, New Year, BHs, Sat, Sun
Directions: Ground floor of Broadgate Circle

1 Lombard Street

Modern

Bank on sophisticated dining at luxurious prices

In the shadow of the Bank of England, 1 Lombard Street is a sleek City operation. A former City banking hall, it combines a neo-classical interior with contemporary design. There's a buzzy, informal brasserie with circular bar and domed skylight up front, while the intimate, discreet, fine-dining restaurant at the rear is the luxury focus of the enterprise. Here a classical backdrop sets the stage for the elegant décor and furnishings. Like the restaurant's surroundings, the food is unashamedly expensive, the appealing repertoire dotted with luxury and sophistication, with the kitchen's modern approach – underpinned by a classical French theme – delivering high quality in refined, well-presented, clear-flavoured dishes of precision and flair. A mignon of veal served with a green pea compôte à la Française, autumn truffles, girolles and a Chablis velouté shows the style.

1 Lombard Street, EC3V 9AA
Tel: 020 7929 6611
Email: hb@1lombardstreet.com
Website:
www.1lombardstreet.com
Chef: Herbet Berger
Owners: Jessen & Co

Times: 12–2.30/6–10, Closed Xmas, New Year, BHs, Sat, Sun, D 24 Dec
Directions: Opposite Bank of England

Addendum

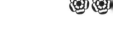

Modern European

Skilled modern cooking in slick, boutique hotel

The modern, yet elegant restaurant, Addendum, contributes to the overall cutting-edge design at this new City hotel. Dark chocolate-coloured fixtures and fittings, amber lighting, clever use of mirrors, leather seats and booths, and tables turned out in their best whites fill the room, while service is slick from a friendly team of equally impeccably presented staff. Skilled, passionate cooking focusing on stunning ingredients, seasonality and crisp, clear flavours is the kitchen's style. Menus offer real value and quality, with classic dishes benefiting from modern twists, and there's plenty of luxury too.

Apex City of London Hotel,
No 1 Seething Lane, EC3N 4AX
Tel: 020 7977 9500
Email: reservations@
addendumrestaurant.co.uk
Website:
www.addendumrestaurant.co.uk
Chef: Darren Thomas
Owners: Norman Springford

Times: 12–2.30/6–9.30, Closed 23 Dec–3 Jan, BHs, Sat, Sun
Prices: Main £16.75–£21.50
Directions: Follow Lower Thames St, left onto Trinity Square, left onto Muscovy St, right onto Seething Ln, opposite Seething Ln gardens

Chamberlains Restaurant

Modern British, Seafood

Market-fresh fish beloved of City slickers

23/25 Leadenhall Market,
EC3V 1LR
Tel: 020 7648 8690
Email: info@chamberlains.org
Chef: Glen Watson
Owners: Chamberlain & Thelwell

Colourful Leadenhall Market, thronging with City workers at midday and early evening, makes a relaxed setting for this seafood restaurant. It sits beneath the restored Victorian glass roof of the old market, alongside the cobbled walkway, with excellent views of the exquisite architecture from the first floor and mezzanine dining areas. You can also eat more casually in the basement wine bar, or bag a table outside on warmer days. The owners, Chamberlain and Thelwell are fish suppliers to the trade and, with deliveries right up to opening times, freshness is guaranteed. Try a starter of lobster bisque with collops of lobster and chopped dill, followed by sesame seared tuna with caponata and grilled Mediterranean vegetables. There's plenty of meat too, though the speciality fish and chips remains popular.

Times: 12/9.30, Closed Xmas,
New Year & BHs, Sat, Sun
Prices: 3 Course Fixed D £19.95
Main £19–£35
Directions: Telephone for
directions

Prism Restaurant and Bar

Modern International 🍾 NOTABLE WINE LIST

Eclectic dining opposite Leadenhall Market

147 Leadenhall Street, EC3V 4QT
Tel: 020 7256 3888
Website: www.harveynichols.com
Chef: Jonathan Warner
Owners: Harvey Nichols

The Square Mile houses several restaurants, but few as impressive as this one. Once the Bank of New York, its lofty ceiling and vast spaces make a palatial backdrop for fine dining. For a more discreet experience there is the Conservatory, separated from the main restaurant and ideal for meals à deux. The menu offers a lively choice of dishes inspired from around the globe, with the accent on detail and flavour. Starters like ballontine of rabbit, date and Parma ham, with a rabbit velouté and celeriac remoulade make a punchy prelude to chargrilled swordfish, borlotti bean and sweet pepper ragout, with chorizo-stuffed baby squid. Owned by Harvey Nichols, their established quality is stamped throughout.

Times: 11.30–3/6–10, Closed
25 Dec, BHs, Sat, Sun
Prices: Main £18–£24
Directions: Please telephone
for directions

Restaurant Sauterelle

French

Stylish French cuisine in the Royal Exchange building

Set on the first-floor mezzanine of the Royal Exchange, Restaurant Sauterelle overlooks the bustling courtyard interior, where the Grand Café and many world-famous jewellers and retailers ply their trade. The atmosphere is fittingly chic, while service is correspondingly efficient, welcoming and professional. The carefully prepared, straightforward but classy, classic regional French cuisine uses the freshest produce from the markets and sits well with the surroundings. Typically, start with rock oysters with champagne velouté, follow with suprême of halibut with a fricassée of wild mushrooms, sauce verte and fresh truffles, or perhaps Chateaubriand steak with roast field mushroom and béarnaise sauce, and finish with pear tart Tatin with crème fraîche.

The Royal Exchange, EC3V 3LR
Tel: 020 7618 2483
Email:
alessandrop@danddlondon.com
Website: www.danddlondon.com
restaurants/sauterelle/home
Chef: Darren Kerley
Owners: D & D London

Times: 12–2.30/6–10, Closed BH
Sat, Sun
Prices: Main £16.50–£21.50
Directions: In heart of business
centre. Bank tube station exit 4

The Chancery

Modern European

Enjoyable brasserie-style dining in legal land

This aptly named, intimate, modern, glass-fronted restaurant (sibling to the Clerkenwell Dining Room, see page 21) is secreted away close to Lincoln's Inn and Chancery Lane, set among the narrow streets and historic buildings of the law community. Contemporary black leather chairs and white linen blend seamlessly with polished mahogany floors, black woodwork and white walls hung with mirrors and modern abstract art. There's a bar downstairs, while the dining space – split into two sections with arched openings – is as modern, crisp, confident and clean-cut as the well-executed cooking. Expect the likes of roast monkfish with chorizo, razor clams and saffron emulsion, or perhaps fillet of beef served with oxtail tortellini, Savoy cabbage and Madeira jus in the good-value, fixed-price menus.

9 Cursitor Street, EC4A 1LL
Tel: 020 7831 4000
Email:
reservations@thechancery.co.uk
Website: www.thechancery.co.uk

Times: 12–2.30/6–10.30, Closed
Xmas, Sat, Sun
Directions: Situated between High
Holborn and Fleet St

Refettorio

Italian

Authentic Italian concept in chic surroundings

Sleek, stylish and contemporary, Refettorio blends comfortably with the swish modernism of the Crowne Plaza Hotel. The L-shaped room has a long bar, high windows hung with Venetian blinds and polished-wood floors and tables. Smart, brown leather booth-style seating provides discreet dining along one wall, while young black-clad staff are suitably attentive. Authentic Italian food; excellent breads, a superb array of impeccably-sourced regional cheeses, hams and salamis, home-made pasta and an all-Italian wine list provide the impressive backdrop to an appealing menu of straightforward but accomplished and well-presented dishes. Start with selection of cured meats and cheeses followed by steamed sea bass with fennel salad and lemon perhaps.

Crowne Plaza Hotel, 19 New Bridge Street, EC4V 6DB
Tel: 020 7438 8052
Email: loncy.refettorio@ichotelsgroup.com
Website: www.refettorio.com
Chef: Mattia Camorani
Owners: Parallel/Crowne Plaza

Times: 12–2.30/6–10.30, Closed Xmas, New Year, BHs, Sun, L Sat
Prices: 3 Course Fixed D £45–£65 Main £8.50–£22
Directions: Situated on New Bridge St, opposite Blackfriars underground (exit 8)

White Swan Pub & Dining Room

Modern, Traditional British

Busy, upmarket gastro-pub with a smart dining room

Beyond the bar of this tastefully restored pub is a mezzanine area, available for drinks parties, and a formal first-floor dining room. Decked out with white-clothed tables, its handsome wooden floors, contemporary chairs, banquettes and mirrored ceiling cut an upmarket edge. Friendly and attentive service adds to the experience. The menu combines classics alongside more esoteric dishes; think braised rabbit tortellini with cep foam and vichy carrots, or red wine braised monkfish cheeks with gremolata mash and deep-fried leeks. Desserts might feature chocolate sponge with hot fudge and white chocolate sorbet, while daily specials provide additional interest.

108 Fetter Lane, EC4A 1ES
Tel: 020 7242 9696
Email: info@thewhiteswanlondon.com
Website: www.thewhiteswanlondon.com
Owners: Tom & Ed Martin

Times: 12–3/6–10, Closed 25 Dec, 1 Jan and BHs, Sat, Sun (except private parties)
Prices: Main £15–£18.50
Directions: Fetter Lane runs parallel with Chancery Lane in the City of London and it joins Fleet St with Holborn

35

North London

Waterlow Park, Highgate

Almeida Restaurant

French 🍷 NOTABLE WINE LIST

Conran eatery serving rustic French food

30 Almeida Street, Islington,
N1 1TD
Tel: 020 7354 4777
Email: almeida-reservations@
conran-restaurants.co.uk
Website:
www.almeida-restaurants.co.uk
Chef: Ian Wood
Owners: Sir Terence Conran

Just down from Highbury Corner on the way to Islington, the Almeida is one of the cosiest eateries in the Conran empire, combining rustic French cooking with a fashionably muted décor. Relax over a drink in the intimate bar, and then move through to the expansive dining area, where a theatre kitchen puts all the culinary action on show. There is an extensive menu on offer with dishes distinguished by a pared down approach – including a tapas-style menu – that lets top-notch ingredients shine through. Straightforward starters and mains show the style; choose crayfish and coriander salad with saffron dressing, or perhaps seared scallops with endive marmalade, cucumber and olive salad, with blackcurrant delice and apple compôte to finish.

Times: 12–2.30/5.30–11, Closed 25–26 Dec, 1 Jan, Good Fri, 17 Apr
Prices: 3 Course Fixed D £17.50–£27
Directions: Turn right from station, along Upper St, past church

---

The Drapers Arms

Modern European

Convivial gastro-pub in trendy Islington

44 Barnsbury Street, N1 1ER
Tel: 020 7619 0348
Email: info@thedrapersarms.co.uk
Website:
www.thedrapersarms.co.uk
Chef: Mark Emberton
Owners: Paul McElhinney,
Mark Emberton

Gastro-pub in a smart residential area of Islington; a lovely building with wooden floors and comfy sofas. A central door opens into the bar area with long wide spaces on either side for tables. The place is packed Sunday lunchtime with young families, older couples and groups of friends. The restaurant upstairs occupies the same large space with a fireplace at either end. Cooking is modern and seasonal with influences from around the world. Try twice-cooked pork belly with Thai spiced salad, followed by maize-fed chicken with roast tomato couscous and tzatiki. Desserts include the likes of apple and walnut Bakewell with crème fraîche.

Times: 12–3/7–10.30, Closed 24–27 Dec, 1–2 Jan, L Mon–Sat, D Sun
Prices: Main £11.50–£15.50
Directions: Just off Upper St, situated between Angel/Highbury & Islington tube stations, opposite town hall

Fifteen London

Italian, Mediterranean v NOTABLE WINE LIST

Funky, informal, not-for-profit restaurant

Jamie Oliver's pioneering culinary venture into youth training – as seen on TV – is still going strong, with current offshoots in Cornwall, Amsterdam and Melbourne. Tucked away in a cobbled side street in the fashionably down-at-heels margins of the Old Street area, this unpretentious, warehouse-style place still pulls in the crowds and tourists. On the ground floor there's a laid-back, buzzy trattoria for lighter meals, while the restaurant is in the basement. Here there's an open kitchen, mural-covered walls and brown leather banquettes or chairs. The cooking's approach is Italian-Mediterranean, driven by quality fresh, seasonal ingredients and straightforward simplicity on a daily-changing repertoire (six-course tasting affair only at dinner); take chargrilled Welsh lamb with marinated aubergine, Italian spinach and an anchovy-rosemary dressing.

13 Westland Place, N1 7LP
Tel: 0871 330 1515
Website: www.fifteen.net
Chef: Jamie Oliver,
Andrew Parkinson
Owners: Fifteen Foundation

Times: 12–2.45/6.30–9.30,
Closed Xmas, New Year
Prices: Main £20–£25
Directions: Exit 1 from Old St tube station, walk up City road, opposite Moorfields Eye Hospital

---

Frederick's Restaurant

Modern European

Fashionable food in contemporary setting

Tucked away in Islington's antiques quarter, the Victorian façade of this well-established restaurant opens into a smart and stylish bar and restaurant. A large conservatory and al fresco dining area are complemented by painted and plain brick walls, clothed tables and suede chairs, while modern art and clever lighting all add to the ambience. The equally modern menu offers plenty of choice and includes some traditional dishes with a modern twist, as well as some vegetarian options. For mains, try fillet of beef with Roquefort, roasted tomatoes and crushed new potatoes, and double chocolate pudding soufflé to finish.

Camden Passage, Islington,
N1 8EG
Tel: 020 7359 2888
Email: eat@fredericks.co.uk
Website: www.fredericks.co.uk
Chef: Adam Hilliard
Owners: Louis Segal

Times: 12–2.30/5.45–11.30,
Closed Xmas, New Year, BHs,
Sun (ex functions)
Prices: 3 Course Fixed D £17
Main £12–£19.50
Directions: From Angel underground 2 mins walk to Camden Passage. Restaurant among the antique shops

The House

Modern British

Enjoyable, simple cooking in a relaxed environment

63-69 Canonbury Road,
N1 2DG
Tel: 020 7704 7410
Email: info@inthehouse.biz
Website: www.inthehouse.biz
Chef: Jeremy Hollingsworth
Owners: Barnaby & Grace
Meredith/Jeremy Hollingsworth

Behind a redbrick façade lies this cosy neighbourhood restaurant which has quite a local following. Wooden floors, whitewashed walls and simple artwork give the dining room a light and airy feel during the day. In the evening, locals gather around the comfortable bar sofas and well-spaced dining tables. The menu features skilful, simple dishes using organic produce (wherever possible). Try Loch Fyne smoked salmon with buckwheat blinis to start, then maybe sea bass with a ragout of borlotti beans and baby onions with braised fennel, and finish with warm Valrhona chocolate pudding served with espresso ice cream. Everything from the breads to ice creams is freshly made.

Times: 12–2.30/6–10.30, Closed L Mon
Directions: Behind town hall on Upper St Islington. Between Highbury Corner and Essex Rd

The Real Greek

Greek

Popular, bustling, earthy, authentic Hoxton Greek

15 Hoxton Market, N1 6HG
Tel: 020 7739 8212
Email:
admin@therealgreek.demon.co.uk

The name sums it up; a fashionable, authentic, unpretentious Greek outfit located on the market square between two old buildings. While retaining some of this old charm, stripped-wood floors, closely packed plain wooden tables, an open kitchen and youthful, friendly service fit the bill, while the adjoining Mezedopolis (a wine and mezedes bar) cranks up the volume. The lengthy menu (in English and Greek) draws on the plentiful Greek larder, delivering simple, robust and colourful authentic dishes, packed with mezedes (appetisers) and partnered by Greek wines. A typical meal might begin with crevettes saganaki with Ismir-style meat dumplings served with trahana to follow.

Times: 12/11, Closed 24–26 Dec, BHs, Sun
Prices: Main £13.50–£17.50
Directions: Situated in square behind Holiday Inn on Old St. From tube station walk down Old St pas fire station then 1st left 1st right to the back of inn

Upper Glas

Swedish

Swedish restaurant in a new location

359 Upper Street, N1 0PD
Tel: 020 7359 1932
Email: glas@glasrestaurant.com
Website:
www.glasrestaurant.co.uk
Chef: Rafael Nabulon
Owners: Anna Mosesson

This Scandinavian restaurant was formerly known as Glas and was located in SE1. Now housed in a listed Victorian tram shed building, and much bigger than before, the interior could be described as authentic Swedish, with antique paintings and modern chandeliers. On offer are a traditional three-course menu and a grazing menu, both using much high quality produce. Of course you can expect herring on the menu – perhaps spiced Matjes herring with sour cream, chives and onion, and there could be smoked venison with beetroot salad and horseradish, or West Coast seafood cappucino with warm langoustine salad.

Times: 12–3/5.30–11, Closed
Xmas, Etr, Sun
Prices: Main £9–£16.50
Directions: Please telephone for
directions

The Bull Pub & Dining Room

British, French

Lively modern gastro-pub offering confident cooking

13 North Hill, N6 4AB
Tel: 0845 456 5033
Email: info@inthebull.biz
Website: www.inthebull.biz
Chef: Jeremy Hollingsworth,
Andres Alemany
Owners: J E Barnaby Meredith

This contemporary, informal gastro-pub (sister to The House at Islington on page 40), situated in a two-storey Grade II listed building, has a buzzy central bar and smart dining area with an open hatch to the kitchen. (Upstairs are private function facilities and a games room.) Polished-wood floors, leather banquettes and modern art create a relaxed, upbeat vibe, while at the front there's a terrace for fair-weather dining. Confident modern British cuisine is the thing here, with the emphasis on simplicity, freshness and quality produce. The carte comes supplemented by blackboard specials and includes an express lunch option, so there's something for everyone; take roast sea bass served with chorizo, new potato, baby spinach and saffron caramel, or perhaps a cherry clafoutis and chocolate sauce finish.

Times: 12–3.30/6–10.30, Closed
L Mon, D 25 Dec
Prices: Main £12–£25
Directions: 5 min walk from
Highgate tube station
Parking: 3

41

Morgan M

Modern French v NOTABLE WINE LIST

Top-notch French cooking in intimate surroundings

The unassuming frontage is in keeping with the restrained elegance of chef-patron Morgan Meunier's intimate eatery. The dining room has burgundy walls, while white linen cloths and elegant table appointments complete the upbeat tone. Service is polished and attentive, and Morgan circulates tables at the end of service. His is real French cooking, technically brilliant using top-quality seasonal ingredients (much brought in fresh from France) and cooked with passion. Think roasted fillet of turbot with petit farci of crab, carrot and ginger risotto and a light carrot jus, or perhaps roasted Anjou squab pigeon, with parsnip purée, braised pear and crispy pepper potato in a red wine jus. Morgan's compact carte comes bolstered by his signature six-course tasting option (including a superb vegetarian alternative), while the wine list takes a patriotic French line. Lunch is quieter but offers good value.

489 Liverpool Road, Islington, N7 8NS
Tel: 020 7609 3560
Website: www.morganm.com
Chef: M Meunier & S Soulard
Owners: Morgan Meunier

Times: 12–2.30/7–10.30, Closed 24–30 Dec, Mon, L Tues, Sat, D Sun
Prices: 3 Course Fixed D £34

Islington

The Lock Dining Bar

The Lock Dining Bar

Modern British

Great value destination

Heron House, Hale Wharf, Ferry Lane, N17 9NF
Tel: 020 8885 2829
Email: www.thelock06@btconnect.com
Website: thelock-diningbar.com
Chef: Adebola Adeshina
Owners: Adebola Adeshina, Fabrizio Russo

This chic eatery, just a few minutes walk from Tottenham Hale station, has the feel of a New York loft house, is decked out with North African furnishings and the walls are hung with works of art by local painters. An open-plan kitchen delivers a menu of modern British dishes with a focus on seasonal produce. Starters might include the likes of baked polenta fritter and Crottin goat's cheese dressed with truffle emulsion, or pan-fried scallops with plantain, and garlic froth, followed by pan-fried fillet of dorade with sautéed potatoes and slow caramelised onions. Finish with deep-fried rice pudding beignets with mixed berry sauce. It's all reasonably priced, particularly at lunchtime, and great value for money.

Times: 12–2.30/6.30–10, Closed L Sat (except match days), D Mon, Sun
Prices: 3 Course Fixed D £19.50–£25 Main £10.50–£22
Directions: Telephone for directions
Parking: 20

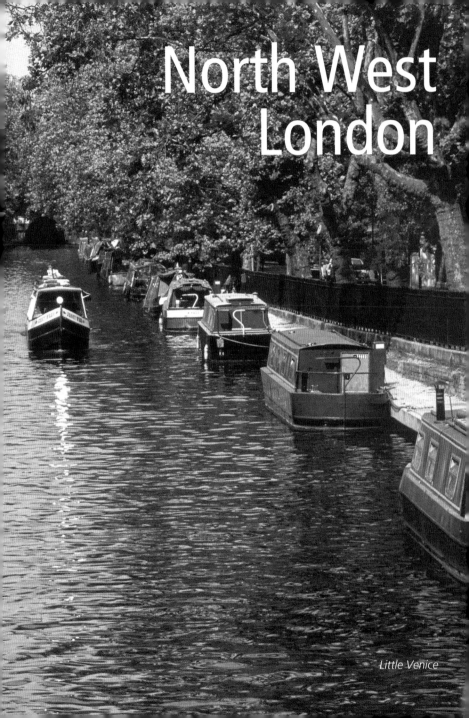

North West London

Little Venice

La Collina

Italian

Authentic Italian cooking in Primrose Hill

17 Princess Road,
Chalk Farm, NW1 8JR
Tel: 020 7483 0192

It's a rare London eatery that manages to capture all the flavour and authenticity of Italian cooking back home. La Collina is a period-style building close to picturesque Primrose Hill, with white-washed walls, linen-clothed tables, wooden chairs and stripped wooden floorboards. Dine upstairs and watch the fashion-concious passers-by, or downstairs, where an open kitchen lets you in on the culinary action. Friendly, attentive staff create a warm informal environment. The kitchen delivers fresh, vibrant mainly Northern dishes with Piedmontese influences that are homely and full of flavour. Tuck into the likes of chestnut noodles with wild boar ragu, or grilled tuna with stewed peppers.

Times: 12–2.30/6–11,
Closed Xmas wk, L Mon–Fri

Dorset Square Hotel

Modern British

Relaxed bar-restaurant with cricketing roots

39-40 Dorset Square, NW1 6QN
Tel: 020 7723 7874
Email: info@dorsetsquare.co.uk
Website: www.dorsetsquare.co.uk
Chef: Martin Halls
Owners: LHP

Standing on the original site of Lords cricket ground, this smart Regency townhouse hotel is home to the popular lower-ground floor Potting Shed Restaurant and Bar – a split-level affair with skylights and a warm, sunny feel. The gardening theme is developed with an array of terracotta pots and seed boxes across one wall, while a cricketing mural adorns another wall. The cooking is predominantly British with contemporary twists. The seasonal menu is kept simple and wholesome, focusing on accurate flavours. Tuck into a tender rump of lamb with garlic cream potatoes, or a Dorset blue cheese and leek tart with grape chutney, followed by a glazed lemon tart with fresh raspberries.

Times: 12–3/6–10.30, Closed
25 Dec, BHs, L Sat, D Sun
Prices: 3 Course Fixed D
£22.50–£25 Main £11.50–£19.50
Directions: Telephone for
directions

Gilgamesh

Pan-Asian

Eclectic range of dishes in mega-lavish surroundings

Camden Stables Market, Chalk Farm Road, NW1 8AH
Tel: 020 7482 5757

This £12m, Babylonian-inspired, mega-lavish, elaborately decorated, restaurant/bar/tearoom/private lounge offers more of a 'food theatre' experience than out-and-out restaurant with its fantastic atmosphere and all this in Camden! Think a huge bar of lapis stone, constantly-changing lighting and a vast retractable roof, while seating is a mix of high bar stools, banquettes and foot stalls that come paired with matching-height, solid-wood tables. The menu is classic Ian Pengelley and so fits the bill, with Pan-Asian cuisine swiftly served by knowledgeable and friendly staff. The eclectic mix takes in the likes of sashimi, tempura, dim sum and Gilgamesh signature dishes like hoba miso Chilean sea bass.

Times: 12–2.30/6, Closed L Mon–Thurs, D Fri–Sun

Novotel London Euston

Modern European

Modern hotel restaurant with a wide-ranging carte

100–110 Euston Road, NW1 2AJ
Tel: 020 7666 9080
Email: h5309-fb@accor.com
Website: www.novotel.com
Chef: Denzil Newton
Owners: Accor UK Business & Leisure

Centrally located, this popular purpose-built hotel offers a wide range of facilities, including Mirrors restaurant and bar. The restaurant's décor is stylish and contemporary with lots of glass, neutral woods, large potted fig trees and colourful upholstery combining to create a sense of space set around a carvery and open kitchen. The atmosphere is vibrant and the service is good. Featuring modern European cooking, and combining the classics with global influences, the menu includes a terrine of Iberico ham, gammon and lobster with Bramley apple purée and golden raisins, and dry aged Scottish rump with salt beef hash and fried quail's egg.

Times: 12–2.30/6–10.30, Closed L Sat, Sun, BHs
Prices: 3 Course Fixed D £21.95 Main £12.50–£19.95
Directions: 5 mins walk between King's Cross and Euston Station, opposite British Library. 1m from Regent's Park

Odette's

Odette's

British, European v

Intimate neighbourhood restaurant

Owned by music promoter and nightclub owner Vince Power and refurbished by designer Shaun Clarkson, Odette's has a friendly vibe with a modern 'boudoir'-style interior. Service is attentive but relaxed, while the kitchen shows pedigree in the capable hands of Welsh chef Bryn Williams (ex Le Gavroche and the Orrery). His light, modern approach delivers with unfussy presentation, clear flavours and a focus on quality seasonal ingredients. The repertoire of fixed-price menus – including a six-course tasting option and vegetarian offering – might deliver the likes of roasted rack and braised shoulder of Elwy Valley lamb served with its own jus, pine nuts and courgette, or perhaps pan-fried turbot with cockles and oxtail, while a warm Valrhona chocolate fondant served with milk ice cream, or poached rhubarb crumble accompanied by a rhubarb sorbet and ginger custard might catch the eye at dessert.

130 Regent's Park Road,
NW1 8XL
Tel: 020 7586 8569
Email: odettes@vpmg.net
Website:
www.odettesprimrosehill.com
Chef: Bryn Williams
Owners: Vince Power

Times: 12–2.30/6.30–10.30,
Closed 25 Dec, Mon (incl BHs),
D Sun
Prices: 3 Course Fixed D
£21.95–£25 Main £15–£25
Directions: Telephone for
directions

Sardo Canale

Italian

Authentic Italian cuisine in a surprising setting

42 Gloucester Avenue, NW1 8JD
Tel: 020 7722 2800
Email: info@sardocanale.com
Website: www.sardocanale.com
Chef: Claudio Covino
Owners: Romolo & Bianca Mudu

This unusual restaurant is located in a new building, designed around an old tunnel and tower dating back to 1850. The original brick tunnel with cobbled stones was used by horses pulling barges in the nearby Grand Union Canal. It's certainly a novel place to find a modern Italian restaurant, serving up regional Italian cooking using fresh ingredients and authentic Sardinian recipes. Service is formal, but the atmosphere is relaxed and friendly, so take some time to peruse the extensive Italian menu, complete with English subtitles. Signature dishes include linguine al granchio – a pasta sauce made of fresh crab meat with extra virgin olive oil, parsley and fresh chillies, and for dessert try frozen coffee cream with mascarpone.

Times: 12–3/6–11, Closed 25–26 Dec, BHs, L Mon
Prices: 3 Course Fixed D £30
Main £12–£17.50
Directions: Please telephone for directions

The Winter Garden

Modern British

Stunning atrium restaurant

The Landmark London,
222 Marylebone Road, NW1 6JQ
Tel: 020 7631 8000
Email: restaurants.reservation@thelandmark.co.uk
Website: www.landmarklondon.co.uk
Chef: Gary Klaner
Owners: Jatuporn Sihanatkathakul

Former headquarters of British Rail and one of the last great railway hotels, the building is over 100 years old. The Winter Garden is a stunning open-plan, naturally lit restaurant situated at the base of an eight-storey atrium complete with palm trees, which also features the sophisticated Mirror Bar. At night, the restaurant turns into a more intimate affair. A selection of modern British dishes is offered on a menu featuring fresh quality produce. Typical starters might include shellfish bisque with vodka crème fraîche, while a main course of pine nut-crusted rack of lamb is accompanied with basil mash, Provençal vegetables and shallot jus. Desserts might include rhubarb and vanilla baked Alaska with rhubarb compôte.

Times: 11.30–3/6–11.30
Prices: Main £15–£40
Directions: M25 turn on to the A40 and continue 16m following signs for West End. Continue along Marylebone Rd for 300 mtrs. Restaurant on left
Parking: 75

Manna

International Vegetarian v

Charming, fun and informal vegetarian restaurant

4 Erskine Road, Primrose Hill,
NW3 3AJ
Tel: 020 7722 8028
Email: yourhost@manna-veg.com
Website: www.manna-veg.com
Chef: Matthew Kay
Owners: S Hague, R Swallow,
M Kay

Believed to be the oldest vegetarian dinner restaurant in England, Manna was founded in the 1960s to bring a gourmet experience to vegetarians and vegans. Top-quality organic ingredients are used in uncomplicated but imaginative dishes that take their inspiration from around the world. Think a kashmiri curry of potato, okra, cauliflower and yogurt topped with almonds and served with rice, aubergine chutney and poppadoms, or perhaps a black bean taco – a corn tortilla filled with spicy black beans and served with grilled sweet potato, chilli corn rice, blackened tomato sauce, leaf salad, guacamole and sour cream. A takeaway service is also available.

Times: 12.30–3/6.30–11,
Closed 25 Dec–1 Jan (open New Year's Eve), L Mon–Sat
Prices: Main £9.50–£13.25
Directions: Telephone for directions

Hendon Hall Hotel

Modern European

Dramatic setting for modern bistro fare

Ashley Lane, Hendon, NW4 1HF
Tel: 0208 20 33341
Email: info@hendonhall.com
Website: www.hendonhall.com
Chef: Paul Sage

In more recent times, this historic mansion has been a girls' school and an RAF convalescent home, but returned to being a hotel after World War II. A dramatic, theatrical, Gothic dining room awaits, complete with a rich décor of deep reds, grand columns, high-back seating, polished-wood tables and crisp white napery. Service is delightful, while the crowd-pleasing menu offers a cosmopolitan bistro-style that's driven by quality, locally-sourced produce. Here chicken and mushroom pie or a Caesar salad might shimmy up alongside the likes of calves' liver served with caramelised onions and sage, or perhaps eight-hour lamb with roasted garlic potatoes, while desserts could feature a pineapple tart Tatin or millefeuille of white and dark chocolate.

Times: 12–2.30/7–10
Prices: Main £13–£20
Directions: M1 junct 2. A406. Right at lights onto Parson St. Next right into Ashley Lane, Hendon Hall is on right
Parking: 70

Singapore Garden Restaurant

Singaporean, Malaysian

Oriental with a mix of Chinese and Singaporean dishes

83–83a Fairfax Road, West Hampstead, NW6 4DY
Tel: 020 7328 5314
Website:
www.singaporegarden.co.uk
Chef: Kok Sum Toh
Owners: Hibiscus Restaurants Ltd

Situated in a parade of upmarket shops close to Finchley Road tube, this modern restaurant has contemporary décor and a sophisticated feel. The Lim family has built up a loyal clientele, drawn by the animated ambience and by the menu which includes a variety of authentic dishes inspired by Chinese, Malay and Singaporean cuisine. Typical dishes include starters like kuay pie tee – crispy pastry cups with bamboo shoots, chicken and prawns – followed by the likes of black pepper and butter crab, or beef rendang – slow-cooked beef in thick coconut sauce. There is a decked area outside for dining in warm weather.

Times: 12–2.45/6–10.45, Closed 4 days at Xmas
Prices: 3 Course Fixed D £23.50–£38.50 Main £7.20–£29
Directions: Off Finchley Rd, on right before Belsize Rd rdbt

Sabras Restaurant

Indian Vegetarian v

Surati restaurant serving exclusively vegetarian cooking

263 High Road, Willesden Green, NW10 2RX
Tel: 020 8459 0340

In a high street location with glass shop front looking onto the street, the interior of this restaurant is well-lit with light white and cream decor. For over 30 years it has served exclusively vegetarian cuisine from the Surati region of India, cooked with enthusiasm and skill. With a well-established reputation, the specialist cuisine draws a wide following to enjoy dishes like Ragda patish (spiced potato cake with a mild yellow pea sauce) and Makai Kaju (sweetcorn, sweet peppers and cashew nuts in a tomato sauce). If you enjoy Indian cuisine and fancy trying something a bit different this would be an excellent choice.

Times: 6–10, Closed 25–26 Dec, BH Mon, Mon, L all week
Directions: Telephone for directions

South East
London

South Bank

The Anchor & Hope

Traditional European

Lively gastro-pub with attitude

36 The Cut, SE1 8LP
Tel: 020 7928 9898
Email:
anchorandhope@btconnect.com

This popular gastro-pub is packed as soon as the doors open and, as there's no booking, it's a case of turning up early and waiting for a table. Wooden floors, bare walls, an open kitchen and a buzzy, lively yet relaxed atmosphere set the scene. A heavy curtain separates the bar from the restaurant area, though it's a similarly sociable affair with close-set tables that you may have to share. The menus show an equally rustic simplicity with their fresh quality ingredients and uncompromising flavours. Perhaps try cabbage, white bean and preserved pork soup, or rare roast venison, duck fat potato cake, bacon and chestnuts, with a pear and almond tart or pannacotta and rhubarb to follow.

Times: 12–2.30/6–10.30, Closed BHs, 25 Dec–1 Jan, Sun, L Mon
Directions: Telephone for directions

Baltic

Eastern European

Stylish, authentic Eastern European restaurant

74 Blackfriars Road, SE1 8HA
Tel: 020 7928 1111
Email: info@balticrestaurant.co.uk
Website:
www.balticrestaurant.co.uk
Chef: Peter Resinski
Owners: Jan Woroniecki

A striking chandelier made of shards of amber dominates this otherwise minimalist open-plan restaurant. Light pours in through the roof windows, while beams give a rustic feel to the stylish space. Vodka cocktails, jazz and an extensive Eastern European menu appeal to a trendy, friendly crowd. Start with blini and caviar, smoked eel and bacon salad, or Polish black sausage with pickled cabbage. Mains take in roast saddle of wild boar and cranberries, wiener shnitzel with beetroot and shallot salad, and pan-fried sea bass with fennel and tomatoes. Nalesniki (crêpes stuffed with sweet cheese, almonds and raisins) is an appealingly authentic way to finish.

Times: 12–3.30/6–11, Closed Xmas, 1 Jan, BHs
Prices: 3 Course Fixed D £28.50
Main £13.50–£18.50
Directions: Opposite Southwark station, 5 mins walk from Waterloo

Cantina del Ponte

Italian

Trendy riverside Italian

The Butlers Wharf Building,
36c Shad Thames, SE1 2YE
Tel: 020 7403 5403
Email:
cantina@conran-restaurants.co.uk
Website: www.conran.com/eat

A heated terrace overlooking the river Thames affords plenty of opportunities for people- and boat-watching alike. Inside a large mural of a Mediterranean marketplace gives an indication of the gastronomic experience in store. The lengthy, seasonally-changing menu comprises a good range of rustic Italian dishes with strong, robust flavours. Tuck into the likes of pumpkin and prosciutto gnocchi, grilled grey mullet or veal osso buco. A decadent chocolate and pistachio tart with pistachio ice cream could be washed down with a glass of Vin Santo. Factor in the sunset over Tower Bridge and you have the recipe for a very romantic evening.

Times: 12–3/6–11, Closed
24–26 Dec
Directions: SE side of Tower
Bridge, on riverfront

Cantina Vinopolis

Mediterranean

Delightful dishes to complement the wine cellar tours

1 Bank End, SE1 9BU
Tel: 020 7940 8333
Email: info@cantinavinopolis.com
Website:
www.cantinavinopolis.com
Chef: Moges A Wolde
Owners: Claudio Pulge,
Trevor Guppier

The wine-related attraction, Vinopolis, is located in the cavernous old railway vaults on Bankside by the Thames, with a large glass entrance and cocktail lounge. The restaurant is set against a backdrop of vaulted arches with an open-plan kitchen at the far end. Produce comes fresh from Borough Market next door and is carefully prepared, accurately cooked and served in traditional style with influences that embrace French, Italian and North African cuisine. A tian of grilled Mediterranean vegetables and mozzarella cheese with herb and balsamic vinaigrette, or Spanish black pudding with chorizo and potato salad and shallot vinaigrette deliver simple and true flavours, while desserts take in the likes of upside-down apple and polenta cake with vanilla ice cream. The wine list reflects Vinopolis expertise and offers great value.

Times: 12–3/6–10.30, Closed BHs,
D Sun
Prices: Main £10.50–£18.50
Directions: 5 min walk from
London Bridge on Bankside
between Southwark Cathedral
& Shakespeare's Globe Theatre

Champor-Champor

Modern Pacific Rim

Creative Malaysian cooking in ethnic surroundings

62–64 Weston Street, SE1 3QJ
Tel: 020 7403 4600
Email:
mail@champor-champor.com
Website:
www.champor-champor.com
Chef: Adu Amran Hassan
Owners: Champor-Champor Ltd

Champor-Champor means 'mix-and-match' in Malay, and this applies to the bohemian décor as well as the food of this intimate and atmospheric restaurant. Forgive the side street location behind London Bridge Station as, once through the door, vivid colours, tribal artefacts and Buddhist statues mingle with modern art and the whiff of incense in the busily decorated space. The creative cooking follows the theme, with its mix of Asian flavours grafted on to Malay roots; think cream of Cantonese roast duck soup and roast fillet of ostrich with black pepper sauce and sweet potato mash.

Times: 6.15–10.15, Closed
Xmas-New Year (7 days), Etr
(5 days), BHs, L Times may vary
Prices: 3 Course Fixed D £26–£30
Directions: Joiner St exit. Left
onto Saint Thomas St & 1st right
into Weston St, restaurant 100yds
on left

The County Hall Restaurant

Modern British

Stunning Thames setting in the heart of Westminster

London Marriott Hotel,
Westminster Bridge Road,
SE1 7PB
Tel: 020 7902 8000
Website: www.marriotthotels.
com/marriott/lonch
Chef: Craig Carew-Wootton
Owners: Marriott International

Formerly the members' reading room of County Hall, the restaurant here is a high-ceilinged, oak-panelled room facing the Palace of Westminster and Big Ben, looking out across the River Thames. It's a wonderful setting by day or by night and the formal feel is reflected in high levels of staffing and classical, but friendly and informative, service. The dishes on the fixed-price menu and carte are modern British with European influences. Main courses might include fillets of John Dory with brown shrimp risotto, broad beans and basil sauce, or pumpkin gnocchi, wilted spinach, goat's cheese and walnut sauce.

Times: 12–2.30/6–10.30, Closed
D 26 Dec
Prices: 3 Course Fixed D £23–£25
Main £16–£25.50
Directions: Situated next to
Westminster Bridge on the South
Bank. Opposite Houses
of Parliament

The Fire Station

Modern European

Bustling gastro-pub close to Waterloo station

150 Waterloo Road,
SE1 8SB
Tel: 020 7620 2226
Email: firestation.waterloo@
pathfinderpubs.co.uk
Website:
www.pathfinderpubs.co.uk

Converted brick-built fire station with a bar area at the front and particularly large windows – once the drive-in doors for the fire engines – with a spacious dining area and an open-plan kitchen to the rear. Rough red-brick walls are adorned with fire service paraphernalia. It is an unpretentious pub setting offering speedy service of fresh, seasonal, quality food, mostly cooked to order – Fire Station fish platter (to share as a main course), roast pork belly, crème brûlée – to a crowd of regulars. Food is served from midday, and bar snacks are also available. There's an extensive list of easy drinking, good value wines.

Times: 12–3/5.30–11
Directions: Adjacent to
Waterloo station

The London Eye

57

Magdalen

European

Classy, new restaurant with French-influenced cooking

With its burgundy décor, bentwood chairs, mirrors and enormous sprays of fresh flowers, there is a deceptively French feel to this popular two-storey restaurant. The food, however, has a British foundation with European influences and the daily-changing menu is fiercely seasonal, with much of the produce sourced from nearby Borough Market. There are Mediterranean flourishes in a starter of hot foie gras with caramelised blood oranges or a main course of roast cod with white beans and garlic leaves, while pork and pigeon terrine, venison and trotter pie and treacle tart and cream are gutsy dishes with a strong British accent. A notable, French-biased wine list includes many options by the carafe.

152 Tooley Street, SE1 2TU
Tel: 020 7403 1342
Email: info@magdalenrestaurant.co.uk
Website: www.magdalenrestaurant.co.uk
Chef: James Faulks, Emma Faulks, David Abbott
Owners: Roger Faulks & James Faulks

Times: 12–2.30/6.30–10.30, Closed Xmas, BHs, 2wks Aug, Sun, L Mon
Directions: 5 min walk from London Bridge end of Tooley Street. Restaurant opposite Unicorn Theatre

The Oxo Tower Restaurant

Modern European v

A 'top of the world' feel with innovative food

Echoing the design of a 1930s ocean liner, this stylish modern restaurant is beautiful in its simplicity. Situated on the eighth floor with glass down both sides, it features a unique louvred ceiling with blue neon lights which creates a beautiful moonlit effect in the evenings. There's also a long open terrace enabling diners to take full advantage of the stunning views over the Thames and St Paul's, and leather-clad bars, slate tables and original art all add to the luxurious feel. The innovative menu features a series of classics with a twist, as well as a sprinkling of dishes combining Mediterranean/Pacific Rim and French/Asian ingredients. Tempting descriptions highlight each dish's many component parts, as in a starter of salt-and-pepper cuttlefish with watermelon, or sea bass with confit garlic-braised haricot beans, roasted cherry tomatoes and truffle oil mascarpone.

8th Floor, Oxo Tower Wharf, Barge House Street, SE1 9PH
Tel: 020 7803 3888
Email: oxo.reservations@harveynichols.co.uk
Website: www.harveynichols.com
Chef: Jeremy Bloor
Owners: Harvey Nichols & Co Ltd

Times: 12–2.30/6–11, Closed 25–26 Dec, D 24 Dec
Prices: Main £16.50–£26
Directions: Between Blackfriars & Waterloo Bridge

Le Pont de la Tour

Traditional French

Wharfside restaurant with unbeatable views

A popular waterfront wharf location with stunning views of Tower Bridge, especially at night when it's floodlit. The terrace is busy in summer as diners flock to watch the action on the river, while inside diners seem to step into the luxury world of a cruise liner. Smart table settings, clean lines and well-dressed staff set the tone for some serious cooking. The French menu offers an extensive choice of dishes, drawing on traditional ingredients like a terrine of foie gras maison with Armagnac jelly to start. There's lots of fresh fish, crustacea or caviars, while meat options might feature a rump of lamb with spiced aubergine caviar and sauce vièrge. There's an impressive and extensive wine list, too.

The Butlers Wharf Building,
36d Shad Thames, SE1 2YE
Tel: 020 7403 8403
Website:
www.lepontdelatour.co.uk
Chef: James Walker
Owners: Conran Restaurants

Times: 12–3/6–11
Prices: Main £13.50–£35.50
Directions: SE of Tower Bridge

The Oxo Tower Restaurant

Roast

British 🍷 NOTABLE WINE LIST

Airy modern restaurant above Borough Market

The Floral Hall, Borough Market,
Stoney Street, SE1 1TL
Tel: 020 7940 1300
Email: info@roast-restaurant.com
Website:
www.roast-restaurant.com
Chef: Lawrence Keogh
Owners: Iqbal Wahhab

Borough Market provides the atmospheric setting for this first-floor establishment, with views of the hubbub below from the bar and over to St Paul's Cathedral from its glass-fronted dining room. The floral portico featured in the dining room was bought from Covent Garden for £1 by Borough Market trustees. Menus make good use of quality produce in classic British dishes. Think roast Banham chicken with bread sauce and Ayrshire bacon, Inverawe smoked Loch Etive trout with watercress and lemon, or roast Welsh black sirloin. Breakfast and afternoon tea are served, and there's a superb cocktail list.

Times: 12–3/5.30–11, Closed
D Sun
Prices: Main £12.95–£25
Directions: Please telephone
for directions

RSJ *The Restaurant on the South Bank*

Modern British

Perfect pre-theatre dining

33 Coin Street, SE1 9NR
Tel: 020 7928 4554
Email: sally.webber@rsj.uk.com
Website: www.rsj.uk.com

Long-established, simple, modern restaurant, popular with media types and theatre- or concert-goers from the adjacent South Bank. Friendly staff keep everything moving efficiently with an eye on performance times. The menu changes monthly or more frequently, reflecting a passion for fresh seasonal produce. With Loire Valley wines a speciality, there are wine events from time to time. The cuisine makes good use of fine quality ingredients to deliver carefully prepared, attractively presented dishes, like wild halibut served with truffled wild mushroom coquiette, and perhaps a raspberry crème brûlée to finish.

Times: 12–2/5.30–11, Closed
Xmas, 1 Jan, Sun, L Sat
Directions: Telephone for
directions

Chapter Two

Chapter Two

Modern European

Prominent and stylish heathside restaurant

This little gem is a place you'll want to return to again and again. Chic, modern and split-level, the glass-fronted restaurant's small ground-floor dining room is visible from the street, while a spiral staircase connects it to a basement space and bar. Decked out with slashes of vibrant colours, lightwood floors and chrome, mirrors add to the feeling of lightness and space, while banquette seating and high-backed chairs bear out the modern styling. Service is equally slick, but friendly and well informed. The kitchen's approach is thoroughly imaginative, with accurate, skilful cooking displaying culinary pedigree, utilising produce of high quality and delivering clean flavours – and all this at affordable prices. Expect the likes of wild halibut with coco beans and a fumet of fennel and shellfish, and desserts such as a hot chocolate fondant with blackberry coulis and stout and currant ice cream.

43-45 Montpelier Vale,
Blackheath Village, SE3 0TJ
Tel: 020 8333 2666
Email:
richard@chaptersrestaurants.co.uk
Website:
www.chapterrestaurants.co.uk
Chef: Trevor Tobin
Owners: Selective Restaurants
Group

Times: 12–2.30/6.30–10.30,
Closed 2–4 Jan
Prices: Main £11.95–£12.95
Directions: 5 mins from Blackheath
Village train station

61

Laicram Thai Restaurant

Thai v

Authentic Thai in a cosy setting

1 Blackheath Grove,
Blackheath, SE3 0DD
Tel: 020 8852 4710
Chef: Mrs S Dhirabutra
Owners: Mr D Dhirabutra

This Thai restaurant of long-standing is in the centre of Blackheath village, enjoying a fine reputation in the area for good food and being easy on the wallet. The décor has a homely feel, with understated Thai touches such as prints of the Thai royal family on the walls and typically welcoming and friendly service from the staff. The menu consists largely of mainstream Thai dishes such as green curry, prawn satay, fishcakes, phat Thai noodles goong pau (grilled prawns in a spicy sauce), and pla neung (steamed sea bass with lime sauce and fresh chilli).

Times: 12–2.30/6–11,
Closed Xmas & BHs, Mon
Prices: Main £5.80–£13.90
Directions: Off main shopping street, in a side road near the Post Office. Opposite station, near library

---

Rivington Bar & Grill

British, European v

Buzzy surroundings for simple British food

178 Greenwich High Road,
Greenwich, SE10 8NN
Tel: 020 8293 9270
Email:
greenwich@rivingtongrill.co.uk
Website: www.rivingtongrill.co.uk

Right next to the Greenwich Picture House, this converted pub – sibling to the sister establishment of the same name in Shoreditch (see entry on page 31 – delivers the blueprint lively, informal brasserie act. It's decked out in informal style, with dark wooden floors, white-washed walls and white paper-clothed tables, which offer the perfect backdrop for the kitchen's simple, seasonal, modern British cooking. With a separate vegetarian menu available, quality raw materials shine in dishes like Wetherall's Blackface mutton and turnip pie, or perhaps Glen Fyne steak and chips, and a Bakewell tart to finish. There's a small alfresco terrace and a mezzanine level above the ground floor.

Times: 12–3/6.30–11

Beauberry House

French, Japanese v

Contemporary French meets oriental fusion food

Gallery Road, SE21 7AB
Tel: 020 8299 9788
Website: www.circagroupltd.co.uk
Chef: Jerome Tauvron
Owners: Ibi Issolah

Pure white décor – with tables all turned out in their best whites and set against a juicy orange floor and chairs – provides the stylish setting for this French meets East Asian fusion restaurant. The beautiful Georgian mansion (formerly Belair House) is set in leafy parkland near Dulwich village, its revamped interiors respecting the classical features while adding bags of contemporary pizzazz. Outdoor terraces abound for alfresco dining with views over gardens and lawns, while service is attentive and informed. The kitchen's fittingly contemporary approach delivers French cuisine with oriental influences using top-quality ingredients; take lobster tempura served with ponzu and wasabi mayonnaise, or flash-fried wagyu beef fillet with black truffles.

Times: 12–3/6–11, Closed Xmas, 1 Jan, Mon, D Sun
Prices: 3 Course Fixed D £17.50
Main £13.50–£22
Directions: Telephone for directions
Parking: 40

Franklins

British

Smart restaurant and popular pub operation

157 Lordship Lane, SE22 8HX
Tel: 020 8299 9598
Email:
info@franklinsrestaurant.com
Website:
www.franklinsrestaurant.com
Chef: Tim Sheehan
Owners: Tim Sheehan & Rodney Franklin

A traditional pub on the outside, Franklins opens off Lordship Lane into a well-frequented locals' bar where the open-all-day policy attracts a posse of regulars. A few paces beyond this atmospheric space is the bright bistro-style restaurant where diners can glimpse all the kitchen drama through a wide hatch. Seasonal produce from in and around the UK dominates the carte, with its daily-changing set lunch menu offering excellent value for money. Traditional English favourites like Old Spot belly with fennel and black pudding, Glamorgan sausages, and mutton faggots with pease pudding will be found alongside guinea fowl with butter beans and chorizo.

Times: 12/12, Closed 25–26, 31 Dec, 1 Jan
Prices: Main £10.50–£18
Directions: Please telephone for directions

The Palmerston

Modern British

Popular gastro-pub close to Dulwich village

91 Lordship Lane,
East Dulwich, SE22 8EP
Tel: 020 8693 1629
Email: thepalmerston@tiscali.co.u
Website:
www.thepalmerston.co.uk
Chef: Jamie Younger
Owners: Jamie Younger,
Paul Rigby, Remi Olajoyegbe

There are pubs aplenty in trendy Lordship Lane, but few have reinvented themselves as successfully as this one. Behind the pastel-painted exterior, the long bar and separate dining area – each warmed by an open fire in winter – are wood-panelled, brightly coloured and welcoming. But the real delight is the food, a homage to fresh, carefully sourced ingredients deftly handled without a hint of artifice. Expect to find potted beef with pickled beetroot, grilled veal chop with celeriac remoulade and sauce charcuterie, and perhaps a homely rhubarb and custard tart with rhubarb compôte to finish. The set lunch is a real bargain.

Times: 12–2.30/7–midnight,
Closed 25–26 Dec, 1 Jan
Prices: Main £11–£16.50
Directions: 2m from Clapham,
0.5m from Dulwich Village, 10min
walk from East Dulwich station

Babur

Indian

Contemporary Indian restaurant

119 Brockley Rise,
Forest Hill, SE23 1JP
Tel: 020 8291 2400
Email: mail@babur.info
Website: www.babur.info
Chef: Enam Rahman & Jiwan Lal
Owners: Babur 1998 Ltd

This popular brasserie has been serving southeast London for over 20 years. Easily identified by the life-size, prowling Bengal tiger on its roof, inside the restaurant has been fully renovated and expanded. The décor is stylish and modern with a contemporary ethnic feel, eye-catching artwork and exposed Victorian brickwork adding to the ambience. The menu includes unusual options such as ostrich and kangaroo and is dotted with tiger heads to indicate the intensity of the chilli heat expected. One head equals hot and two means roaring hot! Start perhaps with ostrich infused with sandlewood and fenugreek, then follow with medallions of monkfish in a spicy tomato masala, or whole lobster with tomato and onion Madeira sauce. The selection of home-made chutneys is exquisite.

Times: 12.30–2.30/6–11.30,
Closed 25–26 Dec
Prices: Main £8.95–£16.95
Directions: 5 mins walk from
Honor Oak Station, where parking
is available

3 Monkeys Restaurant

ndian

Contemporary neighbourhood Indian

136-140 Herne Hill, SE24 9QH
Tel: 020 7738 5500
Email:
info@3monkeysrestaurant.com
Website:
www.30monkeysrestaurant.com
Chef: Raminder Malhotra
Owners: Kuldeep Singh,
Raminder Malhotr

Arranged over two levels with stripped wooden floors, white walls - replete with attractive modern artwork – and furniture draped in white cotton, this is certainly not your run-of-the-mill curry house, but a cool, calm, elegant restaurant. Staff are knowledgeable and happy to make recommendations to those less au fait with the cuisine of the sub-continent, with menus offering a delightful cross-section of authentic regional Indian cuisine. With a state-of-the-art open grill as the centre of attraction, dishes can include methi murgh (chicken sautéed with fresh fenugreek in dry ginger powder flavoured with tomato and onion), or macher malabar (fish stewed in coconut milk with curry leaves and tamarind). Takeaways are also available.

Times: 12–2.30/6–11, Closed Xmas
Prices: 3 Course Fixed D £15.95–£22 Main £7.25–£14.95
Directions: Adjacent to Herne Hill Station

Babur

South West London

Hyde Park

Al Duca

Modern Italian

Straightforward Italian cooking just off Piccadilly

This smart, modern Italian, conveniently situated in St James's, draws the crowds with its affordable pricing, contemporary good looks and buzzy atmosphere. Etched glass, neutral tones and leather banquettes cut a stylish but relaxed edge, while feature wine racks set into the wall catch the eye, and patio-style windows fold back for an alfresco look in summer. Straightforward, unpretentious and enjoyable Italian cooking is the kitchen's style, skilfully combining the freshest ingredients to bring out the best of the wide range of traditional dishes, some with a modern twist. Think braised osso buco with Sardinian couscous and leeks, or perhaps pan-fried fillet of wild sea bass with basil-scented courgettes and grilled radicchio, while pre- and post-theatre menus and an all-Italian wine list bolster the fixed-price carte.

4–5 Duke of York Street,
SW1Y 6LA
Tel: 020 7839 3090
Email:
info@alduca-restaurant.co.uk
Website:
www.alduca-restaurant.co.uk
Chef: Aron Johnson
Owners: Cuisine Collection

Times: 12–2.30/6–11, Closed Christmas, New Year, BHs, Sun
Prices: 3 Course Fixed D £26.50
Directions: 5 mins walk from station towards Piccadilly. Right into St James, left into Jermyn St. Duke of York St halfway along on right

Amaya

Indian v

Entertaining kitchen theatre with South Asian food

The pink sandstone panels, hardwood floors and rosewood furniture of this smart contemporary Indian grill are flooded with light from its glass atrium. Indian statuary and glass plates add to the vibrant ambience created by the open-plan theatre kitchen where chefs marinate meats or labour over tandoors or sigris – charcoal grills. Dishes are mostly Northwest Indian in style but regional dishes also figure, with the emphasis on clean, clear flavours and combinations and modern presentation. Many dishes are offered in small or mains sizes, so you might start with griddled diver-caught king scallops in a light green herb sauce, and to follow, perhaps tandoori monkfish tikka served with fenugreek leaf and turmeric, or grilled lamb chops with ginger, lime and coriander. Finish with a coconut crème brûlée with tamarind sauce.

Halkin Arcade, Motcomb Street,
SW1X 8JT
Tel: 020 7823 1166
Email: amaya@realindianfood.com
Website: www.realindianfood.com
Chef: Karunesh Khanna
Owners: R Mathrani, C Panjabi, N Panjabi

Times: 12–2.30/6–11.15,
Closed 25 Dec
Prices: 2 Course Fixed D £37.50–£55 Main £6.50–£20
Directions: Please telephone for directions

Aslan

Modern British
Modern food in an elevated dining room

Cavendish London, 81 Jermyn Street, SW1Y 6JF
Tel: 020 7930 2111
Email: info@thecavendishlondon.com
Website: www.thecavendishlondon.com
Chef: David Britton, Gretano Monteriso
Owners: De Vere Hotels & Leisure Ltd

Located in the stylish Cavendish London Hotel, the restaurant enjoys an enviable location in the prestigious St James's area of central London. The restaurant is situated on the first floor, with large plate-glass windows that take full advantage of the views, while the dark woods, beige and caramel colour scheme create a relaxed atmosphere. The menu is contemporary modern British with European influences. You might start with pan-fried Scottish sea scallops with Jerusalem artichoke purée, before moving on to the likes of grilled sea bass fillet with crushed potatoes, spinach and saffron dressing.

Times: 12–2.30/5.30–10.30, Closed 25–26 Dec, 1 Jan, L Sat & Sun
Prices: Main £14.50–£21.50
Parking: 60

The Avenue

European
Buzzy, contemporary bar and restaurant

7-9 St James's Street, SW1A 1EE
Tel: 020 7321 2111
Email: avenue@egami.co.uk
Website: www.egami.co.uk
Chef: Richard Bannister
Owners: Image Restaurants

This large, cavernous, starkly minimalist brasserie makes an ever-popular St James's destination, and reverberates with a buzzy atmosphere. High ceilings come decked out with recessed spots, plain white walls donned with large colourful modern art and floors clad in limestone. There's a long bar up front, while trendy dining chairs come in white or grey and tables clothed in white linen. The lengthy brasserie-format menu offers a straightforward, uncomplicated modern approach, blending the more contemporary alongside classics. Take halibut served with crayfish mash and leek frittata, or goujons of cod with tartare sauce.

Times: 12–3/5.45–11.30, Closed 25–26 Dec, 1 Jan, Sun, L Sat
Prices: 3 Course Fixed D £20.95
Directions: Turn right past The Ritz, 2nd turning into St James's St. Telephone for further details

Bank Westminster

Modern British

Ultra-modern, stylish hotel dining, brasserie style

Crowne Plaza London St James,
Buckingham Gate, SW1E 6AF
Tel: 020 7630 6630

Set in the heart of Westminster and the prestigious St James's area
– only a few minutes' walk from Buckingham Palace – the Crowne
Plaza is a fittingly elegant Victorian hotel. Its Bank restaurant is
accessed via the street or hotel lobby, while the adjacent and
stylish Zander cocktail bar boasts the longest bar in town. Bank is
ultra modern too, and shaped in semi-circular format, with glass
windows and one side overlooking a delightful courtyard. The
kitchen deals in fresh, vibrant modern-brasserie-style fare; take
roast monkfish with Serrano ham, served with squid, asparagus
and tomato salsa.

Times: 12-3/5.30-11 (Mon-Sat),
11.30-3 Sun (brunch only)
Directions: Telephone for
directions

Boisdale of Belgravia

British

Traditional, clubby but fun Scottish restaurant

15 Eccleston Street, SW1W 9LX
Tel: 020 7730 6922
Email: info@boisdale.co.uk
Website: www.boisdale.co.uk
Chef: Colin Wint
Owners: Mr R Macdonald

A determinedly Scottish experience is delivered at this Belgravia
restaurant-cum-whisky and cigar bar, with its deep reds and
greens, tartan, dark floorboards and panelled, picture-laden walls.
There is an endearingly clubby atmosphere to its labyrinth of
dining areas and bars, and live jazz adds to the atmosphere in the
evenings. The Caledonian menu supports the theme with Dunkeld
oak-smoked salmon, ravioli of Western Isles king scallops, a daily
game dish, and 28-day matured Scottish beef served with a wide
choice of sauces and accompaniments. Desserts tempt with the
likes of warm pear and fig tart served with prune and Armagnac
ice cream, or hot chocolate cake with Banyuls syrup.

Times: 12–2.30/7–11.15, Closed
Xmas, New Year, Easter, BHs, Sun,
L Sat
Prices: 2 Course Fixed D £17.80
Main £14.50–£28.50
Directions: Turn left along
Buckingham Palace Rd heading W,
Eccleston St is 1st on right

Boxwood Café

British **v** NOTABLE WINE LIST

Upmarket brasserie in high-class hotel

From the Gordon Ramsay stable, this upmarket interpretation of a New York-style café predictably oozes class, located on one corner of The Berkeley Hotel with its own street entrance on Knightsbridge. The elegant dining room is a stylish, split-level basement affair, with a bar and smart table settings. Natural earthy tones parade alongside golds and bronzes and lashings of darkwood and leather, while service is youthful, slick but relaxed, and there's a vibrant metropolitan buzz. The accomplished kitchen's upmarket brasserie repertoire hits the spot, utilising high-quality seasonal ingredients with the emphasis on flavour, innovative combination and stylish presentation; think braised fillet of wild halibut served with baked potato gnocchi, peas, broad beans and courgette flower.

The Berkeley Hotel, Wilton Place, Knightsbridge, SW1X 7RL
Tel: 020 7235 1010
Email: boxwoodcafe@gordonramsay.com
Website: www.gordonramsay.com
Chef: Stuart Gillies
Owners: Gordon Ramsay Holdings Ltd

Times: 12–3/6–11
Prices: Main £16–£28
Directions: Please telephone for directions

Brasserie Roux

French

Stylish brasserie serving rustic French cuisine

This vibrant, elegant, high-ceilinged brasserie set within the Sofitel St James hotel comes with stylish Pierre Yves Rochon design. Its main decorative theme, the cockerel, is the logo of this former banking hall's owners (Cox's & King's) and also, of course, the symbol of France. Bright red leather chairs, pale yellow walls, huge lampshades and bare-wood tables embody the modern, chic but relaxed styling, backed by friendly and knowledgeable service. The traditional, wholesome, unfussy French regional cuisine fits the authentic brasserie style, offering classics that utilise quality produce with flavour at their heart – as in mussels with a light curry sauce, duck cassoulet, lemon sole with hollandaise and clafoutis with prunes and Armagnac.

Sofitel St James London, 6 Waterloo Place, LONDON SW1 SW1Y 4AN
Tel: 020 7968 2900
Email: h3144-fb8@accor.com
Website: www.sofitelstjames.com
Chef: Paul Danabie
Owners: Accor UK

Times: 12–3/5.30–11
Prices: 3 Course Fixed D £15–£24.50 Main £9–£22
Directions: Telephone for directions

Le Caprice Restaurant

Modern European v

Quality cooking in a place that brings out the stars

Arlington House,
Arlington Street, SW1A 1RT
Tel: 020 7629 2239
Website: www.le-caprice.co.uk

This classy restaurant has been a darling of the celebrity circuit for many years. The interior is predominantly black and white, photography by David Bailey, large mirrors and comfortable seating at fairly closely set tables. There are no airs and graces here, and friendly waiting staff treat all guests with the same even-handed respect. Cooking is based on excellent produce and the comprehensive European menu offers comfort eating to appeal to every taste: aubergine and mozzarella ravioli; griddled tiger prawns with wild garlic; pan-fried gilt-head sea bream with lemon and herb butter; chargrilled quails with butternut squash, pancetta and oregano. Sunday brunch is a popular option with pitchers of Bloody Mary or Buck's fizz. Separate vegetarian menu available.

Times: 12–3/5.30–12, Closed 25–26 Dec, 1 Jan, Aug BH, D 24 Dec
Prices: Main £14.25–£26.50
Directions: Arlington St runs beside The Ritz. Restaurant is at end

---

Caraffini

Traditional Italian

Busy, lively traditional Italian

61–63 Lower Sloane Street, SW1W 8DH
Tel: 020 7259 0235
Email: info@caraffini.co.uk
Website: www.caraffini.co.uk
Chef: John Patino, S Ramalhoto
Owners: F di Rienzo & Paolo Caraffini

Close to fashionable Sloane Square, a large white awning picks out this smart and welcoming Chelsea Italian. Frequented by a sophisticated clientele of locals and visitors, its pastel yellow walls are hung with contemporary watercolours and mirrors, and blond-wood floorboards, blue banquettes and upholstered rattan-style chairs help cut a sunny, relaxed atmosphere. The eclectic carte is bolstered by daily specials and all-Italian wines, presented in Italian with English subtitles. Modern overtones are evident in classic regional dishes, with an emphasis on simplicity, freshness and flavour. Take a starter of tiger prawns in hot chilli and olive oil, followed by fresh scallops flavoured with spinach and mushrooms.

Times: 12.15–2.30/6.30–11.30, Closed BHs, Xmas, Sun
Prices: Main £8.75–£20.95
Directions: Please telephone for directions

Le Cercle

Modern French

Discreet restaurant offering modern French food

Close to Sloane Square, this discreet basement restaurant continues to pull in the punters. The dining areas combine a sense of refined intimacy with a surprising spaciousness, accentuated by the high ceilings, neutral colour scheme and artful lighting. The glass-fronted wine cave and cheese room provide suitable stages to highlight two French passions celebrated here, while the menu offers a good overview of the rest of Gallic gastronomy. Dishes such as haddock fillet, smoked carrot emulsion and pickled carrot, or squid ink tagliatelle with shellfish and spinach velouté are cooked with aplomb, with small but perfectly-formed portions and refined presentation. An extensive wine list and the menu have many recommendations for wines by the glass to accompany each course.

1 Wilbraham Place,
SW1X 9AE
Tel: 020 7901 9999
Email: info@lecercle.co.uk
Chef: Thierry Beyris
Owners: Vincent Labeyrie &
Pascal Aussignac

Times: 12–3/6–11, Closed Xmas
& New Year, Sun, Mon
Prices: 5 Course Fixed D £17.50
Main £5.50–£7.50
Directions: Just off Sloane St

The Cinnamon Club

Indian

Sophisticated Indian dining in former library

The former Westminster library makes an unusual setting for a contemporary Indian restaurant. Polished parquet floors, dark wood, high ceilings, domed skylights and a gallery of books retain the building's heritage and old English charm. The restaurant has a clubby feel with high-backed suede chairs and crisp white tablecloths, all very simple and elegant. Traditional Indian cuisine is based around fine ingredients and well-judged spicing. Breakfast, lunch, pre- and post-theatre and carte menus offer a wide selection of dishes. Try dishes such as chargrilled duck breast with cloves and star anise with apple chutney, or wild African prawns baked with 'kasundi' mustard with lemon rice. A good choice of desserts features date pancake with vanilla and toasted coconut ice cream.

The Old Westminster Library,
Great Smith Street, SW1P 3BU
Tel: 020 7222 2555
Email: info@cinnamonclub.com
Website: www.cinnamonclub.com

Times: 12–3/6–11, Closed Xmas,
Etr, BHs, Sun, L Sat
Directions: Take exit 6, across
Parliament Sq, then pass
Westminster Abbey on left.
Take 1st left into Great Smith St

Drones

Drones

Traditional French

Classy Belgravia venue with experience factor

This classic from the Marco Pierre White stable oozes style, glamour and confidence. Walls are lined with black and white photographs of showbiz legends – think David Niven and Audrey Hepburn – while floors are polished parquet, there's leather banquette seating, tables are white clothed and service is slick and attentive. The discreet glass frontage is hung with Venetian blinds, while there's an eye-catching bar and art-deco style wall lighting. The crisply scripted, lengthy menu parades a repertoire of classic French dishes using quality ingredients and an assured, intelligent, straightforward style. Expect Dover sole à la meunière or perhaps a grilled veal chop with sage and butter. Desserts like a Harvey's lemon tart or crème brûlée catch the eye too, while the fixed-price lunch is great value.

1 Pont Street, SW1X 9EJ
Tel: 020 7235 9555
Email: sales@whitestarline.org.uk
Website:
www.whitestarline.org.uk
Chef: Joseph Croan
Owners: Marco Pierre White,
Jimmy Lahoud

Times: 12–2.30/6–11, Closed
26 Dec, 1 Jan, L Sat, D Sun
Prices: Main £14.50–£24.50

The Ebury

British, French

Fashionable, buzzy Pimlico eatery

This large, smart, contemporary bar-brasserie-restaurant certainly stands out from the crowd. On the ground floor there's a lively bar, crustacea counter and stylish, low-slung brown leather seating for more relaxed dining, while the upstairs restaurant has a more formal, romantic feel. An equally modern confection, the upstairs restaurant comes decked out in white linen with cream leather seating, stunning chandeliers and photographs of jazz legends. A glass window allows glimpses into the kitchen, while service is slick, professional and friendly. The refined, modern brasserie-style repertoire is underpinned by a classical French theme, driven by quality ingredients, clear flavours and creative presentation. Take roast rump of lamb served with boulangère potatoes and caramelised onion purée, or hot chocolate fondant with peanut ice cream and honeycomb.

11 Pimlico Road, SW1W 8NA
Tel: 020 7730 6784
Email: info@theebury.co.uk
Website: www.theebury.co.uk

Times: 12–3.30/6–10.30,
Closed 24–30 Dec
Directions: From Sloane Sq Tube left into Holbein Place, then left at intersection with Pimlico Rd. The Ebury is on right on corner of Pimlico Rd & Ranelagh Grove. From Victoria, left down Buckingham Palace Rd, then right onto Pimlico Rd

---

Fifth Floor Restaurant

French, European ⚜NOTABLE WINE LIST

Star-studded dining at top London store

Dine in style on the fifth floor of one of London's most fashionable stores. This contemporary space high above the Knightsbridge traffic is as chic as it is comfortable, with designer white leather chairs and feature lighting creating a relaxed, intimate ambience. The new Swedish-born head chef brings Scandinavian flair to the menus, making the most of seasonal flavoursome ingredients. Lunch, dinner, tasting and weekend brunch menus are all available, as well as a new market menu that utilises produce from the food market. Kick off with Bassett stilton with toasted walnuts, wild rocket and olive oil, followed by Shetland organic cod with marinated white anchovies, mange tout, hazelnut salad and Janson's temptation. Round things off in style with pineapple cannelloni, served with passionfruit mousse, French meringue and mascarpone.

Harvey Nichols, 109-125 Knightsbridge, SW1X 7RJ
Tel: 020 7235 5250
Email: reception@harveynichols.com
Website: www.harveynichols.com
Chef: Jonas Karlsson
Owners: Harvey Nichols Ltd

Times: 12–3/6–11, Closed Xmas, D Sun
Prices: 3 Course Fixed D £24.50–£39.50 Main £14–£25
Directions: Entrance on Sloane Street

Foliage

Modern European NOTABLE WINE LIST

One of the capital's finest

Sitting opposite Harvey Nichols and backing on to Hyde Park, this imposing luxury Knightsbridge hotel fairly bristles with class. To the uninitiated, its liveried doorman and fluttering flags outside might give the impression of a grand Edwardian edifice in the old tradition, yet it's anything but. Sure there's a sumptuous marble foyer, but this is the playground of the young and fashionable, international jetsetter and highflier. Smiling greeting staff are contemporarily dressed, as are the equally fashionable bar and glass-fronted wine-store entrance to Foliage, the signature fine-dining restaurant. Chic, stylish and intimate, the restaurant's theme is all in the name, with Adam Tihany's design conceiving to 'bring the park into the restaurant'. Giant glass wall panels enclose thousands of white silk leaves that come alive with lighting and change colour to echo the seasons, while a split-level floor ensures all have a view of park life. Clean lines, striking flower displays and luxury fabrics and furnishings add to the sophisticated modern tone. These fine details support the dining room's reputation as one of London's finest under chefs David Nicholls' and Chris Staines' sublime cooking. Their approach is via an enticing repertoire of fixed-price menu options that take in a terrific-value lunch jour, carte and tasting offering. Tip-top quality, luxury ingredients grace the intricate cooking showcasing the kitchen's silky technical skills, with well-conceived, well-presented dishes of clean, clear, balanced flavours that live up to the setting and set the tastebuds alight. Think a fillet of Buccleuch beef with 24-hour braised wagyu, oysters, smoked potato purée and pickled Thai shallots, or perhaps pan-fried fillets of John Dory with crushed ratte potatoes, red pepper, tomato and clam vinaigrette and black olive oil.

Mandarin Oriental Hyde Park,
66 Knightsbridge, SW1X 7LA
Tel: 020 7235 2000
Email:
molon-reservations@mohg.com
Website: www.mandarinoriental.
com/london
Chef: David Nicholls, Chris Staines
Owners: Mandarin Oriental Hyde
Park

Times: 12–2.30/7–10.30
Prices: Fixed D £52
Directions: In Knightsbridge with
Harrods on right, hotel is 0.5m on
left, opposite Harvey Nichols

Chris Staines, Foliage

Franco's Restaurant

Italian
A classy reincarnation of an Italian institution

61 Jermyn Street, SW1Y 6LX
Tel: 020 7499 2211
Email: reserve@francoslondon.com
Website: www.francoslondon.com
Chef: Paulo Parlanti
Owners: Jason Philips

Situated in the heart of St James's, this long-established restaurant has returned to Jermyn Street refreshed and revitalised. The perfect location in which to enjoy classically-based Italian food in sumptuous surroundings, a dark green awning overhangs the part-frosted windows and some popular outside tables, while inside there are two interconnecting rooms, the 1940s-style interior complementing the Edwardian façade. You might start with Aberdeen Angus beef tartare, with raw quail's egg and baby asparagus, and for mains try pan-fried mackerel with barba di frate and porcini sauce, or maybe organic salmon, sea bass, or sirloin steak from the grill.

Times: 12–2.30/5.30–12, Closed last wk Dec, Sun, BHs
Prices: 2 Course Fixed D £30–£35 Main £10–£24
Directions: Telephone for directions

The Goring

Traditional British 🍷 NOTABLE WINE LIST
Carefully prepared food in grand hotel setting

Beeston Place, SW1W 0JW
Tel: 020 7396 9000
Email: reception@goringhotel.co.uk
Website: www.goringhotel.co.uk
Chef: Derek Quelch
Owners: Goring Family

A sumptuous and elaborate hotel done out in the grand style, as befits a traditional property in its central London location just behind Buckingham Palace. This family-owned property may be traditional in style but it's anything but stuffy with staff providing friendly and efficient service. David Linley's redesign has created a lighter, modern touch to the grand Victorian dining room, with its sumptuous silks and contemporary centrepiece 'Blossom' chandeliers. Menus are a celebration of all things British, accomplished classics using prime-quality, fresh produce. Think Dover sole (grilled or pan fried) served with new potatoes and spinach, or perhaps steak and kidney pie with cream potatoes, while there are British cheeses from the trolley and puddings like a classic custard tart.

Times: 12.30–2.30/6–10, Closed L Sat
Prices: 3 Course Fixed D £44
Directions: From Victoria St turn left into Grosvenor Gdns, cross Buckingham Palace Rd, 75yds turn right into Beeston Place
Parking: 5

78

Il Convivio

Italian

Stylish Italian dining in upmarket Belgravia

143 Ebury Street, SW1W 9QN
Tel: 020 7730 4099
Email: comments@
etruscarestaurants.com
Website:
www.etruscarestaurants.com
Chef: Lukas Pfaff
Owners: Piero & Enzo
Quaradeghini

Set in a quiet residential street in trendy Belgravia, this chic split-level restaurant has a few sought-after tables at street level, with the main restaurant and conservatory-style room on the lower level. Deep red walls hung with stone slabs inscribed with quotes from Dante's Il Convivio are set off by modern wooden-backed chairs and cream leather cushions. The upmarket Italian cuisine includes a few unconventional touches that showcase the kitchen's technical ability: a Parma ham starter arrives with home-made sweet pickled vegetables, while mains include Arctic black cod caramelised with balsamic and served with asparagus and Muscat grapes, or salt marsh lamb with black olive sauce and glazed baby turnips. A wide-ranging choice is supplemented by daily specials and an extensive wine list.

Times: 12–2.45/7–10.45, Closed Xmas, New Year, BHs, Sun
Prices: 3 Course Fixed D £32.50
Main £11–£19
Directions: 7 min walk from Victoria Station – corner of Ebury St and Elizabeth St

---

Inn the Park

British

All-day eatery in park setting

St James's Park, SW1A 1AA
Tel: 020 7451 9999
Email: info@innthepark.co.uk
Website: www.innthepark.co.uk

The long, grass-roofed, Scandinavian-style building blends invisibly into the rolling landscape of St James's Park. The cleverly named all-day eatery looks out across the lake to Duck Island and beyond to the London Eye. A café by day, with a counter for quick snacks, it becomes a restaurant at night offering simple, full-flavoured, brasserie-style dishes using quality produce from small suppliers. Expect the likes of ham hock terrine, broad beans, pea shoots and spring onion followed by roasted belly of pork, quince jam and parsnip purée. There is a super decked area for summer alfresco dining.

Times: 12–3/6–10.45, Closed D Sun–Mon (winter)
Prices: 3 Course Fixed D £27–£32
Main £12–£17.50
Directions: 200 metres down The Mall towards Buckingham Palace

Just St James

Modern British

Dining in high style in old St James's

12 St James's Street, SW1A 1ER
Tel: 020 7976 2222
Email: bookings@juststjames.com
Website: www.juststjames.com
Chef: Peter Gladwin
Owners: Peter Gladwin

The lavish, impressive, Edwardian Baroque interior with its marble columns, arched windows and corniced ceilings has been cleverly softened with contemporary styling (think suede banquette seating, modern artwork and a glass lift to a mezzanine gallery) to provide a striking setting for some accomplished modern dining. It used to be a private bank, so don't be shocked at some of the St James's prices, but then the menu comes dotted with luxury. The cooking is self-assured and stylishly presented, so open your account with a ballotine of foie gras, duck salad and toasted brioche, and perhaps baked wild halibut with a herb crust, boulangère potatoes and green beans to follow. A large, glass-topped bar and leather seating completes a class act.

Times: 12–3/6–11, Closed 25–26 Dec, 1 Jan, Sun, L Sat
Directions: Turn right on Piccadilly towards Piccadilly Circus, then right into St James's St. Restaurant on corner of St James's St & King St

Ken Lo's Memories of China

Chinese

Refined Chinese cooking close to Victoria

65-69 Ebury Street, SW1W 0NZ
Tel: 020 7730 7734
Email:
memoriesofchina@btconnect.com
Website:
www.memories-of-china.co.uk
Chef: Kam Po But
Owners: A–Z Restaurants

A well-established and popular Pimlico restaurant with a refined, upmarket feel that owes much to the very stylish table settings. Quality abounds from the starched linen to the chopsticks, and the subtle Chinese décor has a contemporary edge. A lengthy carte showcases the classic Chinese food, backed up by a set menu that offers excellent value for money from the same quality produce and refined presentations. Accurate flavours reflect the skilful handling of good raw ingredients, yielding the likes of fresh scallops steamed in shells with black bean sauce, stir-fried fresh lobster with ginger and spring onion noodles and black pepper, or maybe pan-fried medallions of beef. Service is speedy and efficient.

Times: 12–2.30/7–11, Closed BHs, L Sun
Prices: 3 Course Fixed D £30 Main £11.50–£34
Directions: At junction of Ebury St & Eccleston St

The Lanesborough

International

Park Lane grandee with a leafy conservatory

You can expect world-class luxury, stunning service and crisply-cooked traditional British food at this grand hotel on Hyde Park Corner. Sip an aperitif in the swanky cocktail bar, and then move through to the glass-roofed conservatory restaurant, where a pianist plays softly as you take a seat among exotic palms and trickling fountains, at a table set with the finest crystal and china. Quality ingredients are to the fore on the wide-ranging modern menu, and there's no shortage of skill. Kick off with lobster ravioli with provençale dressing perhaps, followed by Scottish beef fillet with shallot purée and Barolo jus, or braised halibut with rosemary truffle broth. Vegetarian dishes are a speciality – try wild herb couscous with chickpea and spinach beignets, or maybe shallot tatin with roasted squash, porcini and almonds.

Hyde Park Corner, SW1X 7TA
Tel: 020 7259 5599
Email: info@lanesborough.com
Website: www.lanesborough.com

Times: 12–2.30/6–11.30
Directions: On Hyde Park corner
Parking: 50

Luciano

Italian

Classy Italian with a touch of 'Marco' magic

The St James's collaboration between Marco Pierre White and Sir Rocco Forte, Luciano's comes brimful of class and glamour. There's a large chic bar at the front with a mosaic-tiled floor and large windows overlooking St James's Street – just the place for a pre-meal Bellini. The atmospheric restaurant – down a few steps beyond the bar – oozes style and glamour. Think provocative photograph-lined walls, slate pillars, polished-wood floors, burgundy leather banquettes and matching chairs, and eye-catching mood lighting; there's oodles of experience with an art-deco nudge in true Marco style. Smartly attired mainly Italian staff, and an Italian-dominated wine list is impressive too. Cooking is classic Italian using top-notch produce delivering straightforward, full-flavoured dishes; take ravioli of leeks and scamorza, or perhaps roast John Dory with Jerusalem artichoke and tomato.

72–73 St James's Street,
SW1A 1PH
Tel: 020 7408 1440
Email:
info@lucianorestaurant.co.uk
Website:
www.lucianorestaurant.co.uk
Chef: Marco Corsica
Owners: Marco Pierre White

Times: Please telephone for details, Closed 25–28 Dec
Prices: 3 Course Fixed D £22.50
Main £12.50–£25
Directions: Please telephone for directions

Mango Tree

Thai

Contemporary authentic Thai food in a stylish setting

46 Grosvenor Place, Belgravia,
SW1X 7EQ
Tel: 020 7823 1888
Email:
reservations@mangotree.org.uk
Website: www.mangotree.org.uk

This fine-dining Thai restaurant is located in Belgravia and is the sister restaurant to Awana in Chelsea (see entry on page 99). The dining room is large and spacious with a sleek, modern feel, with materials sourced direct from Thailand to create a beautiful and atmospheric setting. The authentic Thai food includes starters such as por pia hang hong (shrimp spring rolls served with a sweet and spicy sauce), or perhaps tod mun pla (spicy fishcakes seasoned with curry and kaffir lime leaf), followed by talay pad med mamuang (stir-fried mixed seafood with cashew nuts), or pla pow (sea bass fillet wrapped in banana leaves on a cress salad with spicy lime and tamarind).

Times: 12.30–3/6–11, Closed Sat

Mint Leaf

Modern Indian

Trendy Indian restaurant offering authentic cuisine

Suffolk Place, Haymarket,
SW1Y 4HX
Tel: 020 7930 9020
Email: reservations@
mintleafrestaurant.com
Website:
www.mintleafrestaurant.com
Chef: K K Anand
Owners: Out of Africa Investments

Located in the basement of a recently converted bank, this modern Indian restaurant makes clever use of wire mesh screens, wooden slats, and ambient lighting. Darkwood walls, leather seating and polished stone floors continue the style, and staff are friendly and attentive. The kitchen's focus is on quality produce and vibrant spicing, using modern presentation. For mains, try minced lamb kofta cooked in cardamom-scented sauce, and for a real treat tuck into some tasty peshwari naan which is really up to the mark. Tempting desserts include apple tart with mango sorbet. The trendy cocktail bar serves snacks until midnight.

Times: 12–3/5.30–11, Closed
25 & 26 Dec, 1 Jan, BHs, Etr Sun,
L Sat, Sun
Prices: 3 Course Fixed D £40–£65
Main £8–£32
Directions: End of Haymarket, on corner of Pall Mall and Suffolk Pl. Opposite Her Majesty's Theatre, 100m from Trafalgar Square

Mitsukoshi

Mitsukoshi

Japanese

Authentic Japanese in department store restaurant

Dorland House, 14–20 Lower
Regent Street, SW1Y 4PH
Tel: 020 7930 0317
Email: lonrest@mitsukoshi.co.jp
Website: www.mitsukoshi-restaurant.co.uk
Chef: Kenji Hirai
Owners: Mitsukoshi (UK) Ltd.

Set in the basement of its namesake Japanese department store just off Piccadilly Circus, Mitsukoshi is very much a traditional-styled Japanese. Descend the stairs to the popular sushi bar, or down a further tier to the main dining room, decked out in simple, light, neutral tones with booth-style areas set with dark lacquered tables. The kitchen deals in fresh, quality ingredients and a broad selection of authentic Japanese cuisine. Sushi, sukiyaki and shabu-shabu are the main specialities, with plenty of set-meal options on offer too. Otherwise expect grilled beef fillet with teriyaki sauce or perhaps deep-fried prawns with tempura sauce.

Times: 12–2/6–10, Closed 25, 26 Dec, 1 Jan, Etr

Mocoto

Brazilian

South American food in striking setting

145 Knightsbridge, SW1X 7PA
Tel: 020 7838 1044
Website: www.mocoto.co.uk

This ambitious new Knightsbridge Brazilian – on the site of the one-time Isola restaurant – comes with a bar on the ground floor and beautifully designed basement restaurant. Calm and neutral, there's plenty of wood, hessian and crisp white linen, while chairs are simple 1960s design covered in soft cowhide. A huge wooden-screen wall runs down one side, while a bar takes up the entire length of the other wall and adds a tropical buzz. The accomplished Brazilian-inspired food suits the surrounds, and is fun, vibrant and well executed, driven by first-rate ingredients and well-considered, distinctive flavours. Take roast king prawns with vapapa sauce, peanut sprouts, okra and coriander, or perhaps pork loin with smoked ribs, sausages, sun-dried beef, braised black beans, kale and farofa.

Times: 12–2.30/6–10.30,
Closed Sun

MU at Millennium Knightsbridge

French, Pacific Rim

Reliable dining in the heart of Knightsbridge

17 Sloane Street, Knightsbridge,
SW1X 9NU
Tel: 020 7201 6330
Email: mju@mill-cop.com
Website: www.millenniumhotels.
com/knightsbridge

Occupying a curvaceous space on the first floor of the fashionable Millennium Hotel in the prestigious shopping area of Knightsbridge, MU combines contemporary design and urban chic with classic colours, imaginative lighting and artwork to dramatic effect without losing a sense of warmth and intimacy. The kitchen concentrates on hearty dishes with a modern edge, focussing on interesting combinations of ingredients. Start perhaps with warm Jerusalem artichoke and sun-dried tomato tart with rocket coulis, followed by confit duck leg with parsnip purée and sweet and sour sauce.

Times: 12–2.30/6–10.30,
Closed Sun, L Sat
Directions: 200yds from
Knightsbridge Stn/near Harrods
Parking: 8

Nahm

Thai v

Top-notch traditional Thai in chic hotel

Located in a discreet and luxurious hotel in Belgravia, Nahm is home to an internationally renown chef and in the evenings the restaurant resounds with the cooing of diners enjoying David Thompson's unforgettable flavours. Slatted wooden panelling creates intimate spaces within a large, bright room, while gold, reds and teak add to the minimalist furnishings. This unassuming décor allows the food to do the talking – backed up by assured and knowledgeable service. The Arharn Thai tasting menu offers the best overview of this sophisticated and extraordinary cuisine. Tickle the palate with a hor mok hoi shell appetiser – red curry of scallops with Thai basil and kaffir lime leaves; then sample dishes such as a salad of crispy pork with squid and chilli jam, gen gari gai (aromatic chicken curry with cucumber relish) or dtom hang wua (oxtail braised with coriander seeds and spring onions).

The Halkin Hotel, Halkin Street, Belgravia, SW1X 7DJ
Tel: 020 7333 1234
Email: res@nahm.como.bz
Website: www.halkin.como.bz
Chef: David Thompson, Matthew Albert
Owners: Halkin Hotel Ltd

Times: 12–2.30/7–11,
Closed 25 Dec & BHs, L Sat & Sun
Prices: 4 Course Fixed D £49.50–£75 Main £8.50–£16
Directions: Halkin Street just off Hyde Park Corner

La Noisette

Modern French

A class act with cooking that embraces the seasons

A serious addition to the London restaurant scene from its opening in 2006 (formerly Pengelley's), this Gordon Ramsay backed venture has the acclaimed chef, Bjorn van der Horst at the helm. Inside exudes style and quality, with service predominantly French, highly professional and appropriately understated. The brown and beige colour scheme uses natural materials to good effect, with an abundant use of wood panelling and slate-effect tiles on walls. The kitchen's modern approach is assured with great emphasis placed on sourcing seasonal ingredients. Dishes exude clean flavours, balance, texture and colour interest, and are delivered via an exceptional range of fixed-price menus that truly explore the seasons. Take black bream en papillote with chestnuts, fig and salsify, and a guanaja chocolate marquise with toasted brioche and praline shake on an autumn repertoire.

164 Sloane Street, SW1X 9QB
Tel: 020 7750 5000
Email:
lanoisette@gordonramsay.com
Website: www.gordonramsay.
com/lanoisette/
Chef: Bjorn van der Horst
Owners: Gordon Ramsay

Times: 12–3/6–10.30, Closed BHs,
2 wks Xmas & New Year, Sun
Prices: 3 Course Fixed D £60–£75
Directions: Sloane St, between
Knightsbridge and Sloane Sq,
attached to Carlton Tower Hotel

One-O-One

French, Seafood

First-rate seafood restaurant

There's more than a hint of goldfish bowl to the curvaceous windows of this chic hotel dining room in the Sheraton Park Tower, and deliberately so, perhaps, since it's one of the finest seafood restaurants in London. Discreet frosted glass puts paid to pedestrian ogling, but a snatched glimpse would reveal an aquatic-inspired blue-and-white interior, with aquamarine leather chairs, a swirling blue carpet and a stainless steel sculpture of a fish. Service is slick and delightfully friendly, and the kitchen never misses a beat; chef Pascal Proyart insists on superb quality ingredients and lets their freshness shine through. Fabulous seafood is the driving force, but there are a few meaty options too, and dishes are all distinguished by classic combinations, clean flavours and moments of inspiration. You can choose from an extensive carte, but with cooking this good, it's worth taking a look at the Menu Gormandise. Try soupe de poisson to start, followed, perhaps, by John Dory and baby squid à la plancha with cassoulet bean purée and braised pork belly, or roast lobster with curry leaf tamarind sauce and lemon coriander rice. When someone fancies fish in London, this is the place that first springs to mind. As we went to press we understand a complete renovation had just taken place, together with a new menu.

Sheraton Park Tower,
101 Knightsbridge,
SW1X 7RN
Tel: 020 7290 7101
Email: darren.neilan@
luxurycollection.com
Website: www.luxurycollection.
com/parktowerlondon
Chef: Pascal Proyart

Times: 12–2.30/7–10.30
Directions: E from station, just after Harvey Nichols
Parking: 60

One Twenty One Two

Modern

Hotel fine dining in the heart of Whitehall

This majestic hotel in the heart of Whitehall sits beside the Thames and enjoys unrivalled views of the city skyline. The interior is impressive, with modern refinement seamlessly woven into the architectural elegance. Paying tribute to its former neighbour, Scotland Yard, the restaurant is named after the Yard's once universally famous telephone number, Whitehall 1212. 'One Twenty One Two' offers contemporary dining in sophisticated but relaxed surroundings, with views over the outdoor terrace. The kitchen shows skill and imagination in a repertoire blending modern with traditional, and a focus on fresh quality produce. Take Dover sole served with new potatoes, baby spinach and a lime butter sauce, or perhaps a classic Chateaubriand for two.

Royal Horseguards Hotel,
2 Whitehall Court, SW1A 2EJ
Tel: 0870 3339 1222
Email:
royalhorseguards@thistle.co.uk
Website:
www.royalhorseguards.com
Chef: Michael Birmingham
Owners: Thistle Hotels

Times: 12–2/6–9.45, Closed L Sat & Sun
Prices: 3 Course Fixed D £27.95
Main £17.50–£32
Directions: From Trafalgar Sq take exit to Whitehall. Turn into Whitehall Place then into Whitehall Court

L'Oranger

French

One of London's most beautiful restaurants

In keeping with its classy St James's address, L'Oranger is an impeccably elegant dinner destination. The long panelled room is adorned with flower displays and antique mirrors, with a domed glass ceiling to let in the light, and there's a pretty courtyard for alfresco dining in summer. Fish is a speciality, but the wide-ranging French menu covers all the bases, featuring a selection of classics brought back to life by the odd modern twist. The food is rich and the flavours are robust and bold. Roasted scallops and smoked duck magret is a typical starter, served with truffle mousse and raspberry vinaigrette dressing, while mains might include cod poached in saffron broth with fennel and aïoli.

5 St James's Street, SW1A 1EF
Tel: 020 7839 3774
Email: oranger.restaurant@
googlemail.com
Website: www.loranger.co.uk
Chef: Laurent Michel
Owners: A to Z Restaurants Ltd

Times: 12–2.30/6–11, Closed BHs, Sun, D Sat
Prices: 3 Course Fixed D £32
Main £26–£32
Directions: Access by car via Pall Mall

St James's Park

Pétrus

Modern European v

Top-of-the-range dining in opulent Knightsbridge Hotel

Oozing sophistication and opulence, Pétrus comes discreetly located off the foyer and beyond the stylish Caramel Room lounge-bar at the luxury Berkeley Hotel – the unobtrusive name on the handles of its tinted-glass doors lets you know you've arrived. As soon as you enter you're cosseted by slick and attentive staff, consummate professionals, though not at all stuffy. Rich, vivid and sexy, the interior is the work of design guru David Collins, the sensual claret colours and textures reflecting that of the world-renowned wine that lends the restaurant its name. Eye-catching features grab the attention – two giant abacuses complete with blown-glass beads act as a screen for the wine chillers, fantastic chandeliers, stunning French blinds, chairs of soft burgundy leather and red velvety walls all seduce. Trolleys for cheeses, liqueurs and, most importantly, the bonbons, with its wonderful selection of sweetmeats, all circle the floor in style and add a sense of theatre to the occasion. There's also a small lounge area for aperitifs and a chef's table in the kitchen for up to eight guests. It's all a bold and striking complement to the impeccable cooking that makes Pétrus a dining magnet on the international culinary map. Marcus Wareing's modern approach is classically based, has great integrity and owes much to the insistence on the absolute best in raw ingredients. The elegant, richly detailed cuisine oozes technical wizardry, precision, balance, clear flavours and wow factor ... this is skill of the highest order! Think grilled Dorset halibut teamed with new season leeks, confit potato, Oscietra caviar and parsley, while dessert might showcase a peanut parfait with rice crisp crunch and Valrhona chocolate mousse. A serious wine list, with a good selection by glass, naturally includes offerings from that namesake château, while set-price lunch continues to offer great value at this level.

The Berkeley, Wilton Place, Knightsbridge, SW1X 7RL
Tel: 020 7235 1200
Email: petrus@marcuswareing.com
Website: www.marcuswareing.com
Chef: Marcus Wareing
Owners: Marcus Wareing at the Berkeley Ltd

Times: 12–2.30/6–11, Closed 1 week Xmas, Sun, L Sat
Prices: Fixed D £60

Quaglino's

Modern European

Vast basement St James's brasserie

16 Bury Street, St James's,
SW1Y 6AJ
Tel: 020 7930 6767
Email: saschak@conran-
restaurants.co.uk
Website: www.quaglinos.co.uk
Chef: Craig James
Owners: Conran Restaurants

Built on the site of the original society restaurant, there's no shortage of glamour and style in this well-established contemporary incarnation. A dramatic marble staircase sweeps down into a cavernous space supported by colourful columns, and there's a bar, live music and ranks of white-clothed tables. The restaurant attracts an animated crowd, which adds to the atmosphere and sense of theatre. Simple seasonal dishes are the staple of the extensive brasserie-style menu: think Chateaubriand with sauce béarnaise, or perhaps a lobster and crab cake with spinach and beurre blanc. A fixed-price lunch and pre-theatre menu are also available.

Times: 12–3/5.30–mdnt, Closed 24–25 Dec, 1 Jan, L 26 & 31 Dec, 2 Jan
Prices: Main £11.50–£32
Directions: Bury St is off Jermyn St

The Quilon

Indian v

Stylish Indian specialising in south west coast cuisine

41 Buckingham Gate, SW1E 6AF
Tel: 020 7821 1899
Email:
info@quilonrestaurant.co.uk
Chef: Sriram Aylur
Owners: Taj International Hotels
Limited

This smart Indian rubs shoulders with the best address in town, set just behind Buckingham Palace and decked out with curry powder yellow seating and a modern décor with oil paintings adding that extra pizzazz. There is also a separate waiting and bar area. The menu has an English-style format (laid out as starters, mains and desserts), while the kitchen specializes in the cooking from the south west coast, with key spices, chillies, peppers and vinegars imported direct from the southern region. Expect the likes of duck breast, pot-roasted with red chilli paste, onion, aniseed and tomato, or marinated tilapia fish fillet wrapped in banana leaves and pan fried.

Times: 12–2.30/6–11, Closed 25–26 Dec
Prices: Fixed D £32–£42.50
Main £17.50–£25
Directions: Next to Crowne Plaza Hotel St James

Quirinale

Modern Italian

High-end Italian a stone's throw from Parliament

A smart, modern interior from design guru David Collins sets the scene at this intimate, upmarket, basement Italian, discreetly tucked away on a pleasant street in the lee of the Houses of Parliament. Mirrors, limed floorboards, pastel shades and cleverly recessed pavement windows create a light, airy space, while white tablecloths, elegant chairs and central banquette seating provide the comforts. The cooking is unashamedly Italian, a mixture of classic and modern, the presentation and flavours as clean-cut and stylish as the surroundings or quality ingredients. The carte comes bolstered by daily specials, while there's an impressive selection of Italian breads, cheeses and wines. Expect home-made tagliolini with celeriac and black truffles, or perhaps baked fillet of John Dory served with a vegetable tagliatelle and basil pesto.

North Court, 1 Great Peter Street, SW1P 3LL
Tel: 020 7222 7080
Email: info@quirinale.co.uk
Website: www.quirinale.co.uk
Chef: Stefano Savio
Owners: Nadine Gourgey

Times: 12–3/6–12, Closed Xmas & New Year, 2 wks Aug, Sat, Sun
Prices: Main £12.50–£17.50
Directions: From Parliament Sq to Lambeth Bridge take 2nd left into Great Peter St, restaurant on left

---

The Rib Room

British v

Robust British cooking in the heart of Knightsbridge

Housed on the ground floor of the towering Jumeirah Carlton Tower Hotel, this buzzy restaurant has a sophisticated and moody, club-like atmosphere, and comes richly furnished with acres of wood panelling, awesome floral displays, seductive lighting, artwork by Feliks Topolski and crisp napery. The service gently balances British etiquette with friendliness. Tantalising aromas waft from the large open 'theatre' kitchen, its repertoire pure British gastronomy driven by the best home-reared produce and the successful blend of traditional and more contemporary style. Enjoy classic signature dishes like calves' liver with spring onion mash and fricassée of lentils, bacon and mushrooms, hard to resist Aberdeen Angus rib of beef with Yorkshire pudding or Rib Room seafood platter. A pianist entertains in the evenings.

Jumeirah Carlton Tower Hotel, Cadogan Place, SW1X 9PY
Tel: 020 7858 7250
Email: JCTinfo@jumeirah.com
Website: www.jumeirah.com
Chef: Simon Young

Times: 12.30–2.45/7–10.45
Prices: Main £24–£64
Directions: From major roads follow signs for City Centre, towards Knightsbridge/Hyde Park/Sloane Sq, then into Sloane St/Cadogan Place
Parking: 70

Roussillon

Modern French

Discreet French restaurant focused on the seasons

There is no doubting the serious aspirations of this Pimlico restaurant with its large curved bay window: a formal and professional French team complete with sommelier matches the fine-dining menus and sophisticated modern ambience. With cream and brown décor and low lighting, the generously-sized, spacious tables are ideal for business lunches or evening get-togethers. A short lunch menu, carte and several specialist menus present classical French dishes based on luxury seasonal ingredients. The cooking is accurate and very imaginative, and there's a rustic style to the presentation. Typical dishes include foie gras terrine with walnut and artichoke salad to start, followed by lobster and sautéed girolle, oven-roasted pigeon with creamed morels, or Highland venison chasseur, with perhaps pineapple delice with caramel ice cream and white chocolate to finish.

16 St Barnabas Street, SW1W 8PE
Tel: 020 7730 5550
Email: michael@roussillon.co.uk
Website: www.roussillon.co.uk
Chef: A Gauthier
Owners: J & A Palmer, A Gauthier

Times: 12–2.30/6.30–11, Closed 24 Dec–5 Jan, Sun, L Sat
Prices: 3 Course Fixed D £48
Directions: Telephone for directions

The Rubens at the Palace

British, European

Fine dining overlooking Buckingham Palace

Just opposite Buckingham Palace, this tourist favourite was the headquarters of the commander in chief of the Polish forces in World War II. The Library restaurant's décor follows its name's theme, and has the intimate feel of a Gentleman's club, with rich embroidered fabrics and large comfortable armchairs. There's an unobtrusive formality to the service, with traditional flourishes, such as smoked salmon being carved at the table. Simple presentation, good-sized portions and quality ingredients are evident throughout the menu, epitomised by dishes like roasted Gressingham duck breast served with fondant potato, glazed apples and an organic cider jus.

39 Buckingham Palace Road, SW1W 0PS
Tel: 020 7834 6600
Email: bookrb@rchmail.com
Website: www.redcarnationhotels.com
Chef: Daniel Collins
Owners: Red Carnation Hotels

Times: 7–10.30, Closed Xmas week, L all week
Prices: Main £19.50–£46
Directions: From station head towards Buckingham Palace

St Alban

Modern Mediterranean

Booking ahead is essential at this hot new restaurant

This hungrily awaited opening from Wolseley duo Chris Corbin and Jeremy King (the pair originally behind The Ivy, Le Caprice and J. Sheekey) has hit the ground running. It's a smart modern affair, from the bright seating to the contemporary graphic murals of household objects lining the frosted glass windows and grey walls. Service is spot on, while the kitchen's modern, simply presented approach (under chef Francesco Mazzei) is inspired by the flavours of his native Italy as well as Spain and Portugal; think tagliata of beef with bone marrow mash potato, or a seafood fregola, and perhaps a vanilla pannacotta ristretto finish. One of the hottest new places of winter 2006, and under such fine parentage, there's already a high celebrity count.

4–12 Lower Regent Street,
SW1Y 4PE
Tel: 020 7499 8558
Website: www.stalban.net
Chef: Francesco Mazzei
Owners: Chris Corbin &
Jeremy King

Times: 12–3/5.30–mdnt, Closed
25–26 Dec, 1 Jan, Aug BH, D 24
& 31 Dec
Prices: Main £9.25–£26
Directions: From Piccadilly Circus
tube station into Regent Street.
Carlton Street 2nd left

Salloos Restaurant

Pakistani

Romantic mews restaurant with a Pakistani menu

Long established, professional and well run, Salloos deserves its undeniable status. It's a real family business, with a touch of luxury and glamour to the interior. Chicken shish kebab is an excellent all-round dish, delivered to the table on a large skewer with peppers and onions, the meat having a great tandoor flavour. Nargisi kofta is another masterful offering: egg coated in minced meat, halved and presented like a narcissus flower with a rich subtly spiced sauce. Warm carrot pudding, covered with real silver leaf and sprinkled almonds, makes an interesting dessert. Service is friendly with formal touches.

62–64 Kinnerton Street, SW1X 8ER
Tel: 020 7235 4444
Chef: Abdul Aziz
Owners: Mr & Mrs M Salahuddin

Times: 12–3/7–11.45, Closed
Xmas, Sun
Prices: Main £9.50–£16.50
Directions: Kinnerton St is
opposite Berkeley Hotel on
Wilton Place

Santini Restaurant

Italian

Sophisticated, family-run Italian restaurant

29 Ebury Street, SW1W 0NZ
Tel: 020 7730 4094
Email:
info@santini-restaurant.com
Website:
www.santini-restaurant.com
Chef: Luca Lamari
Owners: Mr G Santin

A long-established, refined Belgravia Italian restaurant with alfresco terrace dining in summer. Inside, large windows, slatted blinds, light marble floors, pastel walls and suede banquettes and tub-style chairs cut an elegant, modern edge. The carte offers a typically lengthy choice of authentic, seasonally inspired, regional Italian dishes with a strong Venetian accent and emphasis on simplicity, flavour and quality ingredients. Expect home-made tagliolini with fresh hand-picked Cornish crab, and classics like veal chop in breadcrumbs (crisply fried), with tiramisù to finish. Attentive, professional service and good wines ooze Italian appeal too.

Times: 12–3/6–11.30, Closed Xmas, 1 Jan, Etr Sun, L Sat & Sun
Prices: Main £13–£31
Directions: Take Lower Belgrave St off Buckingham Palace Rd. Restaurant on 1st corner on left opposite Grosvenor Hotel

---

The Stafford

British ♠ NOTABLE WINE LIST

Luxurious hotel dining in an exclusive location

16–18 St James's Place, SW1A 1N
Tel: 020 7493 0111
Email:
information@thestaffordhotel.co.u
Website:
www.thestaffordhotel.co.uk
Chef: Mark Budd
Owners: Shire Hotels

Tucked away behind Green Park, this genteel hotel has the feel of a luxurious country house in the heart of St James's. Public areas are comfortable with an understated opulence. The world-famous American bar, known for mixing a mean Martini, displays an eccentric collection of club ties, sporting momentoes and signed celebrity photographs. A simpler menu is offered at lunchtime with a daily special from the trolley Sunday to Friday, generally a roast, and fish on Friday. Luxury ingredients are to the fore on the extensive carte: starters might include a soufflé of lobster and sole with caviar and champagne sauce, or steak tartare, while mains can range from roast wild duck with apple and foie gras, to Chateaubriand.

Times: 12.30–2.30/6–10.30, Closed L Sat
Prices: Main £14.50–£35
Directions: 5 mins St James's Palace

Volt

Modern European

Mediterranean-influenced cuisine at trendy restaurant

There's a nightclub-like vibe about this cool Belgravia newcomer. An elegantly curved dining room radiates around a funky central bar seating area decked out in vivid red, with eye-catching soft purple strip lighting inset into walls and framing the bar. Contemporary chairs, leather banquettes and smartly dressed tables shout style, while three equally chic, intimate dining areas, flanging the main room, can be booked for private dining. The cooking complements the surroundings, its modern Mediterranean approach oozing Italian influence, while excellent home-made breads and petits fours add further appeal. Dishes are clean-cut, clear-flavoured and elegantly presented and use top-quality produce; think home-made rabbit ravioli with wild mushrooms, or perhaps pan-fried veal served with baby fennel, potato galette and white aubergine sauce.

17 Hobart Place, SW1W 0HH
Tel: 020 7235 9696
Email: info@voltlounge.com
Website: www.voltlounge.com
Chef: Santino Busciglio
Owners: Bou Antoun

Times: 12–3/6–11, Closed Xmas, last 2 wks Aug, BHs, Sun, L Sat
Prices: 3 Course Fixed D £24.50
Directions: Behind Buckingham Palace

W'Sens by La Compagnie des Comptoirs

Modern French v

Chic Waterloo dining choice

Inside this Grade II listed building you'll find a long retro-lit marble bar designed by an ex-student of Philippe Starck. This is one of the highlights of the warm, contemporary chic design, featuring a mix of fireplaces, black leather tables and a library. The menu offers French- and Mediterranean-style cooking with influences from North Africa and Asia. Look out for dishes like cured carpaccio and tartare of red salmon, then fillet of beef Rossini, pan-fried foie gras, spinach, potato purée with mixed wild mushrooms and truffle jus. A tasting menu and a vegetarian tasting menu for a whole table are also on offer. At the time of going to press we understand that this restaurant was undergoing a major refurbishment.

12 Waterloo Place,
St James, SW1Y 4AU
Tel: 020 7484 1355
Email: reservation@wsens.co.uk
Website: www.wsens.co.uk

Times: 12–2.30/6.30–11, Closed 2 wks before Xmas, Sun, L Sat
Directions: Telephone for directions

Zafferano

Zafferano

Traditional Italian

Chic and popular Knightsbridge Italian

This stylish Italian draws an adoring crowd. The upmarket surroundings include a chic cocktail bar/lounge and private dining room and there's a relaxed, friendly atmosphere throughout. Dark wood and glass deliver a sophisticated modern edge to the main dining room, where you'll find elegant banquettes and friendly, professional service. Chef Andrew Needham's accomplished dishes allow the freshest, top-notch seasonal ingredients to shine. Flawless execution and colourful presentation feature on the appealing fixed-price menus (with a few supplements). Expect to be seduced by the likes of linguine with lobster and tomato, perhaps grilled monkfish with courgettes and sweet chilli, or a fillet of beef with celeriac and baby leeks, and maybe a bread-and-butter panettone pudding to finish. By popular demand, Zafferano Delicatessen has opened adjacent to the restaurant.

15 Lowndes Street, SW1X 9EY
Tel: 020 7235 5800
Email:
info@zafferanorestaurant.com
Website:
www.zafferanorestaurant.com
Chef: Andrew Needham
Owners: A–Z Restaurants

Times: 12–2.30/7–11, Closed
1 wk Xmas & New Year, BHs
Prices: 3 Course Fixed D £39.50
Directions: Located off Sloane St,
behind Carlton Tower Hotel

Awana

Traditional Malaysian

Authentic Malaysian restaurant and satay bar

85 Sloane Avenue, SW3 3DX
Tel: 020 7584 8880
Email: info@awana.co.uk
Website: www.awana.co.uk
Chef: Mark Read
Owners: Eddie Lim

The name means 'in the clouds' in Malay and this restaurant is the newest venture of Eddie Lim, owner of The Mango Tree in Belgravia (see entry on page 82). The dining room is inspired by traditional Malaysian teak houses and is adorned with lush silk panels, delicate glass screens and burgundy leather seating that will complement the darkwood interior. Modern style is given to authentic Malaysian cuisine too, featuring satay, skewered dishes, starters, soups, curry, grills and stir-fries. Typical dishes include assorted seafood from the satay bar (you can watch the chefs at work) like diver-caught scallops or maybe corn-fed chicken served with home-made spicy peanut sauce, while bestsellers like beef rendang or butterfish wrapped in banana leaf might catch the eye.

Times: 11–3/6–11, Closed 25–26 Dec, 1 Jan, D 24 Dec
Prices: Main £9.50–£25
Directions: Left out of South Kensington station onto Penam Rd. Continue past Fulham Rd and this will lead onto Sloane Av

Bibendum Restaurant

European

Classic and contemporary dishes with Conran style

Michelin House, 81 Fulham Road, SW3 6RD
Tel: 020 7581 5817
Email: manager@bibendum.co.uk
Website: www.bibendum.co.uk

Light, airy and elegant restaurant occupying the first floor of the art deco Michelin building, with its fabulous stained-glass windows portraying Bibendum, the Michelin man, in various poses. It's accessed via the ground-floor oyster bar, which serves all manner of crustacea, and the complex also includes a coffee bar. French and British brasserie dishes are brought up to date, Bibendum-style, at this slick operation, using fresh ingredients and accurate execution: rabbit and chorizo rillettes; braised pork cheeks in Sauternes with apricots and herbs; and blackcurrant, pear and almond tart served with amaretto ice cream. There's a great atmosphere, too, perfect for celebrity spotting, plus attentive, knowledgeable service and a notable wine list.

Times: 12–2.30/7–11.30, Closed Dec 25–26, 1 Jan, D 24 Dec

The Capital

French

Inspired cooking and impeccable service

From the welcoming foyer winter fire to the hotel's understated elegance, The Capital is bound to impress. Secreted away in the heart of Knightsbridge – on a quiet street just around the corner from Harrods and Harvey Nichols – this discreet, luxury boutique hotel thoroughly lives up to its name. Its stylish restaurant is a sophisticated, light and airy affair, delivering a suave but understated look inspired by the 1940s, while the adjoining cocktail bar has a Harry's Bar vibe. Lightwood panelling is partnered by cool, pale-blue velvet upholstered chairs, drapes and blinds in the intimate dining room, while contemporary styled chandeliers hang from high ceilings. Artwork by Dalí and sculpture by Henry Moore further enhance its standing, but add crisp white napery, highly professional table service, a serious wine list and inspired cooking from a formidably talented kitchen, and you have premier-league status. Chef Eric Chavot's cuisine comes close to perfection, sophisticated and utilising the finest-quality ingredients and plenty of luxury. Though his roots are firmly entrenched in the French classical style (inspired by France's South West region), there's nothing staid or straight-laced here, instead a wonderful light, modern approach that comes dotted with some surprise elements. Refinement, balance and good technical skill reign supreme, with dishes delivered dressed to thrill and with flavours clear and pronounced. Take a fillet of sea bass with crushed potatoes and aïoli dressing, or perhaps a saddle of rabbit provençale served with seared calamari and tomato risotto, while a chestnut sponge with matcha tea foam and passionfruit cream might catch the eye at dessert. Superbly made in-house breads, amuse-bouche, pre-dessert and petits fours hold style through to the end, while an excellent-value lunch bolsters the enticing carte and Menu Dégustation.

Basil Street, Knightsbridge,
SW3 1AT
Tel: 020 7589 5171
Email:
reservations@capitalhotel.co.uk
Website: www.capitalhotel.co.uk
Chef: Eric Chavot
Owners: Mr D Levin & Mr J Levin

Times: 12–2.30/7–11, Closed
25 Dec D
Prices: Fixed D £55
Directions: Off Sloane St, beside
Harrods
Parking: 10

Le Colombier

French

Popular French brasserie in the middle of Chelsea

145 Dovehouse Street, SW3 6LB
Tel: 020 7351 1155
Email: lecolombier1998@aol.com
Website:
www.lecolombier-sw3.co.uk
Chef: Nigel Smith
Owners: Didier Garnier

Tucked away just off the Fulham Road in the lee of the Royal Marsden Hospital, this popular, buzzy, traditional French-style brasserie comes brimful of Gallic charm and atmosphere. A blue and cream colour scheme, polished floorboards, white linen and smartly turned-out staff hit all the right notes, while a glass-covered terrace up front offers that all-year-round alfresco touch. The straightforward, well-presented brasserie fare uses quality ingredients and a light touch; expect classics like a fillet of beef with béarnaise sauce or poached brill with hollandaise and perhaps a tarte Tatin or crème brûlée finish.

Times: 12–3/6.30–10.30
Prices: Main £13.50–£22.80
Directions: Please telephone for directions

Eight Over Eight

Pan-Asian

Pan-Asian cooking with real attitude

392 King's Road, SW3 5UZ
Tel: 020 7349 9934
Email: richard@eightovereight.nu
Website: www.eightovereight.nu
Chef: Alex Ziverts
Owners: Will Ricker

The bright red Eight Over Eight logo (it means 'lucky forever' in China) stands out over the pale grey walls of this corner bar/restaurant, divided inside by Japanese-style mock ironwork. The contemporary brown-and-beige look is spare and stylish, with beautiful low-hanging oriental lampshades. The menu takes in the standard Pan-Asian cooking styles, with sushi/sashimi, curries, dim sum, salads, tempura, roasts and specials, but there is nothing bland about the cooking. Expect black cod with sweet miso, perhaps chicken teriyaki with oba sake, or a roast monkfish Thai green curry.

Times: 12–3/6–11, Closed 24–29 Dec, L Sun
Prices: Main £10.50–£21.50
Directions: Telephone for directions

Frankie's Italian Bar & Grill

Italian

Glitzy basement restaurant serving simple Italian food

3 Yeoman's Row,
Brompton Road, SW3 2AL
Tel: 020 7590 9999
Email:
infofrankies@btconnect.com
Website: www.
frankiesitalianbarandgrill.com
Chef: Callum Watson
Owners: Marco Pierre White &
Frankie Dettori

Tucked away in a Knightsbridge side street, the ground-level entrance hardly prepares you for the shimmering basement interior. A collaboration between Marco Pierre White and jockey Frankie Dettori, the glitzy décor oozes Marco class, from mirrored walls and huge revolving disco balls to good-sized tables, leather seating and attentive, informed staff. A chequered mosaic-style floor and small bar complete a sparkling line up, served up to a 1950s backing track and buzzy atmosphere. No fuss, simple Italian food, accurately cooked from fresh ingredients on a straightforward menu of one-price antipasti, pasta, burgers and grills – like escalope of veal Milanese – hits just the right note.

Times: 12–3/6–11, Closed 26 Dec,
D 25 Dec
Directions: Near The Oratory on
Brompton Rd, close to Harrods

Manicomio

Italian

Regional Italian cuisine in stylish surroundings

85 Duke of York Square,
Chelsea, SW3 4LY
Tel: 020 7730 3366
Email: manicomio@btconnect.com
Website: www.manicomio.co.uk
Chef: Bobby Cabral & Tom Salt
Owners: Ninai & Andrew Zarach

The name means madhouse, but that's not a reflection on the current restaurant, rather on its history as a military asylum! Today you'll find rustic chic with exposed brickwork, oak tables and flooring and leather seating. The huge terrace is complemented by a private conservatory-style dining room and courtyard. Authentic regional Italian dishes are prepared simply using fresh ingredients. Home-made pastas and grills are the cornerstones of an interesting and wide-ranging menu. Try tuna tartare with capers, rocket, shallots and lemon, or broad bean and ricotta tortelli, followed by chargrilled tiger prawns with fregola, tomato, chilli and garlic.

Times: noon–3/6.30–10.30,
Closed Xmas & New Year
Prices: Main £9.50–£23.50
Directions: Duke of York Sq
100mtrs along King's Rd from
Sloane Sq

Nozomi

Japanese

Luxury Japanese cuisine in chic Knightsbridge

14–15 Beauchamp Place,
Knightsbridge, SW3 1NQ
Tel: 020 7838 1500
Email: info@nozomi.co.uk
Website: www.nozomi.co.uk
Owners: Marius George

The impressive entrance with its stylish black canopy, two sets of marble steps, and uniformed doorman set an ambitious tone which a visit to this high-class restaurant does nothing to dispel. A cocktail bar furnished with silvery grey leather seating is the first port of call, and then there's the understated elegance of the restaurant with its white silk-lined walls, subtle beige banquettes and crisp white tablecloths. The food, too, leads off in a new and independent direction, though the modern interpretations are underpinned by traditional Japanese themes. Thus the menu is divided into the usual sushi and sashimi, yakitori, tempura, fish, meat and poultry, with luxury items like wagyu beef with mushrooms, shallots and white truffles.

Times: 12–3/6.30–11.30
Directions: Telephone for directions

Racine

French

Brasserie upholding the bourgeois culinary tradition

239 Brompton Road, SW3 2EP
Tel: 020 7584 4477
Chef: Henry Harris
Owners: Eric Garnier, Henry Harris

A neighbourhood restaurant, located across the road from the Brompton Oratory, this establishment is dedicated to French bourgeois cooking. Popular with Knightsbridge shoppers and foodies alike, Racine's success is in the detail. Formally-attired waiters provide correct, unfussy service while the curtained entrance, dark wood floors and leather banquette seating add nostalgic allure to a menu of French culinary classics. Typical dishes are hot foie gras on toast with red wine sauce and a warm duck egg yolk, or grilled rabbit with mustard sauce and smoked bacon. Finish with pear poached in spiced red wine with cinnamon custard or enjoy La Fromagerie French farmhouse cheeses. Booking is essential.

Times: 12–3/6–10.30, Closed 25 Dec
Prices: 3 Course Fixed D £18.50 (until 7.30pm) Main £13.25–£21.50
Directions: Restaurant opposite Brompton Oratory

Rasoi Restaurant

Modern Indian v

Elegant townhouse Indian restaurant – simply the best

Vineet Bhatia's modern, progressive attitude to Indian cuisine is echoed in the décor, rich in vibrant Eastern styling that sets the scene for this intimate but sophisticated experience. Natural tones, silk cushions, and tribal masks create an exotic atmosphere, with contemporary cutlery and crockery, white linen and professional front-of-house service. There's an elegance to the kitchen's technical skill, with fine clarity and balance to vibrant flavours, textures and colours, while presentation is refined, cultured and eye-catching. Luxury ingredients parade on an enticing range of menu options that includes a stunning seven- or nine-course Rasoi Gourmand menu (with or without wine selection). Expect the likes of pan-fried sea bass topped with aubergines cooked in Hyderabadi coconut and peanut masala with steamed rice, or a mango mousse with lemon jelly and strawberry sorbet to finish.

10 Lincoln Street, SW3 2TS
Tel: 020 7225 1881
Email: rasoi.vineet@btconnect.com
Website: www.vineetbhatia.com
Chef: Vineet Bhatia
Owners: Vineet & Rashima Bhatia

Times: 12–2.30/6.30–10.30,
Closed Xmas, New Year, BHs, Sun,
L Sat
Prices: Fixed D £40–£84
Directions: Near Peter Jones and
Duke of York Sq

The Brompton Oratory

Restaurant Gordon Ramsay ✿✿✿✿✿

French

London's finest and Britain's most celebrated chef

While his face is rarely off our TV screens and the Ramsay restaurant empire may have gone global, this Chelsea temple of gastronomy – opened back in 1998 – still remains the mothership of his London operations, delivering the best cooking in the capital. A slick black frontage discreetly marks out the restaurant's entrance, while the extensive refurbishment of the intimate dining room by design guru David Collins is wonderfully stylish and sophisticated, the clean lines cleverly allowing the food centre stage. The cream interior also delivers the contemporarily elegant platform for unparalleled front-of-house service – this is as good as it gets. Slick, professional and polished, charmingly orchestrated by maître d' Jean-Claude Breton, whose unique, magical management style makes you feel like you're the only diners in the room. Enthusiastic explanations of dishes increase anticipation, while there's plenty of help navigating the fabulous wine list, too. Classical dishes with contemporary spin grace the kitchen's tantalising fixed-price repertoire of lunch, carte and seven-course Menu Prestige, which come studded with luxury. Simplicity, integrity and lightness of touch are hallmarks of the approach, coupled with innovation, flair, stunning ingredients, precision and depth of flavour. The superlatives may roll on, but the skills on display are exceptional, with consistency and execution almost faultless. So expect to be wowed by the likes of roasted fillet of halibut with carrot and coriander pappardelle, baby navet, salsify and a passionfruit butter sauce, or best end of Cornish lamb served with confit shoulder, provençale vegetables, baby spinach, black olives and a basil lamb jus, while a Granny Smith parfait with honeycomb, bitter chocolate and champagne foam might catch the eye at dessert. Royal Hospital Road remains as popular as ever, thus bookings can only be made a month in advance, so be ready to hang on the end of the telephone to secure that table. You certainly won't be disappointed, this is one of life's musts!

68 Royal Hospital Road,
SW3 4HP
Tel: 020 7352 4441
Website: www.gordonramsay.com
Chef: Gordon Ramsay,
Mark Askew
Owners: Gordon Ramsay

Times: 12–2.30/6.30–11, Closed
Sat, Sun
Prices: Fixed D £70
Main £85
Directions: At junct of Royal
Hospital Road & Swan Walk

Tom Aikens

Modern French v ▲ NOTABLE WINE LIST

Gastronomic big-hitter of supreme class and distinction

This eponymous, much-heralded Chelsea temple to the serious foodie – surprisingly tucked away in a quiet residential street – just gets better, and has deservedly put Tom Aikens up there among the pinnacle of top London kitchens. It's an understated, discreet setting for a premier leaguer, a one-time pub transformed by Anouska Hempel's design into a dining room dedicated to the theatre of fine dining. Dark wooden floors and window shutters, black leather chairs and white walls dotted with modern artwork set the interior's minimalist, self-confident lines. Bamboo screens, table lamps set high into window frames and sumptuous flower displays further distinguish the room, alongside the crockery, cutlery and slate serving plates and well-directed, professional and knowledgeable service. The presentation of Aikens' fixed-priced menu repertoire (lunch, dinner and tasting option) follows the theme of the clean-lined surroundings, with dishes eye-catchingly laid out under their main ingredient; take 'Oyster', which translates as poached oysters with lemongrass, avocado purée and Gewürztraminer jelly. But it's the successful marriage of classical roots, modern interpretation, first-class ingredients and flamboyant presentation that makes Aikens' food sexy and stand out from the crowd. Attention to detail dominates every aspect with its sheer quality, with ancillaries like breads, amuse-bouche, pre-dessert and breathtaking petits fours (of afternoon-tea proportions) hitting top form. Technical skill and intricate design and presentation pepper inventive, generous-portioned, vibrant dishes, their innovative combinations showering the senses with visual and flavour sensations. Expect roasted fillet of sea bass with brioche crumb, celeriac snail ravioli and parsley gnocchi, or perhaps steamed pigeon teamed with chestnut cannelloni, turnip fondant and chestnut sauce to wow the taste buds, while a suitably extensive, French-themed wine list befits the cuisine. This is zenith-class cooking from one of the country's greatest culinary talents – so do make this Chelsea pilgrimage.

43 Elystan Street, SW3 3NT
Tel: 020 7584 2003
Email: info@tomaikens.co.uk
Website: www.tomaikens.co.uk
Chef: Tom Aikens
Owners: T & L Ltd

Times: 12–2.30/6.45–11, Closed 2 wks Xmas & N Year, lst 2 wks Aug & BHs, Sat, Sun
Prices: Fixed D £65
Directions: Off Fulham Rd (Brompton Rd end)

Tom's Kitchen

British, French

Posh comfort food served in a trendy Chelsea diner

This trendy see-and-be-seen brasserie-style diner near the King's Road is the latest addition to the Tom Aikens empire. Housed in a period-style building with large windows, the brasserie has an informal, upbeat vibe, with light wooden tables and coloured and black-and-white canvasses on whitewashed walls adding to the atmosphere. You can relax with a cocktail in the first-floor bar and games room, and there's also a private dining room with its own lounge. The cooking style is based on English and French brasserie dishes, delivered by an accomplished team. You might start with butternut squash, sage and honey soup, or maybe wild mushroom risotto with sage and pine kernels, and follow with baked fillet of sea bass with red pepper relish, wilted spinach and olive oil mash. Open every day for dinner, and for breakfast and lunch from 7am Monday to Friday, there's also a brunch menu at weekends.

27 Cale Street, SW3 3QP
Tel: 020 7349 0202
Email: info@tomskitchen.co.uk
Website: www.tomskitchen.co.uk
Chef: Guy Bossom
Owners: Tom Aikens

Times: 12–3/6–12, Closed 24–27 Dec, L 28 Dec
Prices: Main £10.50–£25
Directions: Cale St (Parallel to Kings Rd), midway between Chelsea Green and St Lukes Church

---

Toto's

Traditional Italian

Popular, friendly Italian restaurant

Walton House, Walton Street, SW3 2JH
Tel: 0871 332 7293
Chef: Paolo Simioni
Owners: Antonio Trapani

Tucked away at the back of Knightsbridge, this lovely white-painted corner property has a patio/courtyard area where you can lunch alfresco. Inside a mezzanine overlooks the main dining room, taking in the sunny yellow walls, petrol blue chairs and fresh flowers, while a Venetian chandelier makes a striking centrepiece. The friendly service and great Italian cooking make this a very popular destination, packed with locals and those lucky enough to get a table by chance. The extensive menu offers modern Italian cuisine with classical undertones. Carpaccio of milk lamb with basil and white celery hearts sits comfortably alongside gratinated home-made veal cannelloni.

Times: 12.15–3/7–11.30, Closed 25–27 Dec
Prices: Main £12–£25

Trinity Restaurant

British, French

Stylish, relaxed local restaurant of pedigree and class

Trinity sees chef-restaurateur Adam Byatt return to his Clapham roots after a sojourn among the bright lights of WC2 – ex Thyme and Origin at Covent Garden's Hospital media complex, and originally of the much-acclaimed Thyme in Clapham Park Road. Here he's landing back in the Old Town area on the edge of leafy Clapham Common, and has created an exciting, buzzy, neighbourhood venture. Set well back from the road, it catches the eye and the light with its smart exterior and large window frontage. Inside there's a sophisticated, friendly atmosphere, the room decked out with white-clothed tables, elegant cream and chocolate-coloured walls, comfortable cane-backed chairs and soft lighting, all providing a contemporary backdrop to the polished, modern French cooking. There are also distant glimpses of the kitchen, plus a large private-dining 'kitchen table' that offers a closer window on all the action. Service is relaxed and friendly, yet suitably professional and knowledgeable. Adam's appealing menus feature interesting and adventurous combinations alongside some simpler dishes (including a Joint of the Day) on a repertoire that includes his hallmark tasting options. High technique, clear flavours, creative presentation and tip-top produce add to the wow-factor; take 'sea bass – crosnes – artichoke' (which translates to slow-cooked fillet of sea bass served with a ragout of ceps, hazelnuts, crosnes and Jerusalem artichoke soup).

4 The Polygon, Clapham Old Town, SW4 0JG
Tel: 020 7622 1199
Chef: Adam Byatt
Owners: Angus Jones

Times: 12.30–2.30/6.30–10.30,
Closed 24–26 Dec, L Mon
Prices: Main £15–£20

Tsunami

Japanese

Contemporary neighbourhood Japanese restaurant

5–7 Voltaire Road, SW4 6DQ
Tel: 020 7978 1610
Website: www.tsunamijapanese
restaurant.co.uk
Chef: Ken Sam
Owners: Ken Sam

Tucked away down a side street near Clapham Station, this buzzy, stylish neighbourhood Japanese restaurant is a honey pot for a cool crowd. Contemporary seating and lighting, colourful flower displays, an open kitchen and black-clad staff create a vibrant platform for the modern Japanese fusion cuisine. Tempura, sashimi, sushi and oysters each have their own section on the lengthy menu, with the quality ingredients and imaginative presentation also evident in specials like black cod in sweet miso, chargrilled lamb with wasabi pepper sauce, and beef fillet with balsamic teriyaki sauce.

Times: 12.30–4/6–11, Closed 25 Dec–4 Jan, L Mon–Fri
Prices: Main £6.50–£20.95
Directions: Off Clapham High Street

Cambio de Tercio

Spanish

Authentic Spanish cuisine in a lively atmosphere

163 Old Brompton Road, SW5 0LJ
Tel: 020 7244 8970
Website:
www.cambiodetercio.co.uk
Chef: Alberto Criado
Owners: Abel Lusa

Just round the corner from Earl's Park in Old Brompton Road, what appears at first sight to be a small restaurant is actually fairly large inside, with tables stretching back and a bar on one side. Wooden flooring and red, cotton-covered chairs set off the white tablecloths, while lively Spanish music adds to the buzzy atmosphere. Authentic Spanish cuisine is the order of the day, with deep-fried squid with ink and garlic mayonnaise, roast suckling pig Segovian style, and monkfish with smoked pancetta, pine nuts and creamy spinach on a menu written in both Spanish and English.

Times: 12–2.30/7–11.30, Closed 2 wks at Xmas, New Year
Prices: Main £14.50–£18
Directions: Close to junction with Drayton Gardens
Parking: 10

Harrods

Blue Elephant

Traditional Thai

Truly extravagant Fulham Thai

From bustling Fulham Broadway, this extravagant Thai restaurant instantly transports you to another world – the experience is almost like dining in a tropical rainforest. Think lush plants, trickling fountains, bridges spanning koi carp-filled ponds, and truly welcoming Thai staff. Candles twinkle, while the scent of tropical flowers mingles with the heady aroma of exotic herbs and spices flown in fresh to service an equally flamboyant, lengthy menu. 'Pearls of the Blue Elephant' is a selection of starters enabling you to sample a number of classic dishes, including a wonderful filo-wrapped prawn with peanut stuffing. For mains, expect homok talay (a spicy fish stew), or perhaps chiang rai (a very spicy stir-fried pork with chillies, garlic and green peppercorns). Vegetarian dishes are plentiful.

4–6 Fulham Road, SW6 1AA
Tel: 020 7385 6595
Email: london@blueelephant.com
Website: www.blueelephant.com

Times: 12–2.30/7–12, Closed Xmas
Directions: Please telephone for directions

Deep

Seafood

A real treat for fish and shellfish enthusiasts

In a stunning waterside location in Imperial Wharf, the luxurious dining room has floor-to-ceiling windows which make the most of the view and cream upholstery, while alfresco dining can be enjoyed on two terraces complete with café-style chrome tables and chairs. The friendly, switched-on team give attentive service. An interesting combination of mainly French, with Baltic and Scandinavian cooking features on a menu dominated by fish and shellfish. Carefully sourced produce is demonstrated in the amazing range of starters that include mussels steamed in wine and shallots, and ballotine of gravad lax with a fennel salad. Main courses might be a warm smoked trout with horseradish and braised beetroots, or paella 'Deep' style.

The Boulevard,
Imperial Wharf, SW6 2UB
Tel: 020 7736 3337
Email: info@deeplondon.co.uk
Website: www.deeplondon.co.uk
Chef: Mr C Sandefeldt & Mr F Bolin
Owners: Christian & Kerstin Sandefeldt

Times: 12–3/7–11, Closed Mon, L Sat, D Sun
Prices: Main £13–£26
Directions: From underground station take Harwood Rd then Imperial Rd

Saran Rom

Thai **v**

Riverside restaurant specialising in authentic cuisine

Imperial Wharf, The Boulevard,
Townmead Road, SW6 2UB
Tel: 020 7751 3111
Email: info@saranrom.com
Website: www.imperialwharf.
com/saranrom
Chef: Yupa Sontisup
Owners: Mr Kobchok
Negoypaiboon

This chic eatery brings a touch of eastern glamour to west London,
its sumptuous décor paying homage to Thailand's royal palaces.
No expense was spared in its creation and visitors dine amid a
luxurious hotch-potch of silk hangings, 19th-century antiques
and teak carvings. Add a ground floor bar, an outside terrace and
riverside views, and it all adds up to a fantastic location to enjoy
some traditional Thai hospitality. Main courses might include
meaty fare such as panang beef or smoked duck curry, while
vegetarians are well catered for too: a separate menu features the
likes of sweet-and-sour tofu, tom yam hed – the famous hot and
spicy Thai soup – and som tom je (papaya salad with carrots and
peanuts flavoured with lemon and chilli).

Times: 12–3/5–midnight,
Closed 25 Dec, 1–4 Jan
Directions: 1.50m from Stamford
Bridge/Fulham Broadway tube
station
Parking: 100

Yi-Ban Chelsea

Japanese, Chinese
Modern oriental dining at Chelsea Wharf-side location

No 5 The Boulevard, Imperial
Wharf, Imperial Road, SW6 2UB
Tel: 020 7731 6606
Email: michael@yi-ban.co.uk
Website: www.yi-ban.co.uk

A stylish, contemporary restaurant at Chelsea's Imperial Wharf.
The dining area is located beyond a funky bar and teppan-yaki
counter, where voile curtains, dark wood and red pendant lights
give a moody, modern feel. The contemporary oriental cuisine here
encompasses teppan-yaki and Chinese food, the former cooked
at a counter where diners can watch the chef in action. For an
oriental restaurant there is a good selection of desserts.

Times: 6–11, Closed 1 wk from
22 Dec, Sun, L all week
Directions: Please telephone for
directions

The Bentley Kempinski Hotel

French, European

Fine-dining experience in ornate restaurant

No expense has been spared on this luxury townhouse hotel, discreetly set in the heart of residential Kensington. The setting for the fine-dining dinner-only 1880 restaurant is an equally palatial affair. Think elaborate ceilings, crystal chandeliers, silk wall panels and richly-coloured furnishings. The restaurant's sophisticated cooking is notable for its grazing-concept menus, with six-, seven-, eight- and nine-course options all miniature versions of dishes on the substantial, fixed-price carte, while service – from an international team – is slick and professional. Expect sautéed scallops with artichoke purée, grapefruit and vanilla, or marinated octopus carpaccio with piperade and balsamic syrup. Desserts include the likes of crème de menthe and chocolate ravioli, or warm Creole banana and coconut ice cream. And don't forget to save room for the exquisitely made breads and petits fours.

27–33 Harrington Gardens,
SW7 4JX
Tel: 020 7244 5555
Email: info@thebentley-hotel.com
Website:
www.thebentley-hotel.com

Times: 12–2.30/6–10, Closed
Easter & Xmas, BHs, Sun–Mon
Directions: Off A4 Cromwell Rd,
opposite Gloucester Hotel

Brunello

Italian

An opulent setting for classy Italian cuisine

Situated in the Baglioni, a sophisticated Italian hotel overlooking Hyde Park, the Brunello has a truly chic and opulent feel. Oozing luxury and style, the restaurant's huge mirrors, black silk curtains and ornate black Murano glass chandeliers – together with burnished gold velvet seating and large gilded napkin rings – create an almost regal setting for intimate candlelit dining. The extensive carte is divided into antipasti, soups, pasta and risotto, and the fish and meat dishes include seafood and meat from the grill. Innovative interpretations of classic regional Italian dishes include 'modern' style veal chop Milanese, alongside artfully constructed salads like lobster, ceps and watercress with black truffle. Superb ingredients – many from Italy – accompanied by an outstanding wine list and enthusiastic service, keep foodies coming back for more, especially the Italian Sunday lunch.

Baglioni Hotel, 60 Hyde Park Gate
Kensington Road, SW7 5BB
Tel: 020 7368 5700
Email:
l.virgilio@baglionihotels.com
Website: www.baglionihotels.com
Chef: Stefano Stecca
Owners: Baglioni Hotels

Times: 12–2.30/7–10.45
Prices: 3 Course Fixed D £48
Main £10–£40
Directions: Hotel entrance on
Hyde Park Gate facing park &
Kensington Palace

L'Etranger

French, Japanese v

Stylish, contemporary setting for classy fusion cuisine

36 Gloucester Road, SW7 4QT
Tel: 020 7584 1118
Email: axelle@etranger.co.uk
Website: www.circagroupltd.co.uk
Chef: Jerome Tauvron
Owners: Ibi Issolah

Part of a complex with an adjacent wine shop and basement cocktail bar, L'Etranger is chic, sophisticated and elegant. Rich colours, fresh orchid displays, leather chairs and white linen add to the upmarket atmosphere of the restaurant, where service is attentive, professional and Gallic. A strong French influence also dictates the Asian fusion menu, which utilises high-quality core ingredients in innovative, well-presented dishes with a particular nod to Japan; take scallop, beef and prawn shabu shabu with lime leaves, or signature caramelised black cod with miso. There's a serious wine list too.

Times: 12–3/6–11, Closed 25 Dec, 1 Jan, L Sat
Prices: 3 Course Fixed D £16.50
Main £15.50–£49
Directions: 5 mins walk from Gloucester Rd tube station at junct of Queens Gate Terrace and Gloucester Rd

---

Swag and Tails

Modern International

Upmarket Knightsbridge village gastro-pub

10–11 Fairholt Street, SW7 1EG
Tel: 020 7584 6926
Email:
theswag@swagandtails.com
Website: www.swagandtails.com
Chef: Alan Jenkins
Owners: Annemaria &
Stuart Boomer-Davies

Hidden away just across the road from Harrods, this convivial, well-heeled, flower-festooned Knightsbridge mews pub is predictably well groomed. There are stripped floorboards, a winter fire, honeyed-wood furniture, swagged-and-tailed curtains and newspapers to peruse in the bustling bar, while the small, quieter restaurant behind parades a lighter, more contemporary edge. Here cream walls come adorned with attractive prints, while service is attentive and friendly. The same crowd-pleasing, bistro-style menu is served throughout; expect herb-crusted fillet of sea trout with chive mash, buttered spinach and parsley and caper oil, or perhaps date sponge served with caramel sauce and vanilla ice cream to finish.

Times: 12–3/6–10, Closed Xmas, New Year, BHs, Sat, Sun
Prices: Main £9.95–£16.50
Directions: Close to Harrods

Zuma

Modern Japanese

Stylish, cutting-edge Japanese cuisine

5 Raphael Street, SW7 1DL
Tel: 020 7584 1010
Email: info@zumarestaurant.com
Website:
www.zumarestaurant.com

A stone's throw from Harrods and Harvey Nichols in the heart of Knightsbridge, Zuma's cutting-edge modernity and stylish design is matched by its fashionable, glamorous clientele. The innovative Japanese cuisine is conjured from ultra fresh produce to create vibrant flavours in an extensive repertoire of beautifully presented dishes served from the main kitchen, the sushi bar or the robata grill as they are cooked. This parade of dishes is ideal for sharing: thinly sliced sea bass with yuzu, truffle oil and salmon roe, or perhaps rib-eye steak with daikon ponzu sauce and garlic crisps. Desserts include Zuma sorbet with king lychee and coconut biscuit.

Times: 12–2.30/6–10,
Closed 25–26 Dec, 1 Jan
Directions: Telephone for directions

The Food Room

French

Stylish contemporary Battersea dining

123 Queenstown Road, SW8 3RH
Tel: 020 7622 0555
Website: www.thefoodroom.com
Chef: Mr E Guignard
Owners: Eric & Sarah Guignard

Popular, modern, minimalist French eatery in Battersea (sibling to The French Table in Surbiton), decorated in warm, soft muted colours with stylish mirrors, metal and abstract art. This spacious, airy venue – with large windows facing onto the street – comes with relaxed, friendly service and a warm atmosphere. Classic French and Mediterranean dishes vie for selection alongside others with more imaginative flair, all produced using fresh seasonal produce and an emphasis on clear, subtle flavours. Take black tiger prawns, pineapple and sage risotto and curry sauce, or pork fillet in Parma ham with potato and blue cheese timbale and rosemary, and perhaps a rhubarb clafoutis finish with mascarpone ice cream.

Times: 7–10.30, Closed
25–26 Dec, BHs, Sun & Mon,
L all week
Prices: Main £10.50–£16.80
Directions: 10 min from Clapham Junction

Chutney Mary Restaurant

Chutney Mary Restaurant

Indian

Seductive restaurant offering refined Indian cuisine

This highly acclaimed Chelsea eatery has been luring lovers of Indian cooking to the King's Road for almost twenty years now and has a well-deserved reputation for refined and creative cuisine. Antique etchings of India are teamed with mirrors and moody lighting to create a romantic modern setting, while service comes courtesy of a friendly and knowledgeable team. The menu draws inspiration from diverse regions, remaining true to classic recipes as well as introducing the best of modern Indian trends to the UK. Malabar scallop is a typical starter (scallops with a creamy coconut and ginger sauce), while mains might include lamb osso buco, or chicken with blood orange and turmeric. Tasting menu available.

535 King's Road, Chelsea,
SW10 0SZ
Tel: 020 7351 3113
Email: chutneymary@
realindianfood.com
Website: www.realindianfood.com
Chef: Nagarajan Rubinath
Owners: Masala World,
R Mathrani, N Panjabi

Times: 12.30–3/6.30–11.30,
Closed D Xmas
Prices: Main £14.50–£21
Directions: On corner of King's Rd
and Lots Rd; 2 mins from Chelsea
Harbour

Aubergine

Modern French

Accomplished, refined cooking from eminent eatery

The namesake-coloured aubergine canopy and front door make this renowned, well-heeled Chelsea fixture easy to spot on its side street just off the Fulham Road's hustle and bustle, where William Drabble's modern French cuisine continues to shine. Aubergine cruets, dress plates and menus continue the theming inside at generous-sized, white-clothed tables with chocolate undercloths, where the room's muted, subtle tones create a relaxed, understated, stylish mood. Floors are light wood, walls beige ragged-effect hung with abstract artworks, and comfortable high-backed chairs come in cream, apricot and dark red. There's a stunning floral display at the entrance and a small seating area to enjoy aperitifs. The predominantly Gallic service is professional, attentive and friendly, providing the perfect support act for Drabble's refined modern cooking that comes underpinned by a classical theme. Intelligently simple, stylish and self confident, it focuses around the use of the highest quality ingredients (including luxury items), with dishes impressively uncomplicated by unnecessary embellishment. The cooking is accurate, delicate, perfectly timed and balanced and oozes clean, clear flavours. Think roasted John Dory with creamed yellow-leg chanterelles, or perhaps an assiette of pork (braised cheek, roast belly and black pudding) served with a mustard jus, and to finish, a tart Tatin with vanilla ice cream. The repertoire's delivered via a fixed-price menu format of lunch (this three-courses affair – with half bottle of wine and half bottle of mineral water – is considered a bargain), plus an enticing carte and seven-course gourmand option, while peripherals like bread, amuse-bouche and petits fours all hit form.

11 Park Walk, Chelsea, SW10 0AJ
Tel: 020 7352 3449
Email:
info@auberginerestaurant.co.uk
Website:
www.auberginerestaurant.co.uk
Chef: William Drabble
Owners: A–Z Restaurants

Times: 12–2.30/7–11, Closed
Xmas, Etr, BHs, Sun, L Sat
Prices: Fixed D £64
Directions: W along Fulham Rd,
close to Chelsea and Westminster
Hospital

Osteria dell'Arancio

Modern Italian

Great Italian regional food and wine in a lively setting

383 King's Road, SW10 0LP
Tel: 020 7349 8111
Email:
info@osteriadellarancio.co.uk
Website:
www.osteriadellarancio.co.uk
Chef: Giuseppe De Gregorio
Owners: Rachel & Harry Hampson

Smack on the corner of Milman's Street, a green-and-white striped awning and a few fair-weather pavement tables pick out this vibrant, unpretentious, authentic little Italian osteria from the King's Road crowd. Colourful, eye-catching artwork and lighting, and an eclectic medley of unclothed wooden tables catch the sunny Mediterranean mood, while service is equally relaxed and friendly. The rustic, home cooking of the Marche region comes driven by quality ingredients and simplicity. Look out for rigatoni all'amatriciana (with Italian bacon and pecorino cheese), or tagliata con rucola (beef with rocket). An excellent all-Italian wine list completes the package.

Times: 12–3/6.30–11
Directions: Situated next to
Moravian Church in Chelsea's
World's End

The Painted Heron

Modern Indian

Stylish, upmarket and impressive modern cuisine

112 Cheyne Walk, SW10 0DJ
Tel: 020 7351 5232
Email: thepaintedheron@
btinternet.com
Website:
www.thepaintedheron.com

A blue awning and glass frontage picks out this modern Chelsea Indian close to Battersea Bridge. Minimalist décor with black lacquered leather-upholstered chairs, dark slatted blinds and plain white walls adorned with striking modern art deliver a stylish, contemporary edge to this deceptively roomy, split-level restaurant. There's just a hint of the nautical reflecting its Thames-side location, with blond-wood floors and black metal handrails lining steps, together with a small bar, and an alfresco courtyard at the back. High-quality modern Indian cooking, with traditional dishes given contemporary spin and presentation, focuses on fresh ingredients and intelligently subtle spicing. Take black tiger prawns and queen scallops in a hot and sour Goan curry, and perhaps a honey and cinnamon pudding with cardamom ice cream to finish.

Times: 12–3/6.30–11, Closed
Xmas & Etr, L Sat
Directions: Telephone for
directions

Vama

Vama

Indian

Upmarket Indian restaurant on the King's Road

438 King's Road, SW10 0LJ
Tel: 020 565 8500 &
Email: manager@vama.co.uk
Website: www.vama.co.uk
Chef: Andy Varma
Owners: Andy Varma, Arjun Varma

There's a separate party room, bar and waiting area here at Vama,
with the restaurant stylishly decorated in warm colours. Large
floor tiles, carved teak chairs with cushioned seats, rich ochre
walls and large wooden-framed pictures give a fresh, comfortable,
modern feel. Classical North West Indian food, mainly Punjabi, is
showcased using traditional recipes cooked in a clay oven with
authentic marinades. Typical dishes include the likes of bhunna
zeera murg (roasted cumin and black salt-coated chicken combined
with ginger and garlic), while a typical dessert might feature
kishmish samosa (a soft cheese and raisin samosa served with Earl
Grey tea ice cream and chocolate sauce).

Times: 12–4/6.30–12, Closed
25–26 Dec, 1 Jan
Prices: Main £4.50–£16
Directions: About 20 mins walk
down King's Rd
Parking: 25

The Butcher & Grill

Modern, Traditional

A carnivore's delight in warehouse-style surroundings

39-41 Parkgate Road, Battersea,
SW11 4NP
Tel: 020 7924 3999
Email:
info@thebutcherandgrill.com
Website:
www.thebutcherandgrill.com
Chef: David Massey
Owners: Paul Grout, Dominic Ford,
Simon Tindall

With its bustling atmosphere, this Battersea newcomer has quickly made a mark on the south-of-the-river dining scene. As the name suggests, entry to the Grill restaurant is via an impressive, stylish butchery shop and deli/food emporium. Décor is warehouse style, with bare red-brick walls, whitewashed ceilings and wooden tables, chairs and floors, while service is friendly and informative. The food fits the surroundings, with top-notch raw materials prepared with skill and passion. A carnivore's delight, the menu offers a wide range of meat cuts (from T-bone or rib to Barnsley chop) simply delivered with a sauce of your choice (perhaps hollandaise or onion gravy).

Times: 12–3.30/6–11, Closed
25–26 Dec, 1 Jan, D Sun
Prices: Main £6–£17

The Greyhound at Battersea

Modern European   NOTABLE WINE LIST

Stylish gastro-pub with top-notch cuisine and wines

136 Battersea High Street,
SW11 3JR
Tel: 020 7978 7021
Email: eat@thegreyhoundat
battersea.co.uk
Website: www.
thegreyhoundatbattersea.co.uk
Chef: Alessio Brusadin
Owners: Mark & Sharlyn
Van der Goot

The transformation of an old down-at-heels pub on bustling Battersea High Street to chic, trendy local and dining room presses all the right quality buttons. Large flash bar, leather seating, polished-wood floors, with crystal glasses and expensive table appointments place it a cut above your average gastro-pub. Service is attentive, friendly and relaxed, and product knowledge is excellent. Great quality, serious skill and some innovative dishes show the kitchen's fine pedigree and prove a match for the fabulous wine list. Clear flavours, fine presentation, seasoning and balance all hit a high note. Expect a starter of grilled octopus, carrot salad, ginger and white wine sauce and main dishes such as slow-roasted pork belly, Savoy cabbage and potato purée.

Times: 12–3/7–10, Closed
23 Dec–3 Jan, Mon, D Sun
Prices: 3 Course Fixed D £31
Main £9.50–£16
Directions: Located near Battersea
Bridge and Clapham Junction

Ransome's Dock

Modern British

NOTABLE WINE LIST

imple seasonal cooking in waterside setting

35-37 Parkgate Road, Battersea,
SW11 4NP
Tel: 020 7223 1611
Email: chef@ransomesdock.co.uk
Website:
www.ransomesdock.co.uk
Chef: Martin Lam, Vanessa Lam
Owners: Mr & Mrs M Lam

his popular waterside restaurant is located in a former ice cream actory close to Albert Bridge. With its cornflower blue walls and nodern food-and-wine related artwork, this friendly, relaxed venue unpretentious and informal, with snacks and coffees available in ne bar area, while outside dining proves an added summer bonus. ne sourcing of quality, seasonal produce – much of it organic – is aramount to the kitchen's success; take Creedy Carver free-range uck breast served with minted peas, carrots, Jersey potatoes and red wine and orange jus, or slow-roast pork belly with raisin and edro Ximenez sherry, Pardina lentils and green beans. A notable ine list completes the upbeat package.

Times: 12–/6–11, Closed Xmas
Prices: Main £10.50–£23
Directions: Between Albert Bridge & Battersea Bridge
Parking: 20

Battersea

Lamberts

Modern British

Relaxed, modern fine dining with impressive cooking

Balham's Lamberts is a cool, minimalist-vogue, modern venue that, whilst styling itself as a fine-dining restaurant, has a relaxed and comfortable atmosphere. It is a deservedly popular place, with a growing reputation, due to the fresh and vibrant food. No surprise then that the kitchen prides itself on using the freshest seasonal British ingredients, including organic produce, with the majority of meat sourced direct from farms while fish comes straight from day boats. The impressive, well-presented cooking takes a modern approach that suits the surroundings, with old favourites sitting comfortably alongside contemporary interpretations of classics; think Farmer Sharp's Herdwick mutton, wether and lamb, and don't miss the blueberry cheesecake and white chocolate ganache.

2 Station Parade, Balham High Road, SW12 9AZ
Tel: 0208 675 2233
Email: bookings@lambertsrestaurant.com
Website: www.lambertsrestaurant.com
Chef: Chas Tapaneyasastr
Owners: Mr Joe Lambert

Times: 12/7–10.30, Closed 25 Dec, 1 Jan, Mon, L Tue–Fri
Prices: 3 Course Fixed D £20–£25
Main £14–£18
Directions: Just S of Balham station on Balham High Rd

Sonny's Restaurant

Modern

Imaginative cooking in modern surroundings

Tucked away in a parade of shops behind a glass frontage, this smart, long-standing neighbourhood favourite is bigger than it looks from outside. Bright and contemporary, its pale blue-and-white décor comes dotted with opaque glass bricks and peppered with striking modern artwork. White tablecloths, a black floor and modern chairs hit the spot too, while the atmosphere's buzzy and upbeat and the service is friendly and relaxed. The accomplished kitchen's modern European brasserie approach is a skilful, clean-cut affair that delivers quality ingredients, clear flavours and colourful presentation; think braised short rib of beef with parsnip purée, or roast fillet of cod with piperade and thyme, with bitter chocolate fondant and coconut sorbet to finish, accompanied by a delicious pudding wine. Sonny's shop is next door and the café opens at 10.30am.

94 Church Road, Barnes, SW13 0DQ
Tel: 020 8748 0393
Email: barnes@sonnys.co.uk
Website: www.sonnys.co.uk
Chef: Ed Wilson
Owners: Rebecca Mascarenhas, James Harris

Times: 12.30–2.30/7.30–11, Closed BHs, D Sun
Prices: 3 Course Fixed D £21.50
Main £10.25–£18
Directions: From Castelnau end of Church Rd on left by shops

126

The Depot Waterfront Brasserie

Modern British

Popular riverside brasserie

Tideway Yard, Mortlake High Street, SW14 8SN
Tel: 020 8878 9462
Email: info@depotbrasserie.co.uk
Website:
www.depotbrasserie.co.uk

With a Thames-side location, situated in what used to be a stable block, this waterfront brasserie blends rusticity with contemporary styling (think banquette seating around the walls) to give the place both style and character. Simple bare tables, neutral shades and high ceilings complement the look. The menu consists of a good selection of simply constructed modern brasserie-style dishes; a fishcake with baby leaf salad and wasabi dressing, or Parma ham and sage wrapped chicken breast with roasted pumpkin and cherry vine tomatoes, and puddings like baked Alaska or Eton Mess (served with exotic fruits and créme Chantilly).

Times: 12–3.30/6–12,
Closed 24-26 Dec
Directions: Between Barnes Bridge & Mortlake stations

Mortlake

Redmond's

Modern British

Well-executed cooking in a sophisticated setting

170 Upper Richmond Road West,
SW14 8AW
Tel: 020 8878 1922
Email: pippa@redmonds.org.uk
Website: www.redmonds.org.uk

A big blue awning and white-painted frontage distinguish this high-street restaurant in Sheen. It's a fitting setting for chef-patron Redmond Hayward, and wife Pippa leading front of house. The chic, understated dining room is hung with modern artwork, while simple glassware gleams in the mood lighting, and tables are clad in crisp white linen. Top-notch raw materials are competently handled; cooking is sound, and presentation stylish. There are some classic combinations like roast partridge with roast root vegetables, pommes Anna and game port jus, and dishes with a more modern twist like fillets of plaice wrapped in smoked salmon with braised leeks and basil sauce.

Times: 12–2.30/7–10, Closed
4 days Xmas, BH Mons, L
Mon–Sat, D Sun
Directions: Located halfway
between Putney and Richmond.
On the South Circular Road at
the Barnes end of Sheen

La Saveur Restaurant

French

Classic French bistro cooking

201 Upper Richmond Road West,
SW14 8QT
Tel: 020 8876 0644
Email: info@brula.co.uk
Website: www.brula.co.uk
Chef: Bruce Duckett, Steve Gupta
Owners: Bruce Duckett,
Lawrence Hartley

Set in a parade of shops, this long, narrow restaurant has mirrored walls to create a spacious feel to the room which has all the hallmarks of classic neighbourhood French bistros. The tightly packed tables are clad in white linen cloths and the walls are plastered with French art nouveau paintings. With windows that fold back to open up the frontage in good weather, there is also a small decked terrace allowing limited alfresco dining. Using quality ingredients, the food is classic bistro fare in the shape of foie gras de canard with brioche and Madeira and Armagnac jelly, steak frites, halibut à la grenobloise and le petit pot au chocolat.

Times: 12–3/6–10.30, Closed
25–26 Dec, 1 Jan
Prices: Main £10–£23
Directions: A205, turn right at
Mortlake Bridge, continue 160 yds,
at lights turn left, restaurant is
300 yds on right

The Victoria

British, European

Good simple food in a friendly gastro-pub

This stylish gastro-pub is a firm favourite with locals and has seven comfortable bedrooms for foodies from further afield. The pub is bright and airy with white walls, white painted floorboards and leather armchairs. The conservatory restaurant, with well-spaced tables and a wood-burning stove, has French doors opening out on to the patio and the newly made-over garden for summer dining. The menu, with an emphasis on seasonality and quality produce, serves traditional British, French, Spanish, Italian and Mediterranean dishes in a contemporary style, such as purple sprouting broccoli with gorgonzola polenta and romesco sauce, or charolais rib-eye or sirloin steaks with chips and salad. Heart-warming desserts offer up the likes of steamed orange pudding with treacle and Cornish clotted cream.

10 West Temple Sheen,
SW14 7RT
Tel: 020 8876 4238
Email: bookings@thevictoria.net
Website: www.thevictoria.net
Chef: Darren Archer,
Stephen Paskins
Owners: Mark Chester &
Darren Archer

Times: 12–2.30/7–10, Closed
4 days Xmas
Prices: Main £9.95–£21.95
Directions: Between upper
Richmond Road and Richmond
Park, halfway between Putney
and Richmond
Parking: 18

Enoteca Turi

Italian

Seasonal, regional Italian cooking in Putney

A stone's throw from the river, this family-run restaurant brings a genuine taste of Italy to Putney, with its stylish interior, warm rustic Tuscan colours, and wooden floors and wine racks. Inspired by regional Italian cuisine, high-quality seasonal ingredients form the backbone of the cooking. Well-presented dishes are executed with confidence and flair. There's a great set lunch menu with choices like pan-fried mackerel wrapped in pancetta with balsamic dressing to start. For mains, choose between hearty risottos and tasty pasta dishes, like corn-fed chicken breast with parcels of aubergine filled with smoked mozzarella, parmesan and fresh basil, plus fresh San Marzano sauce. The wine list is impressive and suggested wines for each dish are available by the glass.

28 Putney High Street, SW15 1SQ
Tel: 020 8785 4449
Email: enoteca@tiscali.co.uk
Website: www.enotecaturi.com
Chef: Mr B Fantoni
Owners: Mr G & Mrs P Turi

Times: 12–2.30/7–11,
Closed 25-26 Dec, 1 Jan, Sun,
L BHs
Prices: Main £10.50–£19.50
Directions: Opposite Odeon
Cinema near bridge

The Spencer Arms

British

Putney gastro-pub serving food with flair

237 Lower Richmond Road,
SW15 1HJ
Tel: 020 8788 0640
Email: info@thespencerarms.co.u█
Website:
www.thespencerarms.co.uk
Chef: Adrian Jones, Adam Highle█
Owners: Jamie Sherriff

Shabby chic sums up the style of this cosy gastro-pub on the edge of Putney Common, with sofas around the fireside, tongue-and-groove panelling, oak tables, church chairs and ox blood banquette seating. Great British food is freshly prepared and the menu offers honest pub grub dishes of macaroni cheese, English salad, and rib-eye steak on the bone with herb butter. Take leek and potato broth with Welsh rarebit, or perhaps grilled scallops with crayfish and radish and celery leaf, and for dessert tuck into chocolate brownie and rhubarb, or Dundee cake with egg custard. House-made chutneys and pickles are also available to buy.

Times: 12–2.30/6.30–10, Closed 25–26 Dec
Prices: 3 Course Fixed D £20–£27.50 Main £7.50–£17.50
Directions: S over Putney Bridge, take 1st right. Spencer Arms is last building on left on Lower Richmond Rd. Opposite Putney hospital

Talad Thai

Thai

Hearty cooking at a popular Thai restaurant

320 Upper Richmond Road,
Putney, SW15 6TL
Tel: 020 8789 8084
Email: info@taladthai.co.uk
Website: www.taladthai.co.uk
Chef: Suthasinee Pramwew
Owners: Mr Sa-ard Kriangsak

A relaxed and friendly Thai restaurant in a quiet part of Putney, with its own Thai supermarket a few doors away. The modern set up includes wooden tables packed closely together, so this is not somewhere to share intimate secrets. The lengthy traditional menu offers a journey through Thai cuisine, with food listed by type, such as stir fries, curry dishes, noodle dishes etc, and authentic ingredients arrive fresh from Thailand. Expect the likes of gaeng phed – red curry with pork, prawns, beef, chicken or vegetable – and numerous seafood dishes such as ta-lay hot (mixed seafood with hot chilli).

Times: 11.30–3/5.30–11, Closed 25 Dec, 1 Jan
Prices: Main £5.50–£7.75
Directions: Please telephone for directions

Amici Bar & Italian Kitchen

Italian

Authentic Italian dining in a relaxed setting

Overlooking Wandsworth Common, this stylish eatery is already a local favourite. Behind the commanding frontage, a contemporary bar replete with comfy sofas leads seamlessly into the dining area, where the chefs serve up classic, unfussy dishes from the busy open kitchen. Wood panelling inset with coloured glass, Venetian blinds and a stone bath doubling as a bread station all add to the informal atmosphere. Try fritto misto con verdure (fried shrimp, calamari, sea bass and red mullet), followed by risotto with radicchio, gorgonzola and Chianti, and make sure you try the excellent fresh bread. Carte, lunch, Sunday brunch and children's menus are all on offer and in summer you can dine alfresco on the shady terrace.

35 Bellevue Road, Wandsworth
Common, SW17 7EF
Tel: 020 8672 5888
Email: info@amiciitalian.co.uk
Website: www.amiciitalian.co.uk
Chef: Paolo Zara
Owners: Christopher Gilmore

Times: 12–3/6–10.30, Closed
24–26 Dec
Prices: Main £8.50–£15
Directions: A214, situated on
corner of Bellevue Rd

Chez Bruce

Modern French

Memorable dining at Wandsworth big-hitter

Chez Bruce has a savvy following who appreciate Bruce Poole's memorable cuisine. Inside cuts a relaxed, modern edge, with wooden floors and soft lighting. With no drinks area, diners are shown straight to white-linen clad tables, where service is attentive and knowledgeable. The kitchen's accomplished modern approach pays due respect to classical French cooking, with Mediterranean influences, but remains unfussy while focusing on quality, seasonal ingredients. Noteworthy flavours, balance and impeccable skill make for a fine experience. Expect the likes of a fillet of sea bream served with a mushroom duxelle, potato pancake, oyster beignet and dill, while a classic crème brûlée or perhaps a cherry and almond croustade with cinnamon ice cream might head-up desserts. Regularly changing menus, affordable prices (particularly at lunch) and a good wine list complete a consistently classy act.

2 Bellevue Road, Wandsworth
Common, SW17 7EG
Tel: 020 8672 0114
Email: enquiries@chezbruce.co.uk
Website: www.chezbruce.co.uk
Chef: Bruce Poole, Matt Christmas
Owners: Bruce Poole,
Nigel Platts-Martin

Times: 12–2/6.30–10.30, Closed
24–26 Dec, 1 Jan, L 27–31 Dec
& 2 Jan
Prices: 3 Course Fixed D £37.50
Directions: Near Wandsworth
Common station

Kastoori Restaurant

Indian v

Fresh vegetarian dishes made daily from scratch

188 Upper Tooting Road,
SW17 7EJ
Tel: 020 8767 7027
Chef: Manoj Thanki
Owners: Mr D Thanki

Worth the trek from further into London or the suburbs if you're not a local, this welcoming vegetarian Indian presents an assuming face with its bright, closely-packed tables and relaxing colour scheme of yellow, white, grey and blue. A delightful choice of Gujarati dishes is threaded with East African flavours in main dishes like spring onion curry, or Methiringan (fennu and aubergine cooked with coriander and garlic sauce). Remember to ask for the chef's choices and daily specials.

Times: 12.30–2.30/6–10.30,
Closed 25–26 Dec, L Mon & Tue
Directions: Situated between two stations.

Ditto Bar & Restaurant

Modern European

Popular, informal local offering bags of choice

55–57 East Hill, SW18 2QE
Tel: 020 8877 0110
Email: info@doditto.co.uk
Website: www.doditto.co.uk
Chef: Brent Taylor
Owners: Will Oakley

This relaxed, informal bar-restaurant comes conveniently set on the high street just off Wandsworth Common and proves a populist local. Front windows open on to the street – great on hot days or to watch the world go by – while inside comes with well-trodden wooden floors and grey walls enlivened with paintings by a local artist. There's rugged wooden and leather furniture in the bar area, while the restaurant section is decked out with polished wooden tables and suede and leather chairs. The kitchen's simple, well-presented modern approach fits the bill, with a lengthy, crowd-pleasing repertoire offering something for everyone; think pan-fried loin of pork with butter beans, red wine, thyme and chorizo.

Times: noon/11pm, Closed 25 Dec,
1 Jan, L Mon–Fri, D Sun
Prices: Main £12.95–£16.50

Common

Modern European

Country-house hotel dining with imaginative cooking

This elegant, 18th-century house has a long tradition of hosting the rich and famous of London society, and stands overlooking Cannizaro Park – its former grounds. Inside there's a country-house vibe, which extends to the Common dining room that is clad with dark walls and modern artwork. Carpeting, upholstered chairs and clothed tables offer the comforts, while efficient service and stunning views over the grounds lend added bonus. The accomplished kitchen's modern European approach fits the bill, delivering quality fresh produce with skill and plenty of flair; take fillet of turbot poached in red wine and served with pommes mousseline and ceps, and perhaps an apple parfait with Granny Smith apple sorbet.

Cannizaro House, West Side,
Wimbledon Common, SW19 4UE
Tel: 020 8879 1464
Email: info@cannizarohouse.com
Website:
www.cannizarohouse.com
Chef: Christian George
Owners: Bridgehouse Hotels

Times: 12–3/7–10
Prices: 3 Course Fixed D £26.95–£41 Main £14–£22.50
Directions: From A3 (London Rd) Tibbets Corner, take A219 (Parkside) right into Cannizaro Rd, then right into West Side.
Parking: 55

The Light House Restaurant

Modern International

Simple modern cooking in upmarket Wimbledon

Set in a small row of shops in Wimbledon's upmarket village, this relaxed eatery does a brisk trade, particularly at weekends, so reservations are advised. A minimalist modern décor of wooden floors and sand-coloured walls provides a low-key background for some great food. Dishes are simple, rustic creations rooted in Italian cuisine, with influences from further afield, particularly Asia. Mains might include pan-fried cod with saffron and tomato paella, or braised lamb shank with herb tabouleh and pomegranate and mint relish, while puddings are contemporary concoctions such as mango semi-freddo with raspberry pannacotta.

75–77 Ridgway, Wimbledon,
SW19 4ST
Tel: 020 8944 6338
Email:
info@lighthousewimbledon.com
Website:
www.lighthousewimbledon.com
Chef: Chris Casey
Owners: Mr Finch & Mr Taylor

Times: 12–2.30/6.30–10.30,
Closed 24–26 Dec, 1 Jan, Etr Sun & Mon, D Sun
Prices: 3 Course Fixed D £18.50 Main £10.50–£16.50
Directions: From station turn right up Wimbledon Hill then left at mini-rdbt, restaurant on left

We

Oxford Circus

Alastair Little Restaurant

European

Harmonious flavours and vibrant colours in Soho

49 Frith Street, W1V 5TE
Tel: 020 7734 5183
Chef: Juliet Peston
Owners: K Pedersen,
M Andre-Vega

It's well worth seeking out this unassuming shop-fronted restaurant in the heart of bustling Soho. The interior reflects the admirably uncomplicated style of the cuisine, with wooden floors, simple chairs and smartly set tables. Bold pictures add a splash of colour and the unusual ceiling lights are quite a feature. It's a popular place with a warm atmosphere and friendly service. Straightforward modern cooking delivers clear, well-balanced flavours in dishes like lamb chump, pork belly and chorizo with fennel and white beans, and pannacotta with rhubarb and pistachio praline.

Times: 12–3/5.30–11.30, Closed
Xmas, BHs, Sun, L Sat
Prices: 3 Course Fixed D £40
Directions: Near Ronnie Scott's
Jazz Club

Alloro

Italian

A taste of Italy in the heart of Mayfair

20 Dover Street, W1S 4LU
Tel: 020 7495 4768
Email: alloro@hotmail.co.uk
Chef: Daniele Camera
Owners: A–Z Restaurant Ltd

A blue awning and glass frontage picks out this smart, discreet, contemporary Italian just off Piccadilly close to the Ritz. Banquettes and leather chairs, polished dark and lightwood flooring, pastel tones, sculptured laurel leaf-themed artwork (alloro means 'laurel') and smartly attired staff all set a classy tone at this popular restaurant with an interconnecting small bar. The modern Italian cooking delivers simplicity, quality ingredients and a light touch on its fixed-price repertoire and separate bar menu. Think braised veal osso buco with home-made tagliatelle and fresh thyme, and a peach and amaretti biscuit tart finish.

Times: 12–2.30/7–10.30, Closed
Xmas, 4 days Etr & BHs, Sun, L Sat
Prices: 3 Course Fixed D £33
Main £20
Directions: From Green Park
station continue towards Piccadilly,
Dover St is 2nd on left

Piccadilly Circus

Arbutus Restaurant

Modern European

Stunning but simple, affordable food from Soho gem

The successful restaurant duo of Anthony Demetre and Will Smith continues at the Soho Square end of bustling Frith Street. Inside the décor of this high-achiever is understated, while the atmosphere is relaxed and informal and white-tablecloth free in the style of the bistro moderne. The U-shaped dining room has bar-seating too, while service (with Will Smith out front) is friendly but slick and polished. Demetre's modern bistro cooking has obvious pedigree, the style intelligently simple, imaginative and innovative. Flavours are clear and confident, combinations well judged; take a saddle of rabbit with shoulder cottage pie, golden carrots and mustard sauce, or perhaps a vanilla cheesecake served with blueberries. Top-drawer breads, a sensible pricing structure and a cleverly constructed wine list – with wines also available by 250ml carafe – completes an excellent package.

63–64 Frith Street, W1D 3JW
Tel: 020 7734 4545
Email:
info@arbutusrestaurant.co.uk
Website:
www.arbutusrestaurant.co.uk
Chef: Anthony Demetre
Owners: Anthony Demetre,
Will Smith

Times: 12–2.30/5–10.30, Closed
25–26 Dec, 1 Jan
Prices: Main £11.50–£15.95
Directions: Exit Tottenham Court
Road tube station, turn left into
Oxford St. Left onto Soho St, cross
over or continue around Soho Sq,
restaurant is on Frith St 25m on
right

Archipelago

International

Unique, romantic and adventurous dining experience

There's nothing to prepare you on the outside – set on an unremarkable side street not far from the Telecom Tower – for the unique journey of exploration within this tiny, offbeat restaurant. A treasure trove of peacock feathers, golden Buddhas, primitive carvings, bird cages and colourful fabrics and seating are among the riot of exotic memorabilia that fill every inch of the green and red walls; it's dark, romantic and atmospheric. Even the menu is unusual, a ribbon-bound scroll with an ancient map on the back reveals the treasures in store; an equally idiosyncratic safari of accomplished, exotic-named dishes that might include crocodile, peacock, wildebeest or marsupial – perhaps zhug-marinated kangaroo fillet with water spinach, choi and crushed chilli potatoes. Service is knowledgeable, relaxed and friendly.

110 Whitfield Street, W1T 5ED
Tel: 020 7383 3346
Email:
info@archipelago-restaurant.co.uk
Website:
www.archipelago-restaurant.co.uk
Chef: Daniel Creedon
Owners: Bruce Alexander

Times: 12–2.30/6–11, Closed
Xmas, BHs, Sun, L Sat
Prices: 3 Course Fixed D £31.50
–£38.50 Main £13.50–£19.50
Directions: From underground
south along Tottenham Court Rd.
1st right into Grafton Way. 1st left
into Whitfield St

The Athenaeum, Damask

Traditional British

Out with the old and in with the new at this hotel

The sumptuous Athenaeum is discreet in every way but the interior of the building, despite limited space, oozes contemporary style after a designer make-over. It's all change with the food options too, by way of the introduction of 'The Elevenses' menu offered from 11am to 11pm (flexible all-day dining with something for everyone) to complement the set lunch and dinner menus and the retro-chic daily-changing carving trolley. The new Damask Restaurant is a glamorous yet relaxed space, where the likes of risotto of New Forest mushrooms and truffles, grilled new season Dorset lamb with buttered spinach and glazed onions followed by a double-baked chocolate pudding might tempt the palate. Service is of the highest level, superbly hosted and supervised, and smartly attired.

116 Piccadilly, W1J 7BJ
Tel: 020 7499 3464
Email: info@athenaeumhotel.com
Website:
www.athenaeumhotel.com
Chef: David Marshall
Owners: Ralph Trustees Ltd

Times: 12.30–2.30/5.30–10.30
Prices: 3 Course Fixed D £25
Main £15–£28.50
Directions: Telephone for
directions

Archipelago

Automat

American

Stylish dining in American-style brasserie

33 Dover Street, W1S 4NF
Tel: 020 7499 3033
Email: info@automat-london.com
Website:
www.automat-london.com
Chef: Shaun Gilmore
Owners: Carlos Almada

This elegant diner-themed restaurant delivers American-style comfort food to Mayfair. Up front there's a café atmosphere, in the middle an upmarket diner vibe with leather banquette-style booth seating, subdued lighting and lots of wood veneer, while at the back there's a brighter, buzzier space with an open kitchen, white-tiled walls and tables set on different levels. The food is uncomplicated but accomplished, featuring some stereotypical Stateside diner favourites, though dishes benefit from modern interpretation and presentation, and quality ingredients. Take a Manhattan clam chowder, perhaps an Automat burger or New York strip-loin steak, and a Mississippi mud pie finish.

Times: 12–3/6–11, Closed Xmas, New Year, L Sun
Prices: 3 Course Fixed D £26–£50
Main £7–£25
Directions: Dover St is off Piccadill

Bam-Bou

French, Vietnamese, Pan-Asian

Lively restaurant inspired by Indo-China

1 Percy Street, W1T 1DB
Tel: 020 7323 9130
Email: sthompson@bam-bou.co.u
Website: www.bam-bou.co.uk

Located in a Georgian townhouse smack bang in the middle of Fitzrovia, Bam-Bou is a discreet Asian-style restaurant with a French colonial feel. Intimate rooms, replete with authentic artefacts, wood floors, retro lighting and jazzy music, provide the setting for sampling a vibrant ethnic menu that draws on Thai, Vietnamese and Chinese cuisine with a strong Western influence. Menu choice is not over elaborate and sound cooking results in full-flavoured dishes. Service is informal and friendly, with good suggestions on how to enjoy the food. Herb-baked Chilean sea bass with hot and sour greens, or crackling roast belly pork with watercress and spiced jambu are typical mains.

Times: 12–3/6–11, Closed 25–26 Dec, BH Mons, Sun, L Sat
Prices: Main £9–£15.50
Directions: 1 min from Oxford St

140

Barrafina

Spanish

Barcelona-style tapas in the heart of Soho

54 Frith Street, Soho, W1D 4SL
Tel: 020 7813 8016
Website: www.barrafina.co.uk

Tucked away in the middle of Soho, Sam and Eddie Hart have used the iconic Cal Pep tapas bar in Barcelona for inspiration. With no booking policy, prepare to queue in this long, narrow room for the high stools that run around the L-shaped, marble-topped counter. Sip on a glass of fino or manzanilla as you wait for plates of charcuterie or well-cooked authentic hot and cold tapas such as mussels à la plancha, lamb's sweetbreads with capers, tuna tartare, morcilla with piquillo peppers and jamon and spinach tortilla. Staff are lively and friendly.

Times: 12–3/5–11, Closed BHs, Sun

Bar Shu

Sichauanese

One of the Capital's 'hottest' Chinese restaurants

28 Frith Street, W1D 5LF
Tel: 020 7287 6688
Website: www.bar-shu.co.uk

Just over the road from Chinatown, this contemporary looking, glass-fronted Soho Chinese is dedicated to the food of the Sichuan province of Southwest China, famous for the fiery spiciness that comes from its liberal use of chillies and lip-tingling Sichuan peppercorns. The décor is clean-lined and modern, dotted with more traditional touches like red lanterns, authentic wood furniture and objets d'art. Staff are both knowledgeable and helpful, while the kitchen delivers dishes like fire-exploding kidney flowers, Dongpo pork knuckle and a dessert of stewed exotic frog jelly in papaya. But heat's not the whole story here, it's also about the layers of flavour, so look out for the so-called 'fish-fragrant' or 'lychee-flavoured' sauces as well as the 'numbing-and-hot'.

Times: 12 noon–11.30pm

Bellamy's

French

Classy brasserie in quiet Mayfair mews

There's a buzz to this French brasserie that's very appealing – come at lunchtime or for dinner and it's perennially popular. Tightly packed tables foster a sense of occasion, and the staff keep the conversation and service flowing despite the pressure. The food is classic French brasserie fare, simply but competently prepared from top-notch ingredients and delivered with all due ceremony. Expect mains such as turbot réti served with sauce champagne, or sliced entrecote of beef with pommes frites to feature alongside oysters, lobster, caviar and whatever other delights the appealing carte has on offer.

18–18a Bruton Place, W1J 6LY
Tel: 020 7491 2727
Email:
gavin@bellamysrestaurant.co.uk
Website:
www.bellamysrestaurant.co.uk
Chef: Stephane Pacoud
Owners: Gavin Rankin and
Syndicate

Times: 12–3/7–10.30, Closed BHs,
Sun, L Sat
Prices: 3 Course Fixed D £28.50
Main £18.50–£28.50
Directions: Off Berkeley Sq,
parallel with Bruton St

Benares

Indian

Fine dining with cutting-edge cooking

Discreetly set on Berkeley Square, Benares puts on a classy Mayfair performance with its striking contemporary design. A wide staircase sweeps up to a cool, funky bar with a series of water-filled ponds decorated with brightly coloured floating flowers. The slick dining room is decked out with limestone flooring, dark leather banquettes and ebony-coloured chairs with creamy white upholstery. The modern Indian cuisine is as sophisticated as the surroundings. Highly lauded chef-patron Atul Kochhar produces eye-catching food, utilising tip-top, luxury European-style produce. Vibrant cooking, subtle spicing and authenticity fuse East and West. Expect dishes such as sea bass poached in a coconut and tamarind sauce and served with coconut rice, or perhaps grilled lamb chops marinated with cardamom and fennel and served with pomegranate, dates, green beans, feta cheese and mint salad.

12 Berkeley Square, W1J 6BS
Tel: 020 7629 8886
Email: reservations@
benaresrestaurant.com
Website:
www.benaresrestaurant.com
Chef: Atul Kochhar
Owners: Atul Kochhar

Times: 12–2.30/5.30–11,
Closed 23–26 Dec, 27–31 Dec, Sat
Prices: 3 Course Fixed D £25–£45
Main £16.95–£38
Directions: E along Piccadilly
towards Regent St. Turn left into
Berkeley St and continue straight
to Berkeley Square

142

Bentley's Oyster Bar & Grill

Bentley's Oyster Bar & Grill

British, European

Classic seafood powerhouse

When this legendary seafood restaurant came up for sale in 2005, TV chef Richard Corrigan decided to restore it to its former glory. Sensitively refurbished with an eye to its Arts and Crafts heritage, there are green leather booths downstairs in the relaxed oyster bar and more formal tables in the Grill restaurant and private dining rooms, both providing the perfect setting for grazing on native or rock oysters in the shell. Corrigan draws on his Irish roots to deliver a menu of accomplished cuisine, firmly focusing on the freshness of Bentley's fish, meat and game, and allowing the main ingredients to shine through. Typical dishes might include wild sea bass with soft fennel and herbs or steamed Elwy Valley lamb pudding. Black-clad staff provide professional service.

11/15 Swallow Street, W1B 4DG
Tel: 020 7734 4756
Email:
cyril.lommaert@bentleys.org
Website: www.bentleysoyster
barandgrill.co.uk
Chef: Brendan Fyldes
Owners: Richard Corrigan

Times: 12/11.30
Directions: 2nd right after
Piccadilly Circus

143

The Berkeley Square

Modern European

Mayfair fine dining without the pomp

7 Davies Street, Berkeley Square,
W1K 3DD
Tel: 020 7629 6993
Email:
info@theberkeleysquare.com
Website:
www.theberkeleysquare.com

Intimate two-floor restaurant in famous Berkeley Square with a colourful, contemporary décor. Aubergine curtains are teamed with brown leather chairs and lime banquettes, while the walls are hung with bright abstract artworks. Take your seat and choose from a repertoire of fixed-price menus, including a seven-course surprise selection. Whatever you plump for, you're in for some accomplished cuisine – tip-top produce is treated with confident deftness and presented with great elegance, and there's an impressive list of tipples on offer to wash it down. Kick off with seared scallops served with foie gras, parsnip purée and a salsify ragout, and then move on to fillet of Aberdeen Angus beef with Sarladaise potatoes, parsley root purée and baby carrots.

Times: 12–2.30/6–10, Closed
Xmas, New Year, BHs, last 2 wks
Aug, Sun, Sat
Directions: NW end of Berkeley Sq

Blandford Street

Modern British, European

Discreet little restaurant in stylish Marylebone

5–7 Blandford Street,
Marylebone, W1U 3DB
Tel: 020 7486 9696
Email: info@blandford-street.co.uk
Website:
www.blandford-street.co.uk
Chef: Martin Moore
Owners: Nicholas Lambert

An intimate restaurant in upmarket Marylebone, with a smart terrace on the front pavement for summer dining. Customers can linger at the bar just inside the door before heading for their table, where seating is on comfy maroon banquettes or brown leather chairs. The service is as discreet as the setting, and the menus simply executed around the day's catch at Poole, well-hung beef, and other market-fresh quality ingredients. From the set lunch menu you might find an authentic cassoulet of Toulouse sausage, confit duck and salted rare breed pork belly, or a simple mushroom risotto. The evening carte offers a broader range but still delivers good value.

Times: 12–2.30/6.30–10.30,
Closed Xmas, New Year, Etr, BHs,
Sun, L Sat
Prices: Main £10.95–£21.95
Directions: Turn right out
of Oxford St exit, cross road
and down Marylebone Ln to
Marylebone High St. Onto
Blandford St, restaurant on left

144

Brian Turner Mayfair

Modern British

Back-to-basics British cooking in upmarket hotel

Millennium Hotel, 44 Grosvenor Square, Mayfair, W1K 2HN
Tel: 020 7596 3444
Email: annie.mckale@mill-cop.com
Website: www.brianturneronline.co.uk/mayfair.asp
Chef: Brian Turner & Paul Bates
Owners: Millennium Hotels

In contrast to the other smart eateries in this swanky Mayfair hotel, Brian Turner's split-level restaurant – which makes the most of the views across Grosvenor Square – boasts understated retro-chic, decked out in contemporary shades and natural materials. Famed for his interest in traditional British comfort food, cooking is based on simple, wholesome and satisfying British classics, yet dishes are given a light and modern touch. Think spit-roast duck on butternut purée with crisp potato, broad beans and bacon, or Finnebrogue venison loin with potato and parsnip terrine, while a soft-centred chocolate pudding with Jaffa Cake ice cream might catch the eye at dessert.

Times: 12.30–2.30/6.30–10.30, Closed BHs, Sun, L Sat
Prices: Main £15–£42
Directions: Close to Oxford St, Bond St and Park Ln

Butler's

Traditional British

Traditional dining in elegant Mayfair retreat

Chesterfield Mayfair Hotel, 35 Charles Street, Mayfair, W1J 5EB
Tel: 020 7491 2622
Email: fandbch@rchmail.com
Website: www.chesterfieldmayfair.com
Chef: Andrew Fraser
Owners: Red Carnation Hotels

Step through the door of this exclusive hotel and you'll find a luxurious Georgian interior appropriate to its prestigious Mayfair address. A clubby feel pervades the public spaces thanks to high quality antiques, leather chairs, and heavy fabrics, and the elegance continues into Butler's restaurant, a sumptuous room with a strong red and brown décor and a subtle African theme. Dine here or in the light and airy Conservatory, where a traditional British menu offers a good range of straightforward dishes based on high-quality ingredients. Kick things off with a pear, gorgonzola and pecan salad, before tucking into the likes of rump of lamb with herb mash and red wine and bay leaf sauce, or choose from the carving trolley, followed by Eton Mess or sticky toffee pudding.

Times: 12.30–2.30/5.30–10.30
Prices: 3 Course Fixed D £26
Main £17.50–£23
Directions: Exit N side tube station, turn left and then first left (Berkeley St). Continue to Berkeley Sq and then left towards Charles St

Camerino

Camerino

Traditional Italian

Friendly Italian restaurant stamped with originality

16 Percy Street, W1T 1DT
Tel: 020 7637 9900
Email:
info@camerinorestaurant.com
Website:
www.camerinorestaurant.com
Chef: Valerio Daros
Owners: Paolo Boschi

Theatrical from the glamorous fuschia-coloured wall drapes to the Italian welcome and service, Camerino (the name means 'theatre changing room') is well worth the short trek up Tottenham Court Road. You can eat modestly from the set menus or pre-theatre choice, or more extravagantly from the carte, but the market-fresh produce is the same, and so is the expert handling from a forward-looking kitchen team. Modern presentation make the likes of deep-fried eel with black truffle risotto, and roasted pheasant with porcini mushrooms and pheasant look as good as they taste, and desserts are another strength.

Times: 12–3/6–11, Closed 1 wk Xmas, 1st Jan, Etr Day, most BHs, Sun, L Sat
Prices: 3 Course Fixed D £23.50 Main £16–£19.50
Directions: Please telephone for directions

146

Cecconi's

Traditional Italian

All-day Italian cuisine and cutting-edge design

5a Burlington Gardens, W1X 1LE
Tel: 020 7434 1500
Website: www.cecconis.co.uk

In keeping with its swish location, opposite Burlington Arcade, Cecconi's is a chic, stylish modern restaurant that attracts a trendy crowd. An extensive all-day menu means you can come in at any time and enjoy a great range of simple, well-presented dishes offering good value for money, including Italian tapas dishes like octopus with lemon and green olives. Start from 7am with breakfast, or brunch at weekends from 12 until 5. Pop in for a light lunch with choices like crab ravioli, lobster spaghetti, or fettucini with wild boar ragout, or indulge in a leisurely dinner. Main courses include new variations on Italian classics – try wild sea bass with clams, tomato and basil.

Times: 12/midnight, Closed Xmas, New Year
Directions: Burlington Gdns between New Bond St and Savile Row

China Tang

Chinese

Sophisticated Chinese set in luxurious surroundings

The Dorchester, Park Lane, W1A 2HJ
Tel: 020 7629 9988
Email: reservations@chinatanglondon.co.uk
Chef: Ringo Chow
Owners: David Tang

Lavish, opulent and stunning are just a few words to describe this ultra-deluxe Chinese setting in the basement of The Dorchester, where no expense has been spared. There's a lavish cocktail bar and spacious dining room, and the décor is a mix of art deco and traditional Chinese. Interior design is mirrored pillars, stunning glass-fronted artworks, tables with marble inset tops laid with heavy silver chopsticks, hand-carved chairs and deep banquette seating. The classic Cantonese cooking, utilizing top-quality produce, parades on dim sum and carte menus that come dotted with luxuries. Try stirfry lobster in black bean sauce, or deep-fried crab claws stuffed with shrimp mousse.

Times: 11/midnight, Closed 25 Dec
Prices: Main £42
Directions: Please telephone for directions

Cipriani

Italian

A dazzling piece of Venice in Mayfair

25 Davies Street, W1E 3DE
Tel: 020 7399 0500
Website: www.cipriani.com

Arrigo Cipriani's first venture outside Venice – haunt of the fashionable, rich and famous – is ideally located just off Berkeley Square. The modern glass-fronted exterior leads to a large, stylish dining room, where impeccable art deco style meets beautiful Murano chandeliers, and white-jacketed staff offer slick and attentive service. Low, leather-upholstered seating and magnolia tablecloths provide added comfort. Classic, accurate, straightforward Italian cooking – with lots of Cipriani touches, authentic, top-quality ingredients and unfussy presentation – hits the mark in dishes such as tagliatelle with fresh peas starter, followed by beef medallions alla Rossini. Do save room for the dessert selection of cakes and fine breads.

Times: 12–3/6–11.45, Closed 25 Dec
Directions: Please telephone for directions

Cocoon

Pan-Asian

Happening Pan-Asian restaurant

65 Regents Street, W1B 4EA
Tel: 020 7494 7600
Email: reservations@cocoon-restaurants.com
Website: www.cocoon-restaurants.com

Booking is essential at this unreservedly popular restaurant, even on a weekday. The loud clamour of after-work conversation is minimised by the careful placing of tables in hidden nooks and crannies, with the clever use of net curtains effectively screening groups away from each other. You can dine at the sushi bar and watch the chefs at work, or pick and choose from a comprehensive menu that takes in the best of the Asian culinary world. Dim sum, sashimi, teriyaki, tempura, green miso soup are all there, along with some interesting fusion dishes.

Times: 12–2.45/5.30–11.30, Closed 25–26 Dec, 1 Jan
Directions: 1 min walk from Piccadilly Circus

The Cumberland - Rhodes

Modern British

Exciting concept in Marble Arch

Great Cumberland Place, W1A 4RF
Tel: 0870 333 9280
Email:
enquiries@thecumberland.co.uk
Website: www.guoman.com
Chef: Gary Rhodes

A high-ceilinged restaurant split into two dining areas either side of a bar creates a modern and impressive backdrop for some exciting cuisine. Expect British dishes with Gary's influence, simply and well prepared, and a pleasure to eat. The menu offers crowd-pleasing classics and new dishes, taking in the likes of crayfish tails with spring onion and bucatini pasta in tomato and chilli sauce, perhaps followed by braised oxtail with mashed potatoes. And what better than finishing off with a much loved British classic – bread-and-butter pudding.

Times: 12–2.30/6–10.15
Directions: Telephone for directions

Embassy London

Modern European

Modern, sophisticated Mayfair restaurant and club

29 Old Burlington Street, W1S 3AN
Tel: 020 7851 0956
Email:
embassy@embassylondon.com
Website:
www.embassylondon.com

Set behind a modern glass frontage in the heart of the West End, this Mayfair restaurant is as stylish and sophisticated as its address. The ground-floor dining room is a contemporary, split-level affair, with chic bar, floor-to-ceiling windows and small alfresco terrace at the front. Soothing creams and browns, white linen, mirrored surfaces and stunning flower displays cut an understated, upmarket edge. Attentive black-clad staff, a vibrant atmosphere and enticing modern European cooking all fit the bill, too. Expect clear, clean-cut flavours and presentation, balanced combinations and tip-top produce to deliver the likes of tuna and wild oyster tartare with sweet pickled cucumber, followed by roast curried lobster, apple and ginger, with sauce Jacqueline. Dine before descending to the nightclub below.

Times: 12–3/6–11.30, Closed 25-26 Dec, 1 Jan, Good Fri, Sun–Mon, L Oct & Sat
Directions: Just off Burlington Gardens, running between Bond and Regent St

L'Escargot *(The Ground Floor Restaurant)* ❀❀

French ♦ NOTABLE WINE LIST

A winning menu with breathtaking artwork

L'Escargot's art collection alone makes it worth a visit – Chagall, Miró, Warhol, Hockney and Matisse are all represented – and with accomplished French cuisine also on offer, its reputation as a Soho grandee is easy to understand. Classic bistro fare is the order of the day, whisked up from quality seasonal produce and delivered to the table by an obliging serving team who handle the crowds with aplomb. Start with smoked haddock ravioli perhaps, served with creamed leeks and mustard beurre blanc, and then plump for pan-fried calves' liver with pomme mousseline and sauce diable, or sea bream with aubergine caviar and olive jus. There's a full carte at lunch and dinner, and a good-value menu du jour for lunch and pre-theatre dinner.

48 Greek Street, W1D 4EF
Tel: 020 7439 7474
Email: sales@whitestarline.org.uk
Website:
www.lescargotrestaurant.co.uk
Chef: Simon Jones
Owners: Jimmy Lahoud &
Marco Pierre White

Times: 12–2.30/6–11.30, Closed
25–26 Dec, 1 Jan, Sun, L Sat
Prices: Main £12.95–£14.95
Directions: Telephone for
directions

L'Escargot (*The Picasso Room*)

Modern French **V** NOTABLE WINE LIST

Accomplished cuisine in an intimate dining room

Dedicated to Picasso, this dining room boasts a collection of original ceramics by the artist as well as a number of prints. Comfortable leather seating and quality table settings are provided, with service both formal and discreet. Starters featuring snails, frogs' legs and smoked foie gras set the tone for a mainly French dining experience, but if that doesn't appeal you might kick off with seared Cornish scallops with lemon and parsley, or red mullet with cauliflower mayonnaise and roasted langoustines. Mains showcase top British produce such as roasted Dorset lobster with Jerusalem artichoke purée, served with a fricassée of girolles and chanterelles, or fillet of John Dory with braised oxtail, and potato and chive risotto. Desserts may include parfait of bananas with warm chocolate fondant and chocolate sauce. An extensive, French biased wine list echoes the quality of the food.

48 Greek Street, W1D 4EF
Tel: 020 7439 7474
Email: sales@whitestarline.org.uk
Website:
www.lescargotrestaurant.co.uk
Chef: Warren Geraghty
Owners: Jimmy Lahoud &
Marco Pierre White

Times: 12–2.15/7–11, Closed
2 wks from 24 Dec (excluding New
Year), 4 wks Aug, Sun–Mon
Prices: Fixed D £42
Directions: Telephone for
directions

Fino

Spanish · NOTABLE WINE LIST

Fashionable tapas with an authentic range

33 Charlotte Street, W1T 1RR
Tel: 020 7813 8010
Email: info@finorestaurant.com
Website: www.finorestaurant.com
Chef: Jean Philippe Patruno
Owners: Sam & Eddie Hart

An upmarket and lively Spanish restaurant hidden away in a surprisingly bright and airy basement off chic Charlotte Street. High ceilings, pale wood floors, red leather chairs and a contemporary mezzanine bar set the stylish scene for sampling some skilfully cooked tapas. Great for grazing and groups' dining from a daily menu that lists both classic and contemporary offerings, and watch them being prepared in the open-to-view kitchen. Expect robust, gutsy dishes and flavours, such as snails with garlic purée, crispy pork belly, or foie gras with chilli jam. Extremely helpful, well-drilled service.

Times: 12–2.30/6–10.30, Closed Xmas & BH, Sun, L Sat
Prices: Main £8–£20
Directions: Entrance on Rathbone St

Four Seasons Hotel London

Modern European, Asian
Relaxed, contemporary dining

Hamilton Place, Park Lane, W1A 1AZ
Tel: 020 7499 0888
Email: fsh.london@fourseasons.com
Website: www.fourseasons.com
Chef: Bernhard Mayer
Owners: Four Seasons Hotels & Resorts

This is sophisticated dining just a stone's throw from Hyde Park. The well-known Lanes Restaurant is a lovely dark, clubby-feel dining room oozing understated luxury – think stained glass, wood panelling and marble. Spotlights illuminate each table and the wall-to-ceiling shelves showcase some beautiful glassware. Service here is seamless yet unpretentious, with obvious attention to detail. The cosmopolitan menu has Asian influences from the chef's time in the Far East, seen in dishes like lamb nasi goreng and lamb satay with fried egg and spicy peanut sauce. It also includes traditional British favourites like bread-and-butter pudding or cherry crumble. A buzzy bar and regular jazz dinners are a feature, too.

Times: 12–3/6–11
Prices: 3 Course Fixed D £38 Main £22–£35
Directions: Hamilton Place, just of Hyde Park Corner end of Park Lane
Parking: 50

alvin - Bistrot de Luxe

Galvin - Bistrot de Luxe

French NOTABLE WINE LIST

Top-notch cuisine at a classy bistro

66 Baker Street, W1U 7DH
Tel: 020 7935 4007
Email: info@galvinuk.co.uk
Website: www.galvinuk.co.uk
Chef: Chris & Jeff Galvin
Owners: Chris & Jeff Galvin

he brothers Galvin worked in some of London's top kitchens efore going it alone in order to create this classy bistro with a arisian feel. Their name above a grey awning and glass frontage s the only clue as to the pedigree of the place halfway along Baker treet. Panelled walls, black leather banquettes and crisp white nen set the tone, while fans whirl overhead, mirrors adorn the valls, and tantalizing glimpses are offered of the kitchen. Fittingly, he highly accomplished cooking is unmistakeably Gallic, with reat ingredients and superb flavours at value-for-money prices. Duck liver parfait is a typical starter, served with shallot confit, while mains are rooted in traditional cuisine: daube of Denham Estate venison for example, with poached quince and chestnuts, or rôte de porc noir with pommes mousseline and pruneaux d'Agen.

Times: 12–2.30/6–11, Closed
25 & 26 Dec, 1 Jan, D 24 Dec
Prices: 3 Course Fixed D £17.50
Main £11.50–£18.50
Directions: Please telephone for
directions

153

Galvin at Windows

Modern French

Exciting destination restaurant with magnificent views

London Hilton on Park Lane,
22 Park Lane, W1K 1BE
Tel: 020 7208 4021
Email:
galvinatwindows@hilton.com
Website:
www.hilton.co.uk/londonparklane
Chef: Chris Galvin

Unrivalled 360-degree views over the capital's skyline prove an irresistible feature of this 28th-floor restaurant perched atop of the London Hilton on Park Lane. Chris Galvin (see also Galvin – Bistrot de Luxe page 153) oversees André Garrett (ex Orrery) in the kitchens of this slick modern French affair. It's glamorous, swish and contemporary, with leather seating, crisp linen and an eye-catching golden-ribbon feature suspended from the ceiling, while the raised central area allows all a view. The spacious bar enjoys the panorama, too, while the confident, skilful modern French approach is driven by tip-top seasonal ingredients and clean-cut flavours and presentation; take a fillet of Speyside beef served with braised cheek, foie gras and ceps. (Also open for breakfast.)

Owners: Hilton International
Times: 12–2.30/7–10.30, Closed
L Sat, D Sun
Directions: On Park Lane,
opposite Hyde Park

Le Gavroche Restaurant

French ♨ NOTABLE WINE LIST

Mayfair's bastion of French tradition

43 Upper Brook Street, W1K 7QR
Tel: 020 7408 0881
Email: bookings@le-gavroche.com
Website: www.le-gavroche.co.uk
Chef: Michel Roux Jnr
Owners: Le Gavroche Ltd

The Roux brothers' first British venture, Le Gavroche may be 40 years old, but its packed tables testify to its enduring appeal and popularity. Cosseting and opulent, the dining room comes awash with legions of dedicated staff and decorated with rich fittings and furnishings, while tables are set with crisp linen and lavish crystal and silver, all setting the tone for a truly classical French experience. Like the décor, Michel Jnr's superb, skilful cooking drips with luxuries, while blending classical dishes with others that show a lighter touch and more contemporary taste. Beef fillet and foie gras with port sauce and truffled macaroni cheese, or steamed lobster with pasta and a light cream brandy sauce, is rounded off perfectly with a warm bitter chocolate tart with sorbet, trifle and spiced milk chocolate mousse. A tasting Menu Exceptional and a serious, French-dominated wine list wraps up this classy Gallic act.

Times: 12–2/6.30–11, Closed
Xmas, New Year, BHs, Sun, L Sat
Prices: Main £26.80–£46.60
Directions: From Park Lane into
Upper Brook St, restaurant on righ

154

Gordon Ramsay at Claridge's

Gordon Ramsay at Claridge's

European v

Elegant dining and gastronomic flair

This elegant, high-ceilinged restaurant is very grand. Service is expectedly slick and professional and tables elegantly appointed, while there's an intimate bar area, and a 'chef's table' in the heart of the kitchen. Chef Mark Sargeant's highly accomplished, modern haute-European cuisine focuses around top-class seasonal ingredients, the fixed-price repertoire of lunch, carte and six-course tasting option dotted with luxury, the cooking fitting perfectly under the Ramsay stable umbrella. There's an intelligent simplicity that allows main ingredients to shine in clean-flavoured dishes; perhaps roasted John Dory and sautéed langoustines served with baby artichokes, pink fir potatoes, carrot purée and a light fennel sauce, and maybe a buttermilk pannacotta with vanilla biscuit and rhubarb jus to close. Save room for the tasters, inter-courses and petits fours, and choose your wine from a serious wine list.

Brook Street, W1K 4HR
Tel: 020 7499 0099
Email:
gordonramsay@claridges.com
Website: www.gordonramsay.com
Chef: Mark Sargeant
Owners: Gordon Ramsay
Holdings Ltd

Times: 12–2.45/5.45–11
Prices: Fixed D £65
Directions: At the corner of Brook
& Davies St

The Greenhouse

Modern European

Fine dining at a discreet Mayfair address

Talented chef Antonin Bonnet (formerly of Morton's, London) heads-up the highly accomplished kitchen at The Greenhouse, a chic, modern Mayfair-mews restaurant that is kitted out in neutral tones and natural textures, and dotted with a classy collection of nouveau, decorative glass. Bonnet's modern approach is inspired by the highest-quality produce from the markets, putting a creative spin to French and Mediterranean classics on a fixed-price repertoire of lunch, carte and a brace of tasting options. Expect crab and daikon ravioli with spicy Korean red chilli pepper, perhaps followed by seared grey mullet with swede purée and Alenois watercress, and to finish, a choice of millefeuille: vanilla bavaroise and prune ice cream, or clementine and jasmine tea ice cream. A fabulous wine list and various tasters, inter-courses and ancillaries hold interest right through to the end.

27a Hay's Mews, W1J 5NY
Tel: 020 7499 3331
Email: reservations@
greenhouserestaurant.co.uk
Website: www.
greenhouserestaurant.co.uk
Chef: Antonin Bonnet
Owners: Marlon Abela Restaurant
Corporation

Times: 12–2.30/6.45–11, Closed
25–26 Dec, 1 Jan, BHs, Sun, L Sat
Prices: 3 Course Fixed D £60
Directions: Behind Dorchester
Hotel just off Hill St

The Grill (Dorchester Hotel)

Modern British

splendid food in opulent surroundings

This grand, world-renowned hotel's Grill has a whimsical, flamboyantly Scottish feel with large murals of heroic Highlanders on the burnished gold walls, oversized lampshades and colourful tartan chairs. The menu features a few classic grills, such as roast beef from the trolley (with Yorkshire pudding and roast potatoes), but the main thrust takes a modern British approach in the hands of young head chef, Aiden Byrne – a protégé of Tom Aikens, and previously at Danesfield House Hotel in Marlow. Highly accomplished dishes are multi-faceted but deliver well-balanced combinations, driven by tip-top quality ingredients and fresh, clean flavours that are presented with real panache. Think roasted scallops with white chocolate and truffle risotto, pan-fried John Dory served with celeriac, apple and horseradish, or perhaps squab pigeon with pickled cabbage and a sweet garlic-butter sauce.

The Dorchester, Park Lane,
W1K 1QA
Tel: 020 7629 8888
Email:
restaurants@thedorchester.com
Website: www.thedorchester.com
Chef: Aiden Byrne
Owners: The Dorchester Collection

Times: 12.30–2.30/6–11
Prices: Main £19.50–£30
Directions: On Park Ln,
overlooking Hyde Park

The Grill

Traditional English, Continental 🔖 NOTABLE WINE LIST

Elegant, traditional-vogue dining

This landmark Mayfair hotel has emerged from complete refurbishment and retains an air of its original charm with the successful marriage of traditional and contemporary styling. The Grill (the oldest hotel restaurant in London – previously called Restaurant 1837) follows the theme and, whilst modern and stylish in appearance, hasn't lost its Victorian-era elegance. Think oak panelling, moss green leather banquette booths, hanging lanterns and specially commissioned wall lights, linen tablecloths and traditional, highly professional service. The kitchen continues the theme, its modern continental approach likewise tempered by a traditional English note, with a focus on old favourites; think English lamb cutlets from the grill selection, to seared Crinnan scallops with cauliflower purée and braised fennel. Brown's renowned afternoon teas are served in the lounge.

Brown's Hotel, Albemarle Street, W1S 4BP
Tel: 020 7518 4060
Email: reservations.brownshotel@roccofortehotels.com
Website: www.roccofortehotels.com
Chef: Laurence Glayzer
Owners: Rocco Forte Hotels

Times: 12.30–2.30/7–10.30
Prices: 3 Course Fixed D £30
Main £14.50–£26
Directions: Off Piccadilly between Green Park tube station and Bond Street

The Grill

Hakkasan

Hakkasan

Chinese

Exotic Chinese dining in central London

Dark and with a club-like atmosphere, this is an incredibly popular restaurant with a dazzling modern interior that reflects the wealth of Chinese culture: think black lacquer and red calligraphy, with delicate Balinese latticework used to divide up seating areas lit by low-slung spotlights. The lengthy menu is built on Cantonese foundations, with influences from other regions, and includes a dim sum selection (available lunchtime only) as well as a range of 'small eat' snacks, and some specials requiring 24-hour notice, such as Peking duck with Royal Beluga caviar. There are old favourites too, often with a twist, and distinguished by first-class ingredients, dazzling technique and plenty of flair. And if all of that wasn't enough, the cocktail list is great too: a frothy collection of tipples that includes a Purple Emperor, Rose Petal Martini and the intriguingly named, Walking Buddha. Not to be missed.

No 8 Hanway Place, W1T 1HD
Tel: 020 7927 7000
Email: reservation@hakkasan.com
Chef: C Tong Chee Hwee
Owners: Alan Yau

Times: 12–2.45/6–12.30,
Closed 25 Dec, L 26 Dec, 1 Jan,
D 24 Dec
Prices: Fixed D £50–£100
Main £9.50–£52
Directions: From station take
exit 2, then 1st left, 1st right,
restaurant straight ahead

Kai Mayfair

Chinese

Luxurious venue for authentic Chinese cooking

65 South Audley Street, W1K 2QU
Tel: 020 7493 8988
Email: kai@kaimayfair.co.uk
Website: www.kaimayfair.co.uk
Chef: Alex Chow
Owners: Bernard Yeoh

A setting of oriental opulence is provided at this upmarket restaurant, with a décor of rich reds and muted gold and silver. Staff are dressed in military-style jackets finished with a Swarovski crystal emblem of the restaurant's name in Chinese characters. The kitchen prides itself on authenticity with some fairly traditional dishes, but new flavours are created and the repertoire adapted by including non-traditional ingredients. Maybe opt for the enticing 'Mermaids in the Mist' – Chilean sea bass in a light miso-type broth, followed by 'The Drunken Phoenix on the Scented Tree' – a whole spring chicken marinated in a fragrant infusion of cinnamon bark and Chinese wine.

Times: 12–2.15/6.30–11, Closed 25–26 Dec, New Year
Prices: Main £16–£53
Directions: Telephone for directions, or see website

The Langham Hotel

Modern International

Modern international cuisine in a new look restaurant

1c Portland Place, W1B 1JA
Tel: 020 7973 7544
Email: lonmemories@
langhamhotels.com
Website: www.langhamhotels.com
Owners: Langham Hotels

At the time of going to press this restaurant was undergoing a major refurbishment. Designed by the renowned David Collins, this chic new operation will seat approximately 100 people and include two private dining rooms, a cocktail room and a wine corridor. Colour schemes will incorporate powder blues with lime green leather, gold wood and mosaic flooring. The cuisine will be modern international with classical French roots. A new feature will be the off-street entrance that will give the restaurant its own identity and render it extremely accessible for both hotel guests and non-residents.

Times: 12–2.30/6–10.30
Directions: On north end of Regent St, by Oxford Circus

Kai Mayfair

Latium

Italian

Fresh, authentic Italian cooking with service to match

21 Berners Street, W1T 3LP
Tel: 020 7323 9123
Email: info@latiumrestaurant.com
Website:
www.latiumrestaurant.com
Chef: Maurizio Morelli
Owners: Maurizio Morelli,
Claudio Pulze

Given the Latin name for the chef-patron's home town (Latina), this smart, intimate restaurant (one of the Capital's best kept secrets) provides such authentic tastes and atmosphere, you'll feel as though you were in Italy. Maurizio Morelli's unique passion for Italian cuisine has created a great seasonal menu with a strong commitment to sourcing fine Italian produce and delivering authentic flavours with flair and panache. Ravioli is a particular speciality, with a separate menu offering a choice of five fresh filled pasta dishes as starters and mains. Try oxtail ravioli with celery sauce or, alternatively, get that Latin fix via dishes like roasted saddle of lamb with baby artichokes, roast potato and asparagus, or an almond and chocolate tart with Amaretto sauce.

Times: 12–2.45/6–10.30, Closed
BHs, Sun, L Sat
Prices: 2 Course Fixed D £24.50
3 Course Fixed D £28.50

Levant

Lebanese, Middle Eastern

A restaurant with vivid colours, scents and flavours

Jason Court, 76 Wigmore Street,
W1H 9DQ
Tel: 020 7224 1111
Email: info@levant.co.uk
Website: www.levant.co.uk

Leave the sobriety of Wigmore Street behind when you descend the stone stairs of Levant into a scene from the Arabian Nights. Lanterns light the way into an exotic basement where colours are rich, fabrics sumptuous, and the atmosphere seductive and beguiling. A long banquette and separate tables dominate the centre of the room, while cosy private areas offer floor cushions for lounging over the Lebanese cooking. The Middle Eastern spices bring an authentic flavour to hot and cold mezzes, and special treats like slow-roasted whole shoulder of lamb served with a nut pilaf.

Times: 12/midnight, Closed
25–26 Dec
Directions: From Bond St station,
walk through St Christopher's
Place, reach Wigmore St,
restaurant across road

*Lindsay House
Restaurant*

Lindsay House Restaurant

Modern European v

Vibrant flavours in a Soho townhouse

This well-known Soho restaurant is discreetly tucked away behind the doors of an elegant townhouse. The four-storey building dates back to 1740 and, instead of the frontage you might expect in Soho, it's all very low key with a doorbell to be rung on arrival. Inside you'll find elegant traditional-style dining rooms on the ground and first floors, plus a private dining room on the second floor. Diners can choose from an array of menus, including a seasonal lunchtime market menu, garden (vegetarian), tasting option and carte. The cooking style relies on carefully sourced top-quality ingredients and robust simple flavours, hallmarks of Richard Corrigan's Irish roots. Clever combinations and excellent presentation might deliver the likes of pan-roasted brill with wild mushroom linguine, or a loin of West Cork beef served with spinach purée, gratin potatoes and caramelised ceps.

21 Romilly Street, W1D 5AF
Tel: 020 7439 0450
Email: richardcorrigan@
lindsayhouse.co.uk
Website: www.lindsayhouse.co.uk
Chef: Richard Corrigan
Owners: Searcy Corrigan

Times: 12–2.30/6–11, Closed
1 wk Etr, BHs & Xmas, Sun,
L Sat & Sun, D Sun
Prices: Fixed D £56 Main £14–£22
Directions: Just off Shaftesbury
Avenue, off Dean Street

163

Locanda Locatelli

Italian ♦ NOTABLE WINE LIST

Inspired Italian cuisine in chic contemporary setting

This slick, sophisticated and much-vaunted Italian – about the best in the country – is tucked away off Portman Square in the back of the Hyatt Regency Churchill Hotel, and is the haunt of a well-heeled, celebrity crowd. Cream leather banquette seating, concave mirrors and subdued lighting (in the evenings) set the scene at this buzzy, classy David Collins designed restaurant. Its retro yet stylish interior features parquet flooring, grained-wood walls, glass dividers and modern artworks, including pieces by Paul Simonan (of the Clash pop band) and Damien Hirst. The service is as sleek and notable as the décor, Italian staff court customers with flair and passion and have a real appreciation of the food, while chef Giorgio Locatelli glides between tables surveying his clientele and ensuring his delicious food is being enjoyed with the passion shown in its creation. The ingredients are the absolute best and lovingly sourced, and the breads (some nine items, like foccacia, pane carasau, grissini, etc) and pasta are phenomenal. The style is modern northern Italian, and there's a real freshness about the cooking, enhanced by great combinations while nothing is over-worked or too complicated, so flavours sing out. The traditionally laid-out menu offers plenty of choice, so do come hungry and set to go four rounds – antipasta, pasta, main and dessert – to do the ultimate justice to Giorgio's inspired cooking ... it doesn't come better in the Italian format! Think home-made chestnut tagliatelle with wild mushrooms, perhaps pan-fried calves' kidney served with potato purée and ceps, and to finish, maybe a panettone bread-and-butter pudding with panettone ice cream. A sommelier is on hand to help navigate the impressive regionally-focused, all-Italian wine list with its superb vintages from Tuscany and Piemonte. But do book well in advance as it's always busy. This is one not to be missed!

Hyatt Regency London, The Churchill, 8 Seymour Street, W1H 7JZ
Tel: 020 7935 9088
Email: info@locandalocatelli.com
Website:
www.locandalocatelli.com
Chef: Giorgio Locatelli
Owners: Plaxy & Giorgio Locatelli

Times: 12–3/7–11, Closed Xmas, BHs
Prices: Main £12–£28
Directions: Please telephone for directions

Maze

Maze

French, Asian

Grazing in elegance at the heart of Mayfair

Part of the Gordon Ramsay stable, Maze has contemporary and bright décor, with an extensive dining area featuring a glass screen with the restaurant's maze motif. Tables are simply laid, while service is professional and knowledgeable, and there is a chef's table overlooking the main pass. Executive chef Jason Atherton delivers a modern French approach with Asian influences via a grazing-style menu of tapas-style dishes (with six to eight dishes recommended per head). There's also a traditional carte, plus a Sunday roast offering. Expect the likes of Orkney scallops roasted with spices, peppered golden raisin purée and cauliflower, followed by roasted brill with provençale cockle vinaigrette, pistou and baby spinach, and to finish, pain au chocolat (chocolate ganache with caffé latte sorbet, vanilla bread-and-milk mousse). The 'flights of wines' innovation suits the grazing concept perfectly.

10–13 Grosvenor Square, W1K 6J
Tel: 020 7107 0000
Email: maze@gordonramsay.com
Website: www.gordonramsay.com
Chef: Jason Atherton
Owners: Gordon Ramsay
Holdings Ltd

Times: 12–2.30/6–10.30
Prices: 6 Course Fixed D £50
Main £7.50–£10.50
Directions: Entrance off
Grosvenor Sq

Mews of Mayfair

Modern

Chic place to see and be seen with cooking to match

As its name suggests, this lively and contemporary restaurant, set amid Mayfair's premier-league shops, stands in a lovely mews just off Bond Street. There's a bar and terraced tables on the ground floor, while upstairs the main restaurant offers a more sophisticated edge. Smart and modern is the style, set off with a striking black-and-white theme; think white walls and white embossed leather upholstery. Service is friendly but professional. The kitchen's experienced international team delivers refined dishes with a wealth of interesting combinations based around tip-top produce. Expect clear flavours and sound balance in dishes like roast sea bass with artichoke purée and pickled chanterelles, and perhaps vanilla roast figs and pistachio ice cream to close.

10–11 Lancashire Court, W1S 1EY
Tel: 020 7518 9395
Email: info@mewsofmayfair.com
Website:
www.mewsofmayfair.com
Chef: David Selex
Owners: James Robson &
Robert Nearn

Times: 12–3/6–11, Closed 25–26 Dec, New Year, Etr Mon, D Sun
Prices: Main £14.50–£29.50
Directions: Between Brook St & Maddox St. Opposite Dolce & Gabbana

---

Mirabelle

Traditional French

Classic French cuisine with Mayfair glamour

Step through the low-key lobby of this Mayfair grandee and you'll find a glamorous bar and restaurant, complete with art deco mirrors, bold artworks and a resident pianist. Part of the Marco Pierre White empire, it lures a well-heeled crowd with its easy cosmopolitan ambience and classic French dishes. Expect unfussy, flavourful cooking that belies the grand surroundings and has an authentic Gallic feel: sole à la provençale, for example, or braised pig's trotters with morels, pomme purée and sauce Périgueux. Desserts might include prune and Armagnac soufflé or lemon tart, and there's an extensive wine list. Private dining rooms are available with a separate menu and there are some great-value set lunches.

56 Curzon Street, W1J 8PA
Tel: 020 7499 4636
Email: sales@whitestarline.org.uk
Website:
www.whitestarline.org.uk
Chef: Igor Timchishin
Owners: Marco Pierre White,
Jimmy Lahoud

Times: 12–2.30/6–11.30, Closed 26 Dec & 1 Jan
Prices: Main £16.50–£25.50
Directions: Telephone for directions.

Mosaico

Italian

Slick, stylish and modern Mayfair Italian

13 Albermarle Street, W1S 4HJ
Tel: 020 7409 1011
Email: mosaico-restaurant.co.uk

Set beneath the DKNY store opposite Brown's Hotel and just round the corner from The Ritz, this Mayfair Italian couldn't be anything else but sophisticated and upmarket. Think red-leather banquettes or stylish chairs, tables dressed in their best whites and limestone floors. Cream walls, prints of Italian scenes and a mirrored frieze above the seating keeps things light, while staff are slick, attentive and Latin. The kitchen takes an equally stylish, modish approach with a northern Italian slant, using quality ingredients, including textbook pastas and cracking breads and grissini. Expect light, well-presented, clear-flavoured dishes like ravioli filled with artichokes in a light vegetable sauce, or perhaps grilled calves' liver and kidneys with truffle-scented olive oil.

Times: 12–2.30/6.30–10.45,
Closed Sun, L Sat, Xmas, Etr, BHs
Directions: Telephone for further details

Nicole's

Mediterranean

Lunchtime retreat for the chic and well-heeled

158 New Bond Street, W1S 2UB
Tel: 020 7499 8408
Email: nicoles@nicolefarhi.com
Website: www.nicolefarhi.com
Chef: Annie Wayte
Owners: Stephen Marks

A wide stone staircase leads down to the bright, split-level restaurant below Nicole Farhi's fashion store on exclusive Bond Street. And, as you'd expect of a haute-couture eatery, there's a stylish, contemporary edge to match that designer label. A small upper level has a steel and glass bar with more informal tables, while oak floors, brown leather and white linen distinguish the main dining area a few steps down. The cooking takes an assured modern approach, based around simplicity and quality seasonal ingredients. For mains expect the likes of grilled halibut with roasted leeks, crispy potatoes and chanterelles, or perhaps baked garlic- and lemon-crusted cod with crab mash and red chard, followed by a chocolate pot and espresso cookie to finish. The bread selection is excellent. A separate bar menu is also available.

Times: 12–3.30, Closed BHs, Sun,
D all week
Prices: Main £18–£24.75
Directions: Between Hermès & Asprey

Nobu

Japanese

Minimalist and upmarket with outstanding cuisine

Nobu takes up the whole of the first floor of the trendy Metropolitan Hotel with views over Park Lane and Hyde Park. Its interior is ultra sleek and minimalist, with clean lines accentuated by neutral colours, stark tiled floors and leather banquettes and chairs. Service is swift, with friendly and unassuming black-clad staff ready to guide the uninitiated through the lengthy, flexible-styled menu, predominantly aimed at grazing and sharing. The accomplished kitchen's style is Japanese but with the occasional South American twist, in dishes like anti-cucho Peruvian-style spicy rib-eye steak, or Chilean sea bass with moro miso. The focus is on exceptionally fresh produce, with defined and vibrant flavours and impressive presentation, as in the must-have black cod with miso. Finish off with an indulgent chocolate bento box – perfect for sharing. There's also a sushi bar to round up a class act.

The Metropolitan, Old Park Lane, W1Y 4LB
Tel: 020 7447 4747
Email: ecb@ecbpr.co.uk
Website: www.noburestaurants.com

Times: 12–2.15/from 6, Closed L Sat–Sun

Nobu Berkeley Street

Japanese

Modern restaurant with a serious approach to food

The sister of the famous Nobu restaurant off Park Lane (see entry above), this Mayfair newcomer has already established itself as a place to see and be seen. Downstairs a spacious bar serves drinks till the early hours, while the upstairs restaurant is open for dinner only and features a sushi bar with an open kitchen, a wood-burning oven and a 12-seater hibachi table where guests can cook their own food with a chef's assistance. The waiters know their stuff and are happy to guide you through the menu or even choose a surprise selection; alternatively plump for the six-course tasting menu to really do the place justice. Crispy Gloucestershire Old Spot pork with spicy miso is a hit, as is chocolate harumaki (spring rolls) with passionfruit dipping sauce.

15 Berkeley Street, W1J 8DY
Tel: 020 7290 9222
Email: ecb@ecbpr.co.uk
Website: www.noburestaurants.com

Times: 6–1am, Closed 25–26 Dec, L all week
Directions: Telephone for directions

Orrery

Orrery

Modern European

Stunning food and service in equal measures

Above the Conran shop, this first-floor, prestigious restaurant has an etched glass screen depicting the namesake orrery – a mechanical model of the solar system. The pedigree of Terence Conran design is unmistakable; contemporary, streamline and typically understated. Two long rows of tables lined with banquettes and chairs fill the room, where service is as stylish as the surroundings. The cooking style is suitably innovative and creative, intricate, light and contemporary, its roots firmly in the classics. Meticulous presentation, highly accomplished technical skills and top-notch produce pepper the repertoire; think best end of new season lamb with slow-braised shoulder, aubergine purée and olive jus, or perhaps steamed monkfish wrapped in prosciutto with braised oxtail and truffle macaroni. As we went to press, we understand that there was a change of chef taking place.

55-57 Marylebone High Street, W1U 5RB
Tel: 020 7616 8000
Email: oliviere@conran-restaurants.co.uk
Website: www.orrery.co.uk

Times: 12–2.30/6.30–10.30, Closed 25–26 Dec, New Year, Good Friday
Directions: At north end of Marylebone High St

Ozer

Turkish, Middle Eastern

A bustling delight, a stone's throw from Oxford Circus

5 Langham Place, Regent Street,
W1B 3DG
Tel: 020 7323 0505
Email: info@sofra.co.uk
Website: www.sofra.co.uk
Chef: Mustafa Guzen
Owners: Huseyin Ozer

Modern and upmarket, Ozer breaks all the old Turkish restaurant clichés. Deep red, curvy, marble-effect walls, a tiled floor and contemporary ceiling lighting kick things off in style. Up front there's a buzzy bar area, while at the back the restaurant comes decked out in white tablecloths and black or red leather chairs. The atmosphere's vibrant, bustling and loud, with hardworking staff. The array of menu options offer a wide, affordable range of traditional dishes, including excellent meze, as well as some more unusual offerings, and all kicked off by complimentary houmous, olives and bread. It's straightforward but accomplished and well-presented; try a meze platter followed up by lamb kulbasti (tender fillet with oregano).

Times: Noon/mdnt
Prices: 3 Course Fixed D £20.95
Main £6.95–£19.95
Directions: 2 min walk towards
Upper Regent Street.

Passione

Italian

Wonderful flavours from an intimate, lively Italian

10 Charlotte Street, W1T 2LT
Tel: 020 7636 2833
Website: www.passione.co.uk
Chef: Gennaro Contaldo &
Mario Magli

Its pinkish-terracotta and glass frontage seem somewhat unremarkable for a widely esteemed Italian, though the name on the awning perfectly sums up this small but big-hearted restaurant, epitomising chef-patron Gennaro Contaldo's love affair with great food. Green walls are hung with food photographs, while blond-wood floors and chairs add a modern edge to close-set tables and a lively, informal atmosphere; there's an endearing neighbourhood local vibe here. It's not difficult to see why Gennaro is a Jamie Oliver mentor, his regional Italian cooking driven by fresh, high-quality seasonal produce, herbs and simple, clean-flavoured style. Perhaps try tagliatelle with summer truffle sauce, or wild sea bass served with sauté peas and broad beans and marinated samphire.

Times: 12.30–2.15/7–10.15,
Closed 1 wk Xmas, BHs, Sun, L Sat
Prices: Main £21–£26
Directions: 5 min walk from
Goodge St underground station

Pied à Terre

Modern French v ![NOTABLE WINE LIST]

Outstanding, highly refined, modern cooking

Having risen from the ashes of a fire back in 2005, this class act continues to run on top form with some superlative and exciting cooking. The frontage is intimate and unassuming, while the sleek interior is fittingly stylish and glamorous. The décor is contemporary and oozes understated luxury, with cream suede and rosewood furniture and architectural glass combining harmoniously. There's also a bar upstairs to relax both pre- and post-meal, featuring leather seats and art by Hamilton, Blake and Hodgkin. Service is as impeccable as ever, led by excellent host David Moore. Australian chef Shane Osborn continues to deliver his brand of stylish and creative modern French cuisine; it is sophisticated, refined and brimful of class and emphatic flavours, using top-notch luxury ingredients and innovation – technically superb, it ticks all the boxes. The tantalising fixed-price repertoire of lunch, carte and tasting menu (with the option of accompanying wines) promotes an agony of choice, delivering top-drawer dishes. Maybe roasted and poached loin of mid-Devon venison served with a quince purée, pommes soufflé and a sauté of bacon, Savoy cabbage and fresh chestnuts, or perhaps roasted halibut with courgette and basil cream, courgette and truffle fondue, razor clams and a lemon oil emulsion, while dessert might feature a bitter-sweet chocolate tart with stout ice cream and Macadamia nut cream. A stunning range of ancillaries (canapés, amuse-bouche, breads, pre-desserts and petits fours) burst with flavour and attention to detail like everything else here, while an impressive wine list rounds off this highflyer in style.

34 Charlotte Street, W1T 2NH
Tel: 020 7636 1178
Email: info@pied-a-terre.co.uk
Website: www.pied-a-terre.co.uk
Chef: Shane Osborn
Owners: David Moore &
Shane Osborn

Times: 12–2.45/6.15–11, Closed 2 wks Xmas & New Year, Sun, L Sat
Prices: Fixed D £30–£62
Directions: S of BT Tower and Goodge St

172

Patterson's

Modern European

Inventive cuisine in an elegant, stylish setting

Tucked away in a tiny Mayfair street at the top end of Savile Row, Patterson's provides an elegant setting for fine dining, complemented by slick, professional service. The bar area, complete with lobster and tropical fish tanks, leads to a spacious, long, narrow dining room with oak flooring, high-backed leather chairs and white walls enlivened by colourful artwork. You can relax here and peruse the menu's modern approach – underpinned by a classical French theme and founded on carefully sourced, tip-top local and organic produce. Father-and-son team Raymond and Tom produce dishes that surprise and delight with their flavour and presentation. Expect loin of lamb in filo pastry with green spring vegetables and curried crab mousseline, and perhaps a pineapple and crème fraîche sorbet millefeuille with fruit salad to finish.

4 Mill Street, Mayfair, W1S 2AX
Tel: 020 7499 1308
Email: pattersonmayfair@btconnect.com
Website: www.pattersonsrestaurant.com
Chef: Raymond & Thomas Patterson
Owners: Raymond & Thomas Patterson

Times: 12–3/6–11, Closed 25–26 Dec, 1 Jan, Good Fri & Etr Mon, Sun, L Sat
Prices: 3 Course Fixed D £40 Main £17
Directions: Located off Conduit St opposite Savile Row entrance

---

The Providores

Fusion NOTABLE WINE LIST

Complex-flavoured fusion food

Once a Victorian pub, The Providores – smack at the heart of Marylebone High Street – now delivers a buzzy, contemporary, all-day café, wine/ tapas bar operation downstairs and a fine-dining restaurant upstairs. Enjoy breakfast, brunch, coffee and a fascinating menu of tapas-inspired fare below, and an extensive choice of fusion food in the dining room above. Both menus change frequently according to produce and inspiration, but chef-patron Peter Gordon's New Zealand roots shine through with his use of unfamiliar ingredients and combinations in innovative, exciting, well-executed and presented dishes. Take seared kangaroo loin on a five-spice celeriac fritter with Kalamansi tomato chutney and Greek yogurt to start, and perhaps slow-braised duck with Spanish black bean, feta and chipotle chilli spring rolls with tamarind to follow.

109 Marylebone High Street, W1U 4RX
Tel: 020 7935 6175
Email: anyone@theprovidores.co.uk
Website: www.theprovidores.co.uk
Chef: Peter Gordon
Owners: P Gordon, M McGrath, J Leeming

Times: 12–10.30, Closed 24 Dec–3 Jan
Prices: Main £19–£25
Directions: From Bond St station cross Oxford St, down James St, into Thayer St then Marylebone High St

Quo Vadis

Quo Vadis

Modern Italian

Showcase for authentic Italian cuisine and modern art

Although Karl Marx once lived in this building, one of the oldest in Soho, its real claim to fame has been as 'Leo Quo Vadis' – one of London's most respected Italian restaurants, founded in the 1930s by Peppino Leoni. The ground-floor restaurant has stained glass windows and a modern, stylish interior displaying striking works of art by artists like Damien Hirst, Andy Warhol and Modigliani. The modern Italian cuisine is just as impressive, serving up antipasti, pasta, risottos, fish, meat and salad dishes on an authentic and varied Italian menu. Try smoked aubergine 'cannelone' with tuna and crispy parmesan, broth of chicken with chicken tortelloni, enoky mushroom and baby leeks, finishing with peach and pistachio tarte feuillete with pistachio and red wine sauce.

26–29 Dean Street, W1D 3LL
Tel: 020 7437 9585
Email: sales@whitestarline.org.uk
Website:
www.whitestarline.org.uk
Chef: Fernando Corradazzi
Owners: Jimmy Lahoud,
Marco Pierre White

Times: 12–2.30/5.30–11.30,
Closed 24–25 Dec, 1 Jan, Sun,
L Sat
Prices: 3 Course Fixed D £17.95
–£19.95 Main £11–£19

175

The Red Fort

Traditional Indian

Stylish, elegant and contemporary Soho Indian

77 Dean Street, W1D 3SH
Tel: 020 7437 2525
Email: info@redfort.co.uk
Website: www.redfort.co.uk
Chef: Iqbal Ahamad
Owners: Amin Ali

This Soho stalwart may have been around for 20 years, but this stylish, upmarket Indian certainly isn't stuck in a time warp. The entrance leads to either its subterranean Akbar Bar or ground-floor dining room, where restful, neutral tones set the scene alongside walls adorned with authentic artefacts. Banquettes line walls, tables are laid with white linen and the staff are smartly attired. The menu continues the theme, with dishes being primarily Mughal Court/North Western in style, utilising top-notch ingredients. Think monkfish tikka to start, followed by anaari champ – Scottish lamb chops from the grill, in star anise and pomegranate jus – or perhaps zaafrani lobster with saffron and garlic, with raspberry shrikhand (yoghurt) to finish. There are also good-value fixed-price lunch and pre-theatre menus.

Times: 12–2.15/5.45–11.15, Closed 25 Dec, Sat, Sun
Prices: 3 Course Fixed D £16
Main £14–£33
Directions: Walk north on Charing Cross Rd. At Cambridge Circus turn left into Shaftesbury Ave. Dean St is 2nd rd on right

---

Ristorante Semplice

Italian

Classy Italian with a passion for authenticity

10 Blenheim Street, W1S 1LJ
Tel: 0207 4951509

'Semplice' means 'simple' in Italian and that's the mantra of this chic Mayfair eatery, formerly two small restaurants. Highly polished ebony walls with gold carvings, accompanied by leather seating in brown and cream, and an impressive Murano chandelier, set the scene. Top-notch ingredients form the foundation, either garnered from the best British producers, or flown in from home (mozzarella arrives daily). A variety of regional Italian dishes are delivered with an emphasis on flavour. Free-range Italian meat also wows, and arrives at the table in dishes like roasted and pan-fried rabbit with baby carrots, broad beans and artichoke sauce or free-range chicken cooked 'sous-vide' with grilled vegetables and parmesan shavings. Service is slick and very Italian.

Times: 12–2.30/7–10.30, Closed BHs, Sun

The Ritz

The Ritz

Modern British, French

NOTABLE WINE LIST

Sumptuous cuisine from a Piccadilly grandee

150 Piccadilly, W1J 9BR
Tel: 020 7493 8181
Email: enquire@theritzlondon.com
Website: www.theritzlondon.com
Chef: John T Williams
Owners: The Ritz Hotel
(London) Ltd

Renowned as one of the most beautiful dining rooms in Europe, the Ritz restaurant is an opulent confection of Louis XVI furnishings, gold chandeliers, and trompe d'oeil frescos. Dressing up is de rigueur, so break out the glad rags and make the most of the occasion by booking ahead for a table overlooking the patio and park. The menu is as grand as the setting; rooted in classical French cuisine with the odd nod to modern trends, it's crammed with luxury ingredients and big flavours, and offers an array of choice that's sure to cause pleasurable dithering. Take a fillet of beef with truffle and ox-tongue gratin, seared duck livers and hermitage jus, or perhaps rosemary-braised turbot with white asparagus and a chicken and ginger emulsion.

Times: 12–2.30/6–10.30
Prices: 4 Course Fixed D £65–£85
Main £19–£47
Directions: 10-minute walk from
Piccadilly Circus or Hyde Park
Corner

177

The Ritz

Roka

Japanese

Stylish, friendly, funky Japanese grill

Located on bustling Charlotte Street, Roka is a contemporary, ultra-hip Japanese restaurant. Its robata grill (traditional Japanese barbecue grill) takes centre stage, with bar seating all around allowing diners to watch the chefs in the open theatre kitchen, while traditional-style table settings fill the rest of the room. Downstairs, there's a more informal, club-like vibe, with a central bar again, but this time, followed up by sofa-style seating and occasional tables. Service is friendly, upbeat and knowledgeable. The new-wave Japanese cooking is delivered via an extensive menu (backed by a couple of tasting options) designed around the robatayaki grill cuisine, together with a selection of fresh, vibrant sashimi and sushi, all based on top-quality produce. Take sea bream fillet with ryotei miso and red onion, or perhaps beef fillet with chilli, ginger and spring onion from the robata.

37 Charlotte Street, W1T 1RR
Tel: 020 7580 6464
Email: info@rokarestaurant.com
Website: www.rokarestaurant.com
Chef: Rainer Becker, Nic Watt
Owners: Rainer Becker,
Arjun Waney

Times: 12–3.30/5.30–11.30,
Closed 25 Dec, 1 Jan
Prices: 2–3 Course Fixed D
£50–£75 Main £7.90–£55
Directions: 5 min walk from
Goodge St

Salt Yard

Italian, Spanish

Tapas restaurant offering vibrant dishes for sharing

54 Goodge Street, W1T 4NA
Tel: 020 7637 0657
Email: info@saltyard.co.uk
Website: www.saltyard.co.uk
Chef: Benjamin Tish
Owners: Sanja Morris &
Simon Mullins

A very popular tapas restaurant (booking is essential most nights) where you can dine in the relative calm of the basement restaurant or join the hip and noisy crowd eating and drinking in the bar. Downstairs the tables are neatly laid between high-backed leather chairs, and you can watch the kitchen buzz as you sample the fare. It's the same food wherever you sit, and the carefully-sourced ingredients are handled simply and with inspiration by a committed team. Try a hearty octopus and lentil stew in red wine, or a delicate tuna carpaccio with baby broad beans and salsa verde, but don't miss the soft chocolate cake.

Times: 12–3/6–11, Closed BHs,
25 Dec, 1 Jan, Sun, L Sat
Prices: Main £3–£17
Directions: Near Tottenham
Court Rd

Sartoria

Italian

Modern Italian at the heart of Savile Row

Its location on Savile Row has inspired a subtle tailoring theme to this sophisticated, contemporary Conran Italian. Think suited mannequins in the window, crockery with a button logo and a pinking scissor image fronting the menu. Plain white walls come softened by standard lamps, taupe carpeting and modern sofas and chairs upholstered in grey. It's all as sleek and professional as the service and as accomplished and clean cut as the seasonal Italian cooking driven by high-quality ingredients – breaded veal cutlet with a fennel salad, for example. An extensive regional Italian wine list, separate bar area and fixed-price lunch/pre-theatre menu all catch the eye too.

20 Savile Row, W1S 3PR
Tel: 020 7534 7000
Email: sartoriareservations@
conran-restaurants.co.uk
Website: www.conran.com
Chef: Pasquale Amico
Owners: Sir Terence Conran

Times: 12–3/6–11, Closed
25–26 Dec, Sun, L Sat
Directions: Tube to Oxford Circus,
take exit 3, turn left down Regent
St towards Piccadilly Circus, take
5th right into New Burlington St,
end of street on left

Scott's Restaurant

British v

Fashionable, glamorous seafood bar and restaurant

This legendary fish restaurant – relaunched by Caprice Holdings (the people behind The Ivy, Le Caprice and J. Sheekey, see entries) – sees it return to its past glories in great style. The contemporary, fashionable remix of this classic oak-panelled restaurant comes inspired by its heyday, with rich burgundy-leather seating, an exquisite chandelier, specially commissioned modern art and a central crustacea bar in the style of a turn-of-the-century cruise liner. There's a doorman to greet, while table service is slick, attentive and polished. The kitchen uses top-notch ingredients in well-presented dishes, with the likes of oysters, caviar, crustacea, smoked fish, whole fish and meat on the bone finding a place. Think classics like Dover sole (grilled or meunière), lobster (américaine, grilled or thermidor), or maybe pan-fried skate with periwinkles, nut-brown butter and capers.

20 Mount Street, W1K 2HE
Tel: 020 7495 7309
Website:
www.scotts-restaurant.com
Chef: Kevin Gratton
Owners: ICD Ltd

Times: 12–3/5.30–11, Closed
Xmas, Jan 1, Aug BH
Prices: Main £18.50–£26.50
Directions: Just off Grosvenor Sq,
between Berkeley Sq and Park Ln

Sherlock's Bar & Grill

Modern French
Traditional methods for inspirational cuisine

Sherlock Holmes Hotel,
108 Baker Street, W1U 6LJ
Tel: 020 7486 6161
Email:
shh.fb@parkplazahotels.co.uk
Website:
www.sherlockholmeshoteluk.com
Chef: Rachid Hammoum
Owners: Park Plaza Hotels

Situated in a chic boutique hotel, there's no mistaking the links to the famous fictional detective, with paintings and a bronze cast to remind diners of his Baker Street roots. The décor is chic and unfussy with warm colours and modern styling. Interestingly, a mesquite wood-burning stove and a charcoal grill are the main methods of cooking here. The emphasis is on quality ingredients with modern inspiration; think Parma ham rolled monkfish tail served with a potato galette and red pepper caponata, and perhaps a tiramisù or apple tart Tatin finish.

Times: 12–2.30/6–10.30
Prices: Main £14.50–£18.25
Directions: Located on Baker St, close to the tube station

Shogun, Millennium Hotel Mayfair

Japanese
Authentic Japanese food in the heart of Mayfair

Grosvenor Square, W1A 3AN
Tel: 020 7629 9400

This well-established Japanese restaurant is located in the lavishly decorated basement of the Millennium Hotel Mayfair, an impressive Georgian fronted building overlooking Grosvenor Square. Features of its interior décor are kyudo archery arrows, palms and a large statue of a Samurai warrior, and the simple wooden tables are set with bamboo place mats. Discreet service is provided by friendly staff in traditional Japanese attire, and the strength of the Japanese clientele is testimony to the authenticity of the cooking. Shogun produces some of the best Japanese food in the capital including a number of good-value set dinner menus, hand-rolled sushi, zenzai, dobin-mushi, sashimi, tempura, teriyaki and dessert options.

Times: 6–11, Closed Mon

Sketch (Lecture Room & Library)

Modern European V NOTABLE WINE LIST

Technical wizardry offers a unique experience

Remarkably unassuming from outside, with its white-shuttered windows and iron railings, the un-savvy might easily walk on by, save for the evening doorman outside to catch the attention. Once inside though, this one-time HQ of Christian Dior comes brimful of surprises, outrageous flamboyancy and refinement. A collaboration between Mourad Mazouz and Parisian super-chef Pierre Gagnaire, Sketch offers a multi-level food-based extravaganza, which includes the vibrant, ground-floor Gallery brasserie (opulent, exciting and bursting with signature art deco), plus the cool Parlour tea room by day, hyper-trendy bar by night. Throughout, fashionable international designers have created specially commissioned signature pieces that catch the eye. The fine-dining Lecture Room and Library upstairs – two parts of the same space – is elegantly decorated in shades of orange, with ivory walls of studded leather and high ceilings, while thick-piled, brightly coloured carpets and long dangling lampshades cut a somewhat Middle Eastern edge. Well-spaced tables with crisp white linen and feather-cushioned armchairs – in purple and crimson – add comfort, while service is professional, attentive and necessarily knowledgeable of the elaborate dish compositions. Dishes bear the unmistakable creative genius of consultant Pierre Gagnaire's distinctive culinary style (delivered here by head chef and Gagnaire protégé, Pascal Sanchez); it's stunning, exciting, innovative and technically superb. The very best quality fresh produce is transformed into an enormous range of textures and flavours, ensuring a surprise at each turn. It's complex and deeply French, with dishes combining many elements, like a signature starter 'Langoustines Addressed in Five Ways', perhaps a main course of poached fillet of Simmenthal beef in a port bouillon, braised lettuce with beef marrow and pochas beans, condiment, vinegar and sea salt wild mushrooms, while to finish, perhaps another signature offering 'Pierre Gagnaire Grand Desserts' which could arrive as five miniatures. So be prepared to be wowed by the experience and sheer theatre of the place.

9 Conduit Street, W1S 2XG
Tel: 0870 777 4488
Website: www.sketch.uk.com
Chef: P Gagnaire, P Sanchez
Owners: Pierre Gagnaire,
Mourad Mazouz

Times: 12–2.30/7–11, Closed 21 Aug–4 Sep, 25–29 Dec, Sun–Mon, L Sat
Prices: Main £39–£48
Directions: 4 mins walk from Oxford Circus tube station, take exit 3, down Regent St, Conduit St is 4th on right

The Square

Modern French **v** 🍷 NOTABLE WINE LIST

A class culinary act in the heart of Mayfair

Style and sophistication lie beyond the glass frontage of this discreet, chic, premier-league restaurant in a sought-after address just off fashionable Bond Street and its designer boutiques. The expansive dining room – accessed via a small bar – is furnished in slick contemporary style, with terracottas, rich browns, steely blues and creams all harmonising. Parquet floors are set out with clothed tables, their rich brown, floor-length undercloths topped-off with crisp white linen, while striking, vibrant abstract artworks add a splash of colour to the neutral tones. A superb wine list and Philip Howard's bright, intense, memorable cooking prove more than a match for the elegant surroundings and impeccable, professional service. His refreshingly modern approach comes underpinned by a classical French theme; the fixed-priced repertoire, which includes an eight-course tasting option, dotted with luxury items, set to impress any business diner. Cultured dishes impress all, though, displaying an emphasis on well-sourced, top-notch ingredients, interesting combinations and strong, clear flavours, and come dressed to thrill. Consistency, timings, freshness and textures all help the cooking stand out from the crowd too. Take a stunning starter of sea-fresh sauté of langoustine tails and potato gnocchi with field mushroom purée, trompettes de la mort and truffle butter, or perhaps succulent slow-cooked fillet of cod with velvety creamed potato, cauliflower, leek hearts and truffle to follow. Poached pineapple, served with tropical jellies and lime ice cream, might catch the eye at dessert and deliver simplicity at its finest, while peripherals – like a fantastic selection of canapés, breads and petits fours – wrap things up in supreme style.

6–10 Bruton Street, W1J 6PU
Tel: 020 7495 7100
Email: info@squarerestaurant.com
Website:
www.squarerestaurant.com
Chef: Philip Howard
Owners: Mr N Platts-Martin
& Philip Howard

Times: 12–3/6.30–10.45,
Closed 24–26 Dec,1 Jan, L Sat &
Sun, BHs
Prices: Fixed D £65
Directions: Telephone for
directions

So Restaurant

Japanese

Modern Japanese with hints of European cuisine

3–4 Warwick Street, W1B 5LS
Tel: 020 7292 0767
Email: info@sorestaurant.com
Website: www.sorestaurant.com
Chef: Kaoru Yamamoto
Owners: Tetsuro Hama

Contemporary styling – with minimalist use of dark wood, clean lines and artwork – picks this Japanese out from the crowd. The ground floor has a more informal lunchtime, café-style atmosphere, while the basement restaurant comes with dark lacquered tables, high-backed leather chairs and plain walls hung with French wine posters and modern artwork, and is dominated by a glass-wall open-to-view kitchen. The cooking is contemporary – classical Japanese with some European twists – using top-notch ingredients and simple, attractive presentation. Think French foie gras with sautéed Japanese mushrooms, or perhaps Spanish Iberico grilled pork marinated in white miso and served with steamed broccoli.

Times: 12–3/5.30–10.30, Closed Xmas–New Year, Sun
Prices: 3 Course Fixed D £20–£50
Main £9–£36
Directions: Exit Piccadilly tube station via exit 1. Turn left along Glasshouse St, restaurant is situated next to The Warwick

Sumosan Restaurant

Japanese

Authentic Japanese cooking at an upmarket address

26 Albermarle Street, Mayfair, W1S 4HY
Tel: 020 7495 5999
Email: info@sumosan.com
Website: www.sumosan.com
Chef: Bubker Belkhit
Owners: Janina Wolken

This cosmopolitan Japanese restaurant is located in the heart of Mayfair, surrounded by exclusive jewellers, designer clothes shops and fine art vendors. It's a popular venue both with the local business community and those looking for authentic cuisine, and has a pared down modern décor of cool clean lines, parquet flooring, and polished dark wood tables. All the bases are covered, from teppan-yaki and tempura to sushi and sashimi; you can choose from an extensive carte, or plump for the seven-course lunch selection. Kick off with beef tartare with nashi pear and sesame before tucking into the likes of spicy somen noodles with lobster and baby asparagus or lamb chops furikaki.

Times: 12–3/6–11.30, Closed Xmas, New Year, BHs, L Sat–Sun
Prices: Fixed D £45–£79
Main £11–£55
Directions: Please telephone for directions

Taman Gang

South East Asian

Vivacious, upmarket venue with elegant cuisine

Leave the chaos of Marble Arch behind and descend to this exotic, dimly lit, split-level basement bar and dining room packed with Eastern promise. Hand-carved limestone walls, mahogany furniture, lanterns and low banquettes evoke the look and feel of ancient Indonesia. Flickering candles, white orchids, contemporary music and youthful, knowledgeable and attentive black-clad staff add to the trendy, atmospheric vibe. The cuisine fits the surroundings, a fashionable, modern, sophisticated Pan-Asian mix, evoking the flavours of China, Japan and Thailand. Stunning presentation, tip-top ingredients, vibrant flavours and skilful handling form a repertoire that promotes sharing. Expect dishes like wok-flashed salt and pepper prawns with green pepper and spring onion, and Merlot black pepper beef with crispy noodles. Don't miss the Oriental-inspired cocktail list.

141 Park Lane, W1K 7AA
Tel: 020 7518 3160
Email: info@tamangang.com
Website: www.tamangang.com

Times: 12–3.30/6–1, Closed L
Mon–Sat

Tamarind

Indian

Contemporary, classy novelle Indian in Mayfair

The entrance may be a simple door leading on to a staircase, but it delivers you to this sophisticated and glamorous, designer-styled, buzzy basement Indian in the heart of Mayfair, decked out in contemporary, minimalist style and graced by elegantly attired, attentive and friendly staff. Muted metallic colours, low lighting, wooden floors and a glass theatre kitchen add to the sense of style, with the kitchen delivering a medley of traditional and contemporary cuisine – focused around the tandoor oven – and cooked in authentic North-West Indian style. Expect neatly presented, subtle-flavoured dishes to grace an appealing menu; perhaps ajwaini macchi (grilled monkfish in a marinade of ginger, yogurt and saffron), or classic rogan josh.

20 Queen Street, Mayfair,
W1J 5PR
Tel: 020 7629 3561
Email:
manager@tamarindrestaurant.com
Website:
www.tamarindrestaurant.com
Chef: Alfred Prasad
Owners: Indian Cuisine Ltd

Times: 12–2.45/6–11.15, Closed
25–26 Dec, 1 Jan, L Sat, BHs
Prices: 3 Course Fixed D £49.50
–£68 Main £16.50–£23
Directions: Towards Hyde Park,
take 4th right into Half Moon St
to end (Curzon St). Turn left,
Queen St is 1st right

Theo Randall, InterContinental ❀❀❀

Italian

Fresh, vibrant rustic-suave Italian cooking

Overlooking Hyde Park and the London skyline, this deluxe land-mark hotel has undergone a multi-million pound refurbishment and now features former River Café head chef Theo Randall's new eponymous restaurant. Clean lined, modern, sophisticated and relaxed, the long beige and grey dining room uses lots of natural materials like wood and leather, and there's a visible kitchen too. Inspired by his passion for top-quality and seasonal produce, the cooking takes on a rustic-suave theme. Ingredients are cooked with great care and skill, but without unnecessary fuss in well-conceived, well-presented, balanced and clear-flavoured dishes on daily-changing menus. Take the likes of perfectly cooked pan-fried Scottish scallops to start, with parsley and Castelluccio lentils, and perhaps a main course of wood-roasted turbot on the bone with parsley, anchovy and new season asparagus.

InterContinental London,
1 Hamilton Place, Hyde Park
Corner, W1J 7QY
Tel: 020 7318 8747
Email:
reservations@theorandall.com
Website: www.theorandall.com
Chef: Theo Randall
Owners: Intercontinental Hotels
Ltd & Theo Randall

Times: 12–3/6.30–11, Closed
Xmas, New Year, 1st wk Jan, BHs,
D Sun
Prices: Main £9–£10
Directions: Hyde Park Corner rdbt

Regent Street

188

Texture

Modern French

Exciting opening from 2 talented young professionals

Best Western Mostyn Hotel,
34 Portman Square, W1H 7BY
Tel: 020 7224 0028

Located on a quiet corner just off Portman Square in the Mostyn Hotel, a delightful new restaurant has opened. It is the first venture for two young enthusiastic professionals who met whilst working at Le Manoir aux Quat'Saisons – Chef Agnar Sverrisson and manager Xavier Rousset, who has expert wine knowledge and runs a highly polished front of house team. The restaurant has an elegant feel with polished wooden floors, large windows and a simple muted cream décor; it is divided by a large, high bar. The cooking has its roots firmly in the classics with some creative twists and Icelandic influences from the chef's origins. With accomplished technical skills, some diverse textures and immaculate attention to detail in the presentation, expect dishes like Scottich scallops with cauliflower textures, followed by Lancashire suckling pig, slow-cooked for 12 hours, with baby cabbage, squid and bonito sauce.

Chef: Agnar Sverrisson
Times: Please telephone for details
Prices: 3 Course alc £45
Directions: On the corner of
Seymour St and Portman St

La Trouvaille

French

French cooking with a modern twist

12a Newburgh Street, W1F 7RR
Tel: 020 7287 8488
Email: contact@latrouvaille.co.uk
Website: www.latrouvaille.co.uk
Chef: Mr Pierre Renaudeau
Owners: T Bouteloup

Set among the cobbled pedestrian lanes and boutiques off Carnaby Street, the small, two-floored La Trouvaille proves quite the Soho find, as its name implies. On the ground floor there's a buzzy, chic wine bar, while on the first floor the more formal yet relaxed restaurant. The dining room is decked out in white linen, perspex chairs, striking mirrors, stripped floorboards and tall windows. Attentive but relaxed French service and a patriotic wine list add to the upbeat mood. Unconventional French cooking – thoughtful and with easygoing invention and well-sourced ingredients – fits the bill. Think a fillet of Galloway beef cooked in broth and served with seasonal vegetables, parsley jus and wasabi gratiné, or a classic hot chocolate fondant with ginger ice cream finish.

Times: 12–3/6–11, Closed Xmas,
BHs, Sun
Prices: 3 Course Fixed D £33
Directions: Off Carnaby St by
Liberty's

Umu

Umu

Japanese, Kyoto

Sophisticated and offering high-quality Kyoto cuisine

Designer Tony Chi has created his vision of opulent Kyoto styling, with an unobtrusive touch button sliding open the wooden front door onto a sophisticated modern interior. The staff are attentive and helpful in guiding diners through the intricacies of the menu. The cooking – from chef Ichiro Kubota – offers innovative classic and contemporary interpretations of Kyoto cuisine, delivered via a fixed-price lunch option, extensive carte, a separate sushi menu and six tasting options. The sheer quality of ingredients and the freshness, clarity, vibrancy and combinations of flavours strike through in every dish and combine with great attention to detail in superb presentation. So dig deep into your pockets and prepare to be wowed by omakase (chef's choice) or sashimi, grilled toro teriyaki or melt-in-the-mouth Wagyu beef with wasabi, finished off with a stylish dessert of green tea soup and pumpkin ice cream.

14–16 Bruton Place, W1J 6LX
Tel: 020 7499 8881
Website: www.umurestaurant.com
Chef: Ichiro Kubota
Owners: Marlon Abela Restaurant Corporation

Times: 12–2.30/6–11, Closed between Xmas & New Year, BHs, Sun, L Sat
Prices: 4 Course Fixed D £60–£135 Main £8–£55
Directions: Off Bruton St & Berkeley Sq

Vasco & Piero's Pavilion Restaurant

Italian

Taste of Umbria in intimate, family-run restaurant

Conveniently tucked away close to the London Palladium and Liberty, this cosy corner restaurant looks somewhat unassuming from outside, but don't be deceived. Once inside the bijou, family-run eatery, the wonders of real Umbrian food and warm hospitality come to life. Closely packed tables, subtle lighting, a warm terracotta colour scheme and attentive, helpful Italian service add to the authenticity. The chef-patron hails from Umbria and continues to import many speciality products direct from the region, while the kitchen's intelligently simple treatment of high-quality ingredients is key. Menus may change daily and pasta is hand made, but clear, vivid flavours reign supreme in dishes like grilled fillet of wild sea bass with spinach, or hand-made agnolotti (Umbrian-style meat ravioli) with rosemary.

15 Poland Street, W1F 8QE
Tel: 020 7437 8774
Email: vascosfood@hotmail.com
Website: www.vascosfood.com
Chef: Vasco Matteucci
Owners: Tony Lopez,
Paul Matteucci & Vasco Matteucci

Times: 12–3/6–11, Closed
BHs, Sun, L Sat
Prices: 3 Course Fixed D £27–£33
Main £12.50–£19.50
Directions: From Oxford Circus
turn right towards Tottenham
Court Rd, continue for 5min and
turn right into Poland St. On corner
of Great Marlborough St & Noel St

Veeraswamy Restaurant

Indian

Sophisticated Indian with refined traditional cooking

Expect a sophisticated, chic atmosphere at London's oldest Indian restaurant that continues to maintain all the glamour dating from its creation in 1926. Plush, Mogul-style carpets sit on gleaming black Indian granite or darkwood floors, shimmering chandeliers and vibrant coloured lanterns hang from ceilings, adding to the latticed silver screens, silver banquettes or upholstered chairs, and large tables alongside views over Regent Street. Classic Indian dishes from all its regions grace the menu, authentically and freshly prepared with quality ingredients. Take a Kashmiri rogan josh, lobster Malabar curry, or Kerala recipe sea bass fillets with red spices cooked in a banana leaf.

Mezzanine Floor, Victory House,
99 Regent Street, W1B 4RS
Tel: 020 7734 1401
Email: veeraswamy@
realindianfood.com
Website: www.realindianfood.com
Chef: Uday Salunkhe
Owners: R Mathrani, C Panjabi &
N Panjabi

Times: 12–2.30/5.30–11.30,
Closed D Xmas
Prices: 2 Course Fixed D £33
Main £11.50–£25
Directions: Entrance near junct of
Swallow St and Regent St,
in Victory House

Via Condotti

Italian

Classical-based dishes and impeccable service

Tucked away among the fashionable boutiques of Mayfair's Conduit Street (just off Bond Street), this attractive, stylish, friendly Italian comes aptly named after one of Rome's most prestigious shopping streets. Its lilac frontage, awning and planters pick it out from the crowd, while inside there's peach décor, lightwood floors, tasteful posters, expensive leather chairs and dazzling white tablecloths. Service is charming and very Italian, unobtrusive and unpretentious, while the cooking comes based on classical roots with some southern influences – chef Pasquale Amico hails from Campania. There is a pleasant, refreshing simplicity about the food, which showcases quality ingredients, some sourced direct from Italy. Think ravioli filled with scamorza cheese, sun-dried tomato and basil sauce, or roasted rabbit with cacciatore sauce.

23 Conduit Street, W1S 2XS
Tel: 020 7493 7050
Email: info@viacondotti.co.uk
Website: www.viacondotti.co.uk
Chef: Pasquale Amico
Owners: Claudio Pulze,
Richard Martinez, Pasquale Amico

Times: 12–3/6.30–11, Closed BHs, Sun
Prices: 3 Course Fixed D £24.50

Villandry

French, European

Impressive restaurant, quality foodstore and bar

This buzzy and lively bar, restaurant, shop and lunchtime takeout has undergone a stylish refurbishment and re-launch. And, as it prizes the quality of its ingredients, entering the restaurant through its upmarket foodstore really whets the appetite. The glass-fronted, high-ceilinged dining room is chic and modern, with tables dressed in their best whites and friendly yet professional service. The modern approach and accurate cooking makes the most of quality, seasonal produce via classic, brasserie-focused menus; take moules mariniére with crusty bread, or pan-fried Scottish beef fillet with béarnaise. A child-friendly attitude and separate bar menu add to the upbeat package.

170 Great Portland Street,
W1W 5QB
Tel: 020 7631 3131
Email: contactus@villandry.com
Website: www.villandry.com
Chef: David Rood
Owners: Jamie Barber

Times: 12–3/6–10.30,
Closed 25 Dec, D Sun, BHs
Prices: Main £11.50–£32.50
Directions: Entrance at
91 Bolsover St, between
Great Portland St tube station
& Oxford Circus

The Westbury Hotel

Modern European

Accomplished cooking at an exclusive Mayfair hotel

Bond Street, W1S 2YF
Tel: 020 7629 7755
Email:
artisan@westburymayfair.com
Website:
www.westburymayfair.com
Chef: Daniel Hillier
Owners: Cola Holdings Ltd

Built in 1955, this chic hotel – set in the heart of Mayfair just off Bond Street – is styled on the Westbury in New York and is home to the renowned Polo Bar. The large, airy Artisan restaurant overlooks Conduit Street, with its own street entrance, and has a classy contemporary look resplendent in creams and browns, with beautiful inlaid wooden floors, wood panelled walls with frosted glass sheets, stunning chandeliers, crisp white linen and cream leather banquettes and chairs. The menus take an equally stylish and appealing modern approach; take confit shoulder of rabbit with pommery mousseline or roast Scottish scallops with squid ink polenta and chorizo.

Times: 12–2.30/6.30–10.30
Prices: Main £16–£33.50
Directions: Telephone for directions

The Wolseley

European

Bustling domed brasserie offering stylish all-day dining

160 Piccadilly, W1J 9EB
Tel: 020 7499 6996
Website: www.thewolseley.com
Chef: Julian O'Neill
Owners: Chris Corbin & Jeremy King

This European café-style phenomenon continues to be a crowd-pleaser. The former Wolseley car showroom has been reinvented as a buzzing restaurant with a glass-domed roof. The show never stops from 7am to midnight – the menus range from breakfasts to all-day snacks and afternoon tea packages, right through to a full carte including soups, starters, crustacea and caviar, salads, eggs and pasta, fish, entrées and grills, desserts and cakes. The daily-changing plats du jour are of particular note, whether it's wild boar casserole, coq au vin or Lancashire hot pot.

Times: 7am–mdnt, Closed 25 Dec, 1 Jan, Aug BHs, 25 Dec, D 24 Dec, 31 Dec,
Prices: Main £9.50–£33
Directions: 500mtrs from Green Park Underground station

Yauatcha

🏵🏵

Chinese

Oriental cuisine with formal service

15 Broadwick Street, W1F 0DL
Tel: 020 7494 8888
Email: reservations@yauatcha.co
Chef: Mr Soon
Owners: Alan Yau

This Soho restaurant is found in 'The Igeni' building, designed by Richard Rogers, with the interior by Christian Liagre. Features include fish tanks embedded in several walls and one that creates the bar. Two distinct spaces mean a tranquil upstairs tea house serving over 150 teas and various pastries, and a more atmospheric basement Dim Sum restaurant with low seating. Traditional Cantonese cooking, some Japanese and other Oriental specialities are on offer. Relaxed and friendly formal Asian service means well-informed waiters who can create a bespoke menu for you from the lengthy repertoire. Expect 'steamed' dishes like lotus leaf wrapped turbot, 'baked and fried' options like baked venison puff or grilled wagyu beef, and 'stir-fries' like black pepper ostrich.

Times: 12/11.30, Closed 24–25 Dec
Prices: 3 Course Fixed D £40–£6(
Main £9.50–£38
Directions: On the corner of Broadwick and Berwick St

YMing Restaurant

🏵

Chinese **v**

Chinese regional specialities in Theatreland

35–36 Greek Street, W1D 5DL
Tel: 020 7734 2721
Email:
cyming2000@blueyonder.co.uk
Website: www.yming.co.uk
Chef: Aaron Wong
Owners: Christine Yau

Situated in the heart of Soho, this stylish Chinese is less frenetic than its Chinatown neighbours. Duck-egg blue walls with jade carvings surround well-spaced and crisply-clothed tables in the intimate setting of a series of small rooms. Helpful, polite, friendly and polished service makes a good impression, while the uninitiated are guided through the extensive carte and fixed-price menus of Cantonese and regional dishes. Think sizzling lamb with ginger and spring onion, or Gansu duck (a Northwest dish cooked with garlic and a subtle, distinctive flavour of anise), or perhaps salmon steamed with black bean sauce.

Times: Noon–11.45, Closed
25–26 Dec, 1 Jan, Sun
(ex Chinese New Year)
Prices: 3 Course Fixed D £10–£20
Main £5–£26

Old Compton Street, Soho

Yumi Restaurant

Japanese

Authentic Japanese restaurant

110 George Street, W1H 5RL
Tel: 020 7935 8320

Staff are friendly and helpful here and one of the menus is in picture form so guests have an idea of what to order. The rest of the menu is in Japanese and English. Service is formal Japanese with kimono-clothed staff keeping vigil over the predominantly Japanese customers. The main dining area is in the basement with a few private dining areas off the main room. With an array of sushi, sashimi, tempura and terriyaki dishes to choose from, typical main dishes include grilled king fish marinated in miso paste or chicken yakitori.

Times: 5.30–10.30
Directions: Telephone for further details

Assaggi

Italian

Imaginative and authentic Italian

39 Chepstow Place, W2 4TS
Tel: 020 7792 5501
Email: nipi@assaggi.demon.co.uk
Chef: Nino Sassu
Owners: Nino Sassu,
Pietro Fraccari

You'll find this small, colourful restaurant above the fashionable Chepstow Pub in trendy Notting Hill. Large windows give the dining room a fresh, airy feel and its unpretentious décor makes diners feel right at home. Friendly staff offer a warm welcome and invaluable help with translating the menu. It's a great place for people-watching and the Italian food – leaning towards regional Sardinian cooking – is inventive, with the emphasis on flavour and the use of authentic ingredients. Try starters like caposante con salsa allo zafferano (scallops with capers served on a bed of mushroom, courgette and pepper couscous), followed by halibut on a bed of carrots, onion and courgettes, with white chocolate mousse, caramelised orange zest and orange caramel to finish. Simple classics, done extremely well.

Times: 12.30–2.30/7.30–11,
Closed 2 wks Xmas, BHs, Sun
Prices: Main £18.50–£23.90
Directions: Telephone for directions

Island Restaurant & Bar

Modern British

Designer hotel restaurant with seasonal fare

Royal Lancaster Hotel, Lancaster Terrace, W2 2TY
Tel: 020 7551 6070
Email: eat@islandrestaurant.co.uk
Website: www.islandrestaurant.co.uk
Owners: Lancaster Hotel Co Ltd

Enter this contemporary hotel restaurant via the salubrious reception area or directly from the street. Huge plate glass windows overlook the park opposite and there is a sleek bar (with great cocktails) and open-plan kitchen in the split-level dining area. In the evening, crisp white tablecloths and dramatic lighting bring an extra touch of glamour. Quality ingredients are handled with skill to produce a daily-changing choice of dishes, presented in a pleasingly minimalist style. Sourcing from British suppliers, popular dishes sit alongside more sophisticated fare – potted crab and brown shrimps with shellfish mayonnaise, and roast rump of lamb with creamed garlic mash and rosemary jus.

Times: 12/10.30, Closed Xmas, BHs, between Xmas and New Year
Prices: Main £9.95–£28
Parking: 50

Jamuna Restaurant

Indian

Quality Indian in quiet part of town

38A Southwick Street, W2 1JQ
Tel: 020 7723 5056
Email: info@jamuna.co.uk
Website: www.jamuna.co.uk
Chef: Suresh Manandhar

Set rather off the beaten track in a small leafy parade of shops, this neighbourhood Indian is located in what was once a private house. A stylish, minimalist affair, it comes with wooden floors, suede chairs and painted walls decorated with traditional and modern art (all for sale). The lengthy carte (with chilli symbols illustrating medium and hot dishes) shows off the kitchen's skilfully prepared and well-presented food, with its infusion of clean, subtle flavours and combination of traditional and less-common North Indian and regional dishes. Expect the likes of adraki chaampen (lamb cutlets from the tandoor, marinated in ginger, peppercorn, mint and yogurt), or more familiar lamb rogan josh (diced leg of lamb with spices, ginger, yogurt and Kashmiri chilli).

Times: 12–2.30/6–11, Closed 25 Dec–1 Jan, 2 weeks in Aug, Sun, L Sat
Prices: Main £12–£36

Nipa Thai Restaurant

Thai

Authentic Thai cuisine overlooking Hyde Park

The Royal Lancaster Hotel,
Lancaster Terrace, W2 2TY
Tel: 020 7551 6039
Email: nipa@royallancaster.com
Website:
www.niparestaurant.co.uk
Chef: Nongyao Thoopchoi
Owners: Lancaster Landmark Hotel
Co Ltd

This Thai restaurant on the first floor of the large Royal Lancaster Hotel is surprisingly intimate. Decorated in authentic style with teak panelling and original artefacts, its picture windows overlook Hyde Park. Quality dishes, including regional specialities, are offered from an extensive menu, where chilli symbols helpfully indicate spicing levels. Chef's recommendations include a mild Thai omelette with salty turnips, basil leaves and chilli, crispy soft-shelled crab served with spicy mango salad, or a more fiery steamed fish in a spicy lemon sauce. Desserts include a range of ice creams, and tab tim krob – water chestnuts coated with tapioca in coconut milk and syrup.

Times: 12–2.30/6.30–10.30,
Closed week between Xmas and New Year, BHs, Sun, L Sat
Prices: 4 Course Fixed D £27–£32
Main £8.50–£14.50
Directions: Opposite Hyde Park on Bayswater Rd. On 1st floor of hotel
Parking: 50

Royal China

Chinese

Ever-popular, traditional Bayswater Chinese

13 Queensway, W2 4QJ
Tel: 020 7221 2535
Email: royalchina@btconnect.com
Website:
www.royalchinagroup.co.uk

Don't be deceived by the smallish shop front, the spacious dining room extends way back, opulently decked out in black-and-gold lacquered walls, mirrors, and etched glass, or teak screens that create more intimate areas. The large number of Chinese diners is a testimony to its success. Classic Chinese food with quality ingredients (especially seafood) comes together to produce clean-cut dishes and flavours. The extensive menu is bolstered by several set options, with dim sum a favourite and available daily. Expect the likes of Szechuan prawns, perhaps chicken with chilli and black beans, or yeung chow rice with pork and shrimps.

Times: 12/11, Closed 25–26 Dec
Directions: Please telephone for directions

High Road Brasserie

European

Cool, bustling west London brasserie

162–164 Chiswick High Road,
W4 1PR
Tel: 020 8742 7474
Website:
www.highroadbrasserie.co.uk

French windows and canopied pavement seats pick out this urban-chic High Road brasserie, the latest addition to Nick Jones's blossoming empire. Pillars and mirrors, pewter-topped tables, leather banquettes, patchwork-coloured floor tiles and a marble bar make this a light, modern, stylish venue with a very New York air. The food fits the surroundings – informal, modern European brasserie fare on an all-day menu. From breakfast or food to run through the day, to more substantial dishes – like halibut with clams, mussels and saffron, perhaps a seafood platter, or Pyrenean Black Pig chop. (There's also a private members' club and boutique hotel on site.)

Times: 7am–midnight

Sam's Brasserie & Bar

European

Informal brasserie with friendly service, quality food

11 Barley Mow Passage, W4 4PH
Tel: 020 8987 0555
Email: info@samsbrasserie.co.uk
Website:
www.samsbrasserie.co.uk

Secreted away down a narrow walkway just off the Chiswick High Road, this converted, one-time paper factory has a cosmopolitan, New York loft-style edge. Patron Sam (Harrison) previously worked as general manager to Rick Stein's Padstow empire, while chef Rufus Wickham has an impressive track record, too. High ceilings, girders, pillars, industrial piping and cream-painted or bare-brick walls lend that timeless, relaxed urban vibe, while giant oval lampshades, banquettes or black-lacquered chairs and small blond-wood tables fill the vibrant space. There's a smaller mezzanine dining level at the front and a semi-open kitchen to the back, while off to one side, the buzzy bar continues the theme. The cooking delivers simple, clean-cut dishes and flavours driven by top-quality ingredients; take crisp sea bass with sautéed potatoes and horseradish cream.

Times: 12–3/6.30–10.30
Directions: Behind Chiswick High
Rd, next to the green

La Trompette

European

French-inspired cuisine at fashionable, chic restaurant

5–7 Devonshire Road,
Chiswick, W4 2EU
Tel: 020 8747 1836
Email:
reception@latrompette.co.uk
Website: www.latrompette.co.uk
Chef: James Bennington
Owners: Nigel Platts-Martin,
Bruce Poole

Times: 12–2.30/6.30–10.30,
Closed 25-26 Dec, 1 Jan
Prices: 3 Course Fixed D £35–£45
Main £19–£24
Directions: From station follow
Turnham Green Tce to junct with
Chiswick High Rd. Cross road &
bear right. Devonshire Rd 2nd left

Set on a quiet side street in fashionable Chiswick, La Trompette sings its own praises, with a more flamboyant frontage than its neighbours that singles it out from the crowd. Potted box trees and an awning cordon off the small outside dining area with a certain style, replete with heaters and white cloths. The tinted-glass, sliding-door frontage adds a further classy, self-assured note, and, with Nigel Platts-Martin and Bruce Poole as its owners (of Chez Bruce fame, see entry on page 131), there's no doubting this brasserie-style outfit's pedigree. A muted colour scheme prevails over a sophisticated, relaxing interior, decked out in chocolate leather banquettes, smartly dressed tables and light-oak floors. Efficient, knowledgeable and friendly French service adds a reassuring note, while an award-winning wine list provides a star turn alongside a bustling but unpretentious atmosphere. The accomplished modern European cooking continues the evolved take on French cooking under the assured wing of James Bennington, delivered via appealing, daily-changing, fixed-price menus. Simple, brasserie-style dishes, with fresh, quality ingredients take centre stage, showcasing clean, clear flavours, balance, flair and flawless technique. Superb breads (in at least three flavours) accompany a class act. Expect the likes of an inspired dish of baked quail Pithiviers served with a shallot purée and port sauce to open, perhaps a fillet of red mullet with a shellfish and herb risotto, steamed samphire and grilled fennel to follow, and, to finish, blueberry and almond tart with whipped cream.

Le Vacherin

French

Smart Parisian-style bistro serving classic cuisine

Green awnings and full-length windows pick out this slice of leafy Chiswick that's forever France. Blond-wood floors, a mirror-frieze above banquette-lined cream walls, foodie pictures and posters, attentive French staff clad in long white aprons and a backing track of Gallic music, evoke the atmosphere of a smart Parisian bistro. The cooking follows the script, with simple, classic French brasserie fare and an all-French wine list to match. The namesake soft mountain cow's milk cheese, Vacherin (in season November to February) makes a regular appearance on the menu, and organic produce is used wherever possible, with everything from bread to ice cream being made inhouse. Tuck into the likes of Chateaubriand with French beans and béarnaise sauce, or shallow-fried John Dory fillet with caper butter, finished off with a thin fig tart with Vacherin ice cream.

76–77 South Parade, W4 5LF
Tel: 020 8742 2121
Email:
malcolm.john4@btinternet.com
Website: www.levacherin.co.uk
Chef: Malcolm John
Owners: Malcolm & Donna John

Times: 12–3/6–11, Closed
25 Dec, BHs, L Mon
Prices: Main £11.50–£18
Directions: Turn left and
restaurant, 400mtrs on left

Momo

Japanese

Popular restaurant serving traditional Japanese cuisine

14 Queens Parade, Ealing,
W5 3HU
Tel: 020 8997 0206
Chef: Shigeru Kondo
Owners: Mr Kondo

This Japanese restaurant is worth seeking out – it enjoys an excellent reputation with locals for its traditional cooking. Hidden away in a quiet residential area of North Ealing, you'll find it in an urban precinct. The restaurant has exotic décor and you can have a traditional Japanese cooking pot (nabemono) at your table if you wish. The menu, in Japanese and English, is divided into sections covering set meals; sushi; sashimi; various appetisers; seafood including king prawns, squid and mackerel dishes; meat and poultry dishes featuring pork, chicken and beef; vegetable or soybean dishes; and an extensive choice of rice and noodle dishes, all at very reasonable prices.

Times: 12–3/6–11, Closed 2 wk
Xmas, 1 wk Aug, BHs, Sun
Prices: 3 Course Fixed D £19.50
–£27 Main £8.50–£25
Directions: 0.2m from North Ealing
station

Agni

Traditional Indian

Regional Indian cuisine in stylish surroundings

160 King Street, W6 0QU
Tel: 020 8846 9191
Email: info@agnirestaurant.com
Website: www.agnirestaurant.com
Chef: Gowtham Karingi
Owners: Neeraj Mittra &
Gowtham Karingi

Set over two floors, with a relaxed, unfussy bistro style, Agni comes decked out in yellow and gold with a clear Indian theme. This relatively new-kid-on-the-block has pedigree too, with Gowtham Karingi (ex head chef at Zaika and Veeraswamy) and Neeraj Mittra (ex manager at Chutney Mary) at the helm, and service is professional and very friendly. The traditional Indian cuisine is well presented, reflecting the progression of regional Indian food from its ancient roots, with emphasis on quality ingredients, clever spicing and clear flavours. Bags of choice, from a tiger prawn biryani to seafood moilee or chicken tikka tiranga, and to finish, try the beetroot halwa.

Times: 12–2.30/5.30–11, Closed
25 Dec to 1 Jan
Prices: 2 Course Fixed D £12.95
–£14.95 Main £6.50–£12.95
Directions: Telephone for
directions

Anglesea Arms

British, French

Trendy gastro-pub offering simple, robust food

35 Wingate Road, W6 0UR
Tel: 020 8749 1291
Email:
anglesea.events@gmail.com
Chef: Henrik Ritzen
Owners: Michael Mann,
Jill S Sullivan

Plenty of hustle and bustle is always guaranteed at this shabby-chic Hammersmith gastro-pub, popular with trendy locals and students alike. A log fire, wooden floors, Victorian décor and an open-plan – sometimes boisterous – kitchen all add to its laid-back charm. Seasonal produce is evident on the daily-changing blackboard menu, which serves up good, hearty and robust food that hits the mark every time. Perhaps smoked eel and potato pancake, quail's egg and egg beignet or sautéed squid, butterbean purée chorizo and rocket.

Times: 12.30–2.40/5/7–10.30,
Closed 24–31 Dec
Prices: Main £9.50–£17.50
Directions: Off Goldhawk Road.

The Brackenbury

Modern European

Accomplished cooking in a friendly environment

129-131 Brackenbury Road,
W6 0BQ
Tel: 020 8748 0107
Email:
lisa@thebrackenbury.fsnet.co.uk
Chef: Matt Cranston
Owners: Lisa Inglis

Tucked away on a quiet residential street, The Brackenbury is the epitome of the neighbourhood restaurant genre, with its relaxed, friendly approach. A front terrace proves a fair-weather bonus, while inside this pair of one-time shops, it's a split-level affair decked-out with olive green walls, varnished wooden tables and modern chairs or banquette seating. The kitchen's modern European cooking is delivered with a nod to the Mediterranean on regularly-changing menus driven by quality ingredients, colourful presentation and clear flavours. Think roast lamb rump with fondant potato, slow-roast tomato, baby artichoke and an olive jus.

Times: 12.30–2.45/7–10.45,
Closed 24–26 Dec, 1 Jan, Easter
Mon, Aug BH Mon, L Sat, D Sun
Directions: Telephone for
directions

Hammersmith

Chez Kristof

French

Classic French cooking in a neighbourhood bistro

111 Hammersmith Grove,
W6 0NQ
Tel: 020 8741 1177
Email: info@chezkristof.co.uk
Website: www.chezkristof.co.uk
Chef: Richard McLellan
Owners: Jan Woroniecki

This popular neighbourhood restaurant occupies a corner site in a quiet part of Shepherd's Bush. Squeeze on to one of the closely packed tables and tuck into some well executed rustic French dishes. Gallic classics include snails with garlic butter, spatchcock coquelet with olives and lemon, and pot au chocolat. A good choice of crustacea also features, including duchess rock oysters, razor clams, and ragout of cockles and mussels. If you want to eat great French food at home, a visit to the restaurant's delicatessen next door is a must.

Times: 12–3/6–11.15, Closed 24–26 Dec, 1 Jan
Prices: Main £12.50–£17.50
Directions: Please telephone for directions

The Gate

Modern Vegetarian v

Vegetarian restaurant offering inventive cuisine

51 Queen Caroline Street,
W6 9QL
Tel: 020 8748 6932
Email:
hammersmith@gateveg.co.uk
Website: www.thegate.tv
Chef: Adrian Daniel,
Mariusz Wegrodski
Owners: Adrian & Michael Daniel

This is a vegetarian restaurant in an unusual listed building, approached via a church entrance hall. Once inside the room – formerly an artist's studio – it is bright and airy with high ceilings, large windows and dramatic art. The cooking is an inspired alternative to the usual vegetarian choices. It seeks out bold flavours, inventive combinations and fresh ingredients to produce simple but ingenious dishes, with wild mushrooms a speciality. Worldwide influences and modern techniques make this a great choice for vegetarians, vegans and those in search of new tastes. Typical is a root vegetable and chickpea tagine, or wild mushroom fricassee or butternut squash risotto.

Times: 12–3/6–11, Closed 23 Dec -3 Jan, Easter Mon, Sun, L Sat
Prices: Main £8.50–£13.50
Directions: Hammersmith Apollo Theatre, continue down right side for approx 40 yds

The River Café

The River Café   ✿✿✿

Italian

Famous Italian Thames-side trendsetter

Though celebrating over 20 years, people still flock to Rose Gray and Ruth Rogers' famous, Thames-side Hammersmith Italian. It is a modern, minimalist white room (converted from an 18th-century warehouse) comes with plenty of steel and glass and an urban vibe that mixes an informal atmosphere with a fine-dining experience. Light floods in through floor-to-ceiling windows and there's a long stainless-steel open kitchen with wood-burning oven. Menus change twice daily, so there's a sense of spontaneity to the flavour-driven cooking. The authentic, unfussy Italian cuisine – mainly Tuscan and Lombardian influenced – uses only the very best, freshest produce (with many ingredients sourced for their rarity and seasonality) simply treated with skill and panache. Take seared calves' liver with Swiss chard, castelluccio lentils, herbs and crème fraîche, and perhaps an almond and nespoli tart to finish.

Thames Wharf, Rainville Road,
W6 9HA
Tel: 020 7386 4200
Email: info@rivercafe.co.uk
Website: www.rivercafe.co.uk
Chef: R Gray, R Rogers, Sian Owen
Owners: Rose Gray, Ruth Rogers

Times: 12.30–3/7–11, Closed
24 Dec–1 Jan, Easter, BHs, D Sun
Prices: Main £25–£32
Directions: Restaurant in
converted warehouse. Entrance on
S side of Rainville Rd at junct with
Bowfell Rd
Parking: 29

Sagar

Vegetarian, Indian v

Authentic cooking in the heart of Hammersmith

157 King Street, Hammersmith,
W6 9JT
Tel: 020 8741 8563
Chef: Ramadas
Owners: S. Shurmielan

This unpretentious restaurant with a modern glass frontage is set among shops on a busy Hammersmith street. It's a popular place with a lively atmosphere, close-set tables, blond-wood floorboards and walls dotted with Indian artefacts. The kitchen's lengthy vegetarian repertoire offers a good range majoring on dishes from the Udipi region, including starters such as idli (steamed rice cakes) with sambar and coconut chutney, samosas, vegetable kebabs, and main meals incorporating dosas (a must try), uthappams (lentil pizzas), and thalis (a selection of different dishes), plus fresh home-made breads. For dessert, why not try payasam – a hot pudding made with fine vermicelli in milk, cashew nuts and raisins. Dishes are skilfully crafted with clean-cut presentation and distinct flavours and prices are incredibly low for the quality delivered.

Times: 12–2.45/5.30–10.45,
Closed 25–26 Dec
Prices: 3 Course Fixed D
£8.50–£11.50 Main £3.50–£5.75
Directions: 10min from
Hammersmith Tube

Snows-on-the-Green Restaurant

Modern

Vibrant restaurant with accomplished cuisine

166 Shepherd's Bush Road, Brook
Green, Hammersmith, W6 7PB
Tel: 020 7603 2142
Email: sebastian@
snowsonthegreenfreeserve.co.uk
Website:
www.snowsonthegreen.co.uk
Chef: Sebastian Snow
Owners: Sebastian Snow

A green awning and glass frontage picks out this popular, long-established neighbourhood restaurant, set in an arcade of shops opposite Brook Green on the busy road between Hammersmith and Shepherd's Bush. Dark-stained floorboards and sage green paintwork sit comfortably alongside white-clothed tables, while black and white photographs, candles, and friendly and attentive service crank up the atmosphere. The kitchen's modern approach takes on a sunny Mediterranean slant too, cooking with passion, the style robust rather than refined with colourful, clear-flavoured dishes. Think celeriac soup with wild mushrooms to start, followed by pan-fried wild sea trout in a horseradish crust with golden beetroot and pancetta, and espresso crème caramel to finish.

Times: 12–3/6–11, Closed BH
Mon only, Sun
Prices: 3 Course Fixed D £16–£17
Main £13–£17, L Sat
Directions: 300yds from station

Babylon

Modern International

Minimalist chic with extraordinary views

The Roof Gardens, 99 Kensington
High Street, W8 5SA
Tel: 020 7368 3993
Email:
babylon@roofgardens.virgin.co.uk
Website:
www.virgin.com/limitededition

Cracking views over the London skyline from the seventh-floor
decked terrace and sleek, glass-sided dining room – framed by
the lush greenery from the Roof Gardens below – prove a winning
Kensington formula at Richard Branson's Babylon. Contemporary
styling, booths, white linen and a small bar with fish-tank walls,
provides the stylish backcloth for slick, friendly service and those
capital views. The menu's modern approach suits the surroundings
and deals in quality produce; think red wine-braised halibut served
with parsnip mash, baby onions and red wine jus, and to finish,
perhaps organic lemon tart with raspberry crackle sorbet.

Times: 12–3/7–11, Closed 25 Dec
& selected dates in Dec–Jan, D Sun
Directions: From High St
Kensington tube station, turn
right, then right into Derby St
Parking: 15

Belvedere

French, European

Stunning interior and garden views

Abbotsbury Road, Holland House,
Holland Park, W8 6LU
Tel: 020 7602 1238
Email: sales@whitestarline.org.uk
Website:
www.belvedererestaurant.co.uk
Chef: Billy Reid
Owners: Jimmy Lahoud

The orangery in pretty Holland Park is the setting for this achingly
elegant restaurant, a destination in its own right even without
the added attraction of top-notch cuisine. Inspired interior design
evokes a 1920s feel; think sparkling mirrors, ornate wallpaper
and huge oyster-shell lights. Leafy green plants, brown leather
seating, and parquet flooring complete the picture and serve as the
perfect backdrop to the kitchen's understated brasserie cooking.
You'll find something to suit most tastes, from old favourites such
as eggs Benedict, sausage and mash, and rice pudding, to more
sophisticated fare – pheasant with chestnuts, bacon lardons and
morel jus for example, or pork belly with Puy lentils and potato
purée, with pear Tatin and cinnamon ice cream to finish.

Times: 12–2.30/6–10.30,
Closed 26 Dec, 1 Jan, D Sun
Prices: 3 Course Fixed D £18
Main £11.50–£22
Directions: On the Kensington
High St side of Holland Park
Parking: 50

Cheneston's Restaurant

Modern British

Intimate restaurant in elegant townhouse hotel

Milestone Hotel, 1 Kensington
Court, W8 5DL
Tel: 020 7917 1000
Email: bookms@rchmail.com
Website: www.milestonehotel.com

Located opposite Kensington Palace and Gardens, this Victorian mansion has been transformed into a hotel of style and class, with many restored original features. Expect stunning bedrooms, luxurious lounges and a sumptuous dining room with leaded Victorian windows and shining crystal and silverware. As befits the surroundings and the clientele, food is classically based and both cooking style and presentation are simple and unfussy. Typical dishes include an open ravioli of Cornish crab and lobster with lobster ginger broth, pot-roast suprême of guinea fowl with celeriac and parsley mash and morel mushroom sauce, and to finish a warm chocolate tart with white chocolate ice cream. Service is formal and professional from an international team.

Times: 12–3/5.30–11
Directions: M4/Hammersmith
flyover, take 2nd left into
Gloucester Rd, left into High St
Kensington, 500mtrs on left

Clarke's

Modern Mediterranean

The freshest food simply treated with reverence

124 Kensington Church Street,
W8 4BH
Tel: 020 7221 9225
Email: restaurant@sallyclarke.com
Website: www.sallyclarke.com
Chef: Sally Clarke, Liz Payne
Owners: Sally Clarke

Set amongst the well-known antique shops of Kensington Church Street and Notting Hill, you'll find the neat shop front for the restaurant, adjacent to Sally Clarke's famous bread shop. Minimalist décor is chic and modern with crisply starched table linen, and staff are professional and diligent. The restaurant now offers a choice at dinner (three at each turn) and it's no longer necessary to have all four courses (once a set four-course affair), plus there's also a brunch offering on Saturdays from 11am until 2pm. Menus change weekly and are posted on their website each Monday. Ingredients, skill and artistry take priority here, and it is this that makes the cooking so successful and enduring. Modern European-style dishes might include Cornish day-boat monkfish roasted on the bone and served with a relish of Niçoise olives, lovage and young leeks.

Times: 12.30–2/7–10, Closed
8 days Xmas & New Year, Sun,
D Mon
Directions: Telephone for
directions

Eleven Abingdon Road

European

Cool neighbourhood venue off High Street Kensington

11 Abingdon Road,
Kensington, W8 6AH
Tel: 020 7937 0120
Email:
eleven@abingdonroad.co.uk
Chef: David Stafford
Owners: Rebecca Mascarenhas

This light, modern, glass-fronted restaurant is tucked away in a little road just off High Street Ken and proves quite a find; it shares ownership with Sonny's in Barnes. The stylish, restrained, clean-cut interior – with a small chic bar area up front decked out with leopard- and tiger-skin chairs – comes dominated by an eye-catching art collection set to a backdrop of sage-green walls, contemporary lighting, modern darkwood chairs and a friendly, upbeat vibe. Staff dressed in jeans and long black aprons deliver modern, Mediterranean-slant dishes using quality seasonal ingredients; think chargrilled halibut served with slow-cooked fennel, Swiss chard and salsa verde, or perhaps slow-cooked veal shin with risotto Milanese and gremolata.

Times: 12.30–2.30/6.30–11,
Closed 25 Dec, BHs
Prices: 2 Course Fixed D £19.50
Main £10–£17.50
Directions: Telephone
for directions

V&A South Kensington

Kensington Place

Modern British

Busy restaurant with vibrant colour and atmosphere

Watch the world go by at this prominently located and ever-popular Notting Hill haunt. Passers-by also get a good look in through the long plate-glass fascia, while a revolving door leads into a bustling, energetic bar, and the main restaurant is decorated with a striking mural depicting nearby Kensington Gardens. Closely-set tables and colourful wooden chairs are reminiscent of the schoolroom. Well-executed brasserie food, simple and precise, uses top-quality seasonal produce, with old favourites offered alongside more imaginative creations. Fish is a speciality, with dishes like red mullet, potato and olive pancake, followed by steamed sea bass with cauliflower and skate tempura, and chocolate and mascarpone torte served with coffee sauce to finish. The restaurant has its own elegant fish shop next door to cater for your every fishy need, and includes goodies from the restaurant.

201–9 Kensington Church Street, W8 7LX
Tel: 020 7727 3184
Email: kpparty@egami.co.uk
Website: www.egami.co.uk
Chef: Sam Mahoney
Owners: Place Restaurants Ltd

Times: 12–3.30/6.30–11.15,
Closed 24–26 Dec, 1 Jan
Prices: 3 Course Fixed D £24.50
(Mon–Fri) Main £17–£30
Directions: Telephone
for directions

Launceston Place Restaurant

Modern European

Uncomplicated cuisine in a genteel setting

1a Launceston Place,
W8 5RL
Tel: 020 7937 6912
Email: lpr@egami.co.uk
Website: www.egami.co.uk
Chef: Iain Inman
Owners: Christopher Bodker

An upmarket eatery in a leafy part of Kensington, the restaurant is 21 years old and still going strong. It occupies a series of small townhouse rooms, quintessentially English in presentation but with a modern twist. It caters to locals, businessmen and lunching ladies. An accomplished kitchen adopts a modern line – with a nod to the Mediterranean – and delivers a menu of straightforward contemporary dishes. Kick off with sweetcorn and tarragon risotto with excellent bite and consistency, and follow with chicken ravioli, full of flavour, served with wild mushroom cream, with a subtly-flavoured pannacotta given a great kick by red berry compôte for dessert. Book early for lunch, it really buzzes around 1–1.30pm.

Times: 12.30–2.30/6–11, Closed
Xmas, New Year, Etr, L Sat
Prices: 3 Course Fixed D £18.50
Main £16.50–£24.50
Directions: Just south of
Kensington Palace

Royal Garden Hotel

Modern European v
Fantastic views and imaginative cuisine

Situated in fashionable Kensington just a short walk from the Albert Hall, the hotel is built on the site of the former Kensington Palace vegetable plot, hence its name. Norman Farquharson's gastronomic cooking at The Tenth Floor Restaurant is matched only by the stunning views across Kensington Gardens and Hyde Park towards the capital's tallest landmarks. Its huge windows exploit those views, allowing light to flood in. The elegant dining room is a fresh, contemporary space with its own bar and cabaret area; tables are well spaced, and the atmosphere intimate. By day, it feels like a chic insider's haunt; by night it's one of London's most romantic destination restaurants. Modern European cuisine brings together a fusion of traditional cooking techniques and modern twists, with a generous sprinkling of quality ingredients and Asian imports, including lobster, truffles, saffron and oysters, cast across an interesting menu. A separate vegetarian and six-course tasting menu is available. Baked roquefort and leek soufflé with a ruby port reduction might be followed by a main course of pan-fried fillet of John Dory with langoustine and orange sauce, or perhaps saltimbocca of monkfish with Puy lentils, roasted baby onions and red wine jus. Tempting desserts take in the likes of caramel brûlée with pear foam and cranberry muesli cookies, or maybe milk chocolate orange cup served with a tangerine tartlet and orange chutney. There are gastronomic events with guest chefs throughout the year.

2–24 Kensington High Street, W8 4PT
Tel: 020 7361 1910
Email: tenthrestaurant@ royalgardenhotel.co.uk
Website: www.royalgardenhotel.co.uk
Chef: Norman Farquharson
Owners: Goodwood Group

Times: 12–2.30/5.30–11, Closed Etr wknd, 2 wks Aug, 2 wks Jan, BHs, Sun, L Sat
Prices: Main £18.50–£28
Directions: Next to Kensington Palace, Royal Albert Hall
Parking: 200

Timo

Italian v

Chic, authentic Italian dining

343 Kensington High Street,
W8 6NW
Tel: 020 7603 3888
Email:
timorestaurant@tiscali.co.uk
Chef: Franco Gatto
Owners: Piero Amodio

Located in a quiet stretch of fashionable Kensington High Street, this friendly Italian restaurant is worth seeking out for its authentic regional cuisine at reasonable prices. The neutral décor is modern but relaxed, with tan suede chairs and crisply dressed tables, while huge prints add a splash of colour. The traditional Italian menu aims for flexibility, with side orders to supplement the dishes if you've got a big appetite. Go for a starter of buffalo mozzarella with slow-baked tomato and rocket, followed by tagliatelle with prawns, asparagus and cherry tomatoes and, if you have room, a delicious chocolate and hazelnut fondant.

Times: 12–2.30/7–11, Closed Xmas, New Year, BHs, L Sat, D Sun
Prices: 3 Course Fixed D £27–£35
Main £8.50–£21.50
Directions: 5 mins walk towards Hammersmith, after Odeon Cinema, on left of street
Parking: 3

Zaika

Modern Indian v

Lively restaurant serving carefully prepared cuisine

1 Kensington High Street,
W8 5NP
Tel: 020 7795 6533
Email: info@zaika-restaurant.co.uk
Website:
www.zaika-restaurant.co.uk
Chef: Sandjay Dwivedi
Owners: Claudio Pulze,
Sandjay Dwivedi

High ceilings, double-height stone windows and carved arches grace the panelled interior of this former bank, located opposite Kensington Palace. The restaurant is decorated in a rich palette of colours, including the contemporary chairs and banquettes. Blonde-wood floorboards, Indian artefacts, modern lighting and a bar at the front add to the sophisticated styling, while professional, informed service and an impressive wine list complete the upbeat vibe. The kitchen's innovative menu of modern Indian cuisine delivers well-executed, vibrantly-flavoured and creatively presented dishes from quality ingredients, as in tandoori chicken tikki, tandoori monkfish with curry leaf risotto, and chocolate samosas for dessert. The emphasis is on a lighter approach without the use of clarified butter.

Times: 12–2.45/6–10.45, Closed BHs, Xmas, New Year, L Sat
Prices: 4 Course Fixed D £–£40
Main £13.50–£19
Directions: Opposite Kensington Palace

212

E&O

Pan Asian

Buzzy, fashionable oriental-style eatery and bar

A red neon sign and dark exterior picks out this corner-set, trendy bar-restaurant (part of the Will Ricker group – see also Eight Over Eight and Great Eastern Dining Room) close to Notting Hill and Portobello Road, which blends oriental style with modern minimalist décor. Think slatted darkwood, plain white walls, giant oval lampshades, brown-leather banquettes or black-lacquer chairs and polished floorboards. Upfront there's a bustling red-walled bar and, to the side, a few alfresco pavement tables, while everywhere the atmosphere's vibrant and upbeat. The modern pan-Asian fusion menu is divided into sections for grazing and sharing from dim sum to tempura, curries or sashimi, and specials like beef yaki-niku.

14 Blenheim Crescent, W11 1NN
Tel: 020 7229 5454
Email:
eando@rickerrestaurants.com
Website:
www.rickerrestaurants.com
Chef: Simon Treadway
Owners: Will Ricker

Times: 12–3/6–11, Closed Xmas, New Year, Aug BH
Directions: At Notting Hill Gate tube station turn right, at mini rdbt turn into Kensington Park Rd, restaurant 10min down hill

---

Edera

Modern Italian

Good-value, modern and stylish neighbourhood Italian

This clean-lined, minimally styled Holland Park Italian – with glass frontage, awning and a few pavement tables to catch the eye – proves a stylish yet friendly venue. Decked out on tiered levels, it comes with blond-wood floors, light walls and terracotta pillars, while banquette seating, coordinated upholstered chairs and white linen provide the upmarket comforts, backed by attentive Latin staff clad in long black aprons. The kitchen, like the patriotic wine list, draws inspiration from the Italian regions, with the occasional nod to Sardinia. Take home-made veal ravioli with a cherry tomato sauce, or perhaps pan-fried monkfish accompanied by an olive mash and mullet roe. The style is straightforward, clean cut and creatively accomplished, driven by high-quality seasonal ingredients.

148 Holland Park Avenue, W11 4UE
Tel: 020 7221 6090
Email: edera@btconnect.com
Chef: Carlo Usai
Owners: A–Z Ltd/Mr Pisano

Times: 12–2.30/6.30–11, Closed 25–26 & 31 Dec
Prices: Main £7–£20
Directions: Please telephone for directions

The Ledbury

@@@

Modern French  NOTABLE WINE LIST

Highly accomplished French cooking

Set in the heart of residential Notting Hill, The Ledbury has a contemporary and luxurious interior with cream leather chairs and polished parquet floors. Service is professional and attentive without being stuffy or overbearing. The sophisticated cooking, from Oz-born Brett Graham, delivers high technical skill through modern dishes underpinned by a classical French theme, with good presentation, interesting combinations and textures. Peripherals like breads and petits fours all hold form, while the fixed-price lunch (great value), carte and eight-course tasting option are partnered by a high-class wine list. Expect a loin of cod poached in liquorice and served with creamed potato, razor clams and fennel, or perhaps braised veal cheeks zingara with a gratin of macaroni and black truffle, while a pineapple tart Tatin with fromage blanc and a black pepper and lime sorbet might head-up desserts.

127 Ledbury Road, W11 2AQ
Tel: 020 7792 9090
Email: info@theledbury.com
Website: www.theledbury.com
Chef: Brett Graham
Owners: Nigel Platts-Martin
& Philip Howard

Times: 12–2/6.30–11, Closed
24–26 Dec, 1 Jan, Aug BH wknd
Directions: 5 min walk along
Talbot Rd from Portobello Rd, on
corner of Talbot and Ledbury Rd

Lonsdale

Fusion, Modern Asian

Trendy lounge-style eatery with a youthful clientele

48 Lonsdale Road, W11 2DE
Tel: 020 7727 4080
Email:
reception@thelonsdale.co.uk
Website: www.thelonsdale.co.uk

A white frontage and doorman make this evening-only, clubby bar-restaurant stand out from the crowd in residential Notting Hill. There's something of a basement vibe, with bold retro styling, a buzzy, trendy atmosphere and black-clad, youthful service. From its brightly lit cocktail bar to the restaurant area at the back, the Lonsdale strips away conventional fine-dining formalities, its close-set, darkwood tables teamed with burgundy leather banquettes or large stools, while mirror-lined lilac walls, matching low-level lights above table and contemporary music hit all the right notes. In tune with the contemporary surroundings, the kitchen takes an equally fashionable approach, its menu laced with Asian influence; think steamed sea bass served with ginger, spring onions and pak choi.

Times: 6pm–mdnt, Closed 25–26 Dec, 1 Jan, L all week
Directions: One street parallel N Westbourne Grove between Portobello Rd and Ledbury Rd

Portobello Market

Notting Hill Brasserie

Notting Hill Brasserie

Modern European

Chic food, chic décor, chic location

Converted from three Edwardian townhouses, this brasserie oozes quality with its mix of stylish good looks and period features. The swish minimalist décor, modern African art, and confident, friendly service are further enhanced by a separate cocktail bar. The accomplished kitchen impresses with execution and professionalism with both classic and original twists on crisply-scripted menus driven by quality seasonal ingredients. Expect roasted fillet of cod served with parsnip purée and a lightly curried ragout of mussels, or maybe roast loin of venison with sweet potato purée and braised red cabbage, and perhaps a cinnamon crème brûlée with molasses ice cream, or hot chocolate fondant accompanied by hazelnut ice cream to round things off in style. Excellent breads and the likes of amuse-bouche match the upbeat performance, while Sunday lunch is served up with live jazz.

92 Kensington Park Road, W11 2PN
Tel: 020 7229 4481
Email: enquiries@ nottinghillbrasserie.com
Chef: Mark Jankel
Owners: Carlo Spetale

Times: 12–4/7–1, Closed D Sun
Prices: Main £19–£25
Directions: 3 mins walk from Notting Hill station

Ribbands Restaurant

Modern British, French

Relaxed, assured modern dining in Notting Hill

147–149 Notting Hill Gate,
W11 3LF
Tel: 020 7034 0301
Email:
www.ribbandsrestaurants.com
Website:
eat@ribbandsrestaurants.com

This corner-sited Notting Hill Gate venue draws a moneyed neighbourhood crowd. A split-level affair, it comes decked out in fashionable distressed-wood flooring and modern lighting, with walls a mix of brickwork or pale and deep pink panelling. The restaurant is accessed via the bar and reception area, and staff are suitably friendly and attentive. The accomplished kitchen's modern approach deals in quality produce and flavour on a fixed-price repertoire; take roasted duck breast served with Savoy cabbage and a Cassis sauce, while lemon tart with raspberry sorbet might lead-up desserts.

Cibo

Italian

Authentic Italian cooking to linger over

3 Russell Gardens, W14 8EZ
Tel: 020 7371 2085
Email: ciborestaurant@aol.com
Website:
www.ciborestaurant.co.uk

Colourful, offbeat, abstract Renaissance-style nude paintings immediately catch the eye at this small, long-established neighbourhood restaurant close to Olympia. White walls and tablecloths come paired with modern blond-wood chairs and colourful crockery and in summer, the full-length glass-front windows fold back so dining feels almost alfresco. Friendly waiting staff bring plenty of extras, from well-ladened bread baskets to large olives and mini pizzas and petits fours. Menus are in Italian with English subtitles, with fish and shellfish a speciality and home-made filled pasta excellent. The cooking focuses on a straightforward but imaginative style driven by quality ingredients; think duck ravioli with a mushroom sauce, grilled swordfish served with roast baby tomatoes, capers and olives, and a zabaglione or tiramisù finish. As you'd expect, wines are exclusively Italian.

Times: 12.105–2.30/7–11, Closed
Xmas, Etr BHs, L Sat, D Sun
Prices: Main £12.50–£25
Directions: Russell Gardens is a
residential area off Holland Road,
Kensington (Olympia) Shepherd's
Bush

217

Somerset House

West Central
London

Jurys Great Russell Street

Modern European

Elegant 1930s setting for relaxed dining

16–22 Great Russell Street,
WC1B 3NN
Tel: 020 7347 1000
Email:
restaurant_grs@jurysdoyle.com
Website: www.jurysdoyle.com
Chef: Paul O'Brien
Owners: Jurys Doyle Hotel
Group Ltd

Designed by the renowned architect Sir Edwin Lutyens in the 1930s, this impressive Neo-Georgian listed building retains many of its original features and houses a smart, spacious restaurant (named after Lutyens) tucked away in the basement. Its clean, traditional lines are in keeping with the surroundings, as is the adjacent small, classic cocktail bar for aperitifs. The crowd-pleasing menu fits the bill, too, with the likes of braised wild sea bass served with baby fennel, pan-fried gnocchi, pepper confit and chorizo oil, or perhaps a British game plate (wild guinea fowl confit, stuffed quail, Yorkshire venison and port wine sauce). Desserts might include coconut crème brûlée.

Times: 6–10, Closed L all week
Prices: Main £11–£22.95
Directions: Short walk from
Tottenham Court Rd and
tube station

Matsuri High Holborn

Japanese

Traditional Japanese in contemporary setting

Mid City Place, 71 High Holborn,
WC1V 6EA
Tel: 020 7430 1970
Email:
eat@matsuri-restaurant.com
Website:
www.matsuri-restaurant.com
Chef: H Sudoh, T Aso, S Mabalot
Owners: Matsuri Restaurant Group

Futuristic Japanese restaurant occupying a corner site on bustling High Holborn. You'll find a choice of three dining areas that showcase the various styles of cuisine – the sushi counter, the teppan-yaki room and the main dining room with open-plan kitchen. The Japanese ex-pats frequenting this restaurant are a clue to the quality and authenticity of the cooking. Menus are lengthy, yet good ingredients are simply prepared and well presented, with lots of memorable fresh fish. The teppan-yaki set menus provide an overall flavour of Japanese cuisine. The highly acclaimed Wagyu beef has now been added to the menus, and there's a set price Twilight menu available between 6 and 7pm.

Times: 12–2.30/6–10, Closed
25–26 Dec, 1 Jan, BHs, Sun
Prices: 5 Course Fixed D £35–£75
Main £15–£35
Directions: On the corner of Red
Lion St. Opposite the Renaissance
Chancery Court Hotel

The Montague on the Gardens

Modern British

Stylish hotel restaurant with modern cuisine

15 Montague Street,
Bloomsbury, WC1B 5BJ
Tel: 020 7637 1001
Email: bookmt@rchmail.com
Website:
www.montaguehotel.com
Chef: Neil Ramsey
Owners: Red Carnation Hotels

A swish boutique hotel in the heart of Bloomsbury, the Montague has two dining options – the Blue Door bistro or the fine-dining restaurant, the Chef's Table. The latter is a light, airy space with panoramic views over London on three sides and an outside terrace for alfresco dining and summer barbecues. Attentive staff are on hand to make guests feel at ease and the cooking is modern British with some French influences. Expect dishes such as lobster risotto with mascarpone and parmesan crisp, followed by pan-fried sea bream with confit tomato and caviar beurre blanc.

Times: 12.30–2.30/5.30–10.30
Prices: 3 Course Fixed D £25–£50
Main £13.95–£24.50
Directions: 10 minutes from
Covent Garden, adjacent to the
British Museum

Pearl Restaurant & Bar

Modern French v

Stylish restaurant with accomplished cuisine

Renaissance Chancery Court,
252 High Holborn, WC1V 7EN
Tel: 020 7829 7000
Email: info@pearl-restaurant.com
Website:
www.pearl-restaurant.com
Chef: Jun Tanaka
Owners: Hotel Property Investors

The old Pearl Assurance Building has been transformed into a glamorous, metropolitan, destination restaurant. The chic interior includes original marble pillars, while walnut, hand-spun pearls, cream leather chairs, well-spaced tables with expensive settings and a huge wooden wine cave catch the eye, too. Staff – including a sommelier – provide attentive, professional service, while lunch, dinner, tasting option and vegetarian menu all come at fixed prices. The skilful kitchen takes a fresh, modern French approach, delivering exciting combinations with clear flavours driven by high-quality produce. Take a terrine of foie gras, smoked pigeon and ham hock served with baby beetroot, walnuts and pickled shallots to start, perhaps turbot poached in red wine and served with creamed black cabbage and crispy oysters to follow, and to finish, maybe Valrhona chocolate shortbread with tonka bean ice cream.

Times: 12–2.30/6–10, Closed Dec,
BHs, 2 wks Aug, Sun, L Sat
Prices: 3 Course Fixed D £49
Directions: 200 mtrs from Holborn
tube station

The Admiralty Restaurant

French

Contemporary restaurant in Somerset House

Somerset House, The Strand,
WC2R 1LA
Tel: 020 7845 4646
Email:
info@theadmiralityrestaurant.com
Website:
www.theadmiralityrestaurant.com
Chef: Chris Wayland
Owners: Leiths

Its Thames-side setting, off the courtyard at Somerset House, proves a grand prelude to lunch or dinner in the two high-ceilinged dining rooms that once played host to the Naval Headquarters. This delightful venue has recently been refurbished to create a smart and contemporary dining experience. The cooking is French regional with modern twists. Expect duck confit with Puy lentils, or rump of Cornish lamb with dauphinoise potato, flageolet beans and herb jus.

Times: 12–2.30/5.30–10.30,
Closed 24–27 Dec, D Sun
Prices: Main £12.50–£16
Directions: Telephone for directions, see website

Albannach

Modern Scottish 🍷 NOTABLE WINE LIST

Highland chic meets city bustle

66 Trafalgar Square, WC2N 5DS
Tel: 020 7930 0066
Email: info@albannach.co.uk
Website: www.albannach.co.uk
Chef: Thijmen Peters
Owners: Dan Sullam, Niall Barnes

Purple sprouting heather in the windows, kilted staff and, of course, the name provide major clues that you're in a Scottish-themed restaurant. Overlooking Trafalgar Square, the walls of this fabulous mezzanine restaurant are adorned with beautiful photographs of Scotland. The dark wood, open-plan dining areas are perhaps more like a bar or a nightclub than a fine-dining restaurant but it's a style that works, creating an atmospheric place perfect for imbibing generous amounts of whisky or enjoying a foray into eclectic, modern Scottish cuisine with Caledonian produce championed with William Wallace-style fervour. Try the haggis, neeps and tatties with Hermitage sauce, followed by seared West Coast salmon or the rib-eye Buccleuch beef.

Times: 12–3/5–10, Closed 25–26 Dec, 1 Jan, Sun
Directions: SW corner of Trafalgar Sq, opposite Canada House

L'Atelier de Joël Robuchon

French v

Slick, sexy sophistication from French super-chef

This is legendary French super-chef Joël Robuchon's first foray in the UK. Spread over three floors, the ground-floor L'Atelier serves small signature dishes at the kitchen counter. Seating is on high stools around the busy kitchen counter or at high tables. The first-floor dining room, La Cuisine, also has an open kitchen but has conventional tables and carte-menu format. The intimate second-floor Le Bar has a nightclub vibe and completes the trio. Staff are attentive, friendly and informed, while menus in both restaurants offer many similar dishes, but the focus downstairs is strictly on small grazing plates. Consistently innovative and skilled, the cooking is fun too. Fine ingredients and a lightness of touch parade in dishes like pan-fried sea bass served with a lemongrass foam and stewed leeks, or steak tartare with hand-made French fries. (Note there's a limited booking policy downstairs.)

13–15 West Street, WC2H 9HE
Tel: 020 7010 8600
Email: info@joelrobuchon.co.uk
Chef: Frederic Sironin,
Olivier Limousin
Owners: Bahia UK Ltd

Times: 12–3/5.30–11,
Closed 25–26 Dec
Prices: Fixed D £35 Main £15–£45
Directions: Telephone for
directions

Albannach

Bank Aldwych

Modern European

Welcoming brasserie close to Covent Garden

Despite its enormous size, this former bank is welcoming and cosy. The Aldwych entrance leads into a spacious bar area and through to the vibrant restaurant, where a ceiling of hanging green glass panels creates an intimate effect, and colourful murals show old-fashioned seaside scenes. The brasserie food is well thought out, carefully cooked and immaculately presented from breakfast through brunch and lunch to dinner. Wild mushroom risotto and truffle oil, grilled calves' liver with onion gravy, grilled venison with poached pear, and monkfish tail with Laksa broth are among an appealing choice that includes good-value set meals, and even a children's menu.

1 Kingsway, WC2B 6XF
Tel: 0845 658 7878
Email: aldres@bankrestaurants.com
Website: www.bankrestaurants.com
Chef: Damien Pondevie
Owners: Individual Restaurant Company plc
Times: 12–2.45/5.30–11.30, Closed 25–26 Dec, 1–2 Jan, BHs, D Sun
Prices: 3 Course Fixed D £17.50 Main £6.50–£21.95
Directions: From Holborn Tube station turn left onto Kingsway, go to end, cross the road, restaurant on corner of Aldwych & Kingsway

---

Christopher's

Contemporary American

Victorian grandeur meets contemporary American

Situated smack bang in the middle of Covent Garden and theatreland, Christopher's is an American themed establishment with a Martini bar downstairs, private dining and a large restaurant upstairs. The fascinating Victorian building, once London's first licensed casino, features a sweeping stone staircase, high, decorative ceilings and tall windows. Contemporary décor adds bold colours, polished wood floors and striking accessories. The huge menu offers lots of steak, fish and fresh seasonal fare, with starters like Caesar salad, followed by Midwestern veal meatloaf, and New York cheesecake to finish. Theatre and weekend brunch menus are popular options.

18 Wellington Street, Covent Garden, WC2E 7DD
Tel: 020 7240 4222
Email: coventgarden@christophersgrill.com
Website: www.christophersgrill.com

Times: 12–3/5–11, Closed 24 Dec–2 Jan, 25–26 Dec, 1 Jan, D Sun
Directions: Just by Strand, overlooking Waterloo Bridge

Clos Maggiore

Clos Maggiore

Modern French 🍷 NOTABLE WINE LIST

Fine dining in romantic Covent Garden setting

Mulberry-coloured awning and frontage picks out this restaurant (formerly called Maggiore's) from the razzmatazz of Covent Garden. Inside it oozes romance, reminiscent of a stylish country inn in Provence or Tuscany. Think warm colours, a roaring winter fire in a blossom-adorned conservatory-style courtyard with fully opening glass roof. Real box hedging and flowers add to the garden feel, while elegantly laid tables and smoked mirrors all contribute to the romance. Service is impeccable – slick, friendly, and professional. The cooking is modern-focused and underpinned by a classical theme. Classy, sophisticated and driven by high-quality ingredients, this is French cooking at its best. Presentation is simple, portions generous and flavours bold, all accompanied by a fine wine list. Expect roast rack of Elwy Valley lamb with smoked pomme purée, glazed Chantenay carrots with confit lemon.

33 King Street,
Covent Garden, WC2E 8JD
Tel: 020 7379 9696
Email:
enquiries@closmaggiore.com
Website: www.closmaggiore.com
Chef: Marcellin Marc
Owners: Tyfoon Restaurants Ltd

Times: 12–2.30/5–11, Closed 24–26 Dec & 1 Jan, Sun, L Sat
Prices: Fixed D £24.50–£45 Main £15.50–£44.50
Directions: 1 min walk from The Piazza and Royal Opera House

225

Imperial China

Chinese

Sophisticated Cantonese cooking in Chinatown

Its glass doors fronting Lisle Street lead through an inner courtyard complete with waterfall, bridge and pond to the contemporary Chinese-designed, glass-fronted dining room set on two floors. Think modern wood panelling, lighting and artwork to slate, lightwood or blue-carpeted floors. White table linen, upholstered chairs in gold and smartly attired, friendly Chinese staff epitomise the upmarket vibe. The light, sophisticated Cantonese cooking fits the bill, drawing the crowds of Chinese Londoners, with its comprehensive dim sum menu and typically lengthy carte dotted with a few unfamiliar choices. Expect grilled black cod or perhaps stir-fried chicken with cashew nuts.

White Bear Yard, 25a Lisle Street, WC2H 7BA
Tel: 020 7734 3388
Email: mail@imperial-china.co.uk
Website:
www.imperial-china.co.uk

Times: 12/11.30, Closed Xmas
Directions: From station into Little Newport St, straight ahead into Lisle St and right into White Bear Yard

Incognico

French, Italian

Franco Italian food in the heart of theatreland

There's an authentic French brasserie feel to this Shaftesbury Avenue restaurant, a favourite among theatre-goers. The interior is stylishly good looking with leather banquettes, oak panelling, stripped wooden floors and light spilling in from large windows. There's also a spacious bar, and an intimate private dining room in the basement. The food is all about quality raw materials cooked with great assurance. Classic French dishes with an Italian slant are simply presented, including an impressive chicken liver parfait with a rich buttery flavour served with toasted Poulaine bread. Wild salmon fillet with cauliflower purée and red wine sauce proves a good combination for the main course, the fish translucent and supremely fresh. And for dessert, take chocolate pannacotta with griottine cherries.

117 Shaftesbury Avenue, Cambridge Circus, WC2H 8AD
Tel: 020 7836 8866
Email:
incognicorestaurant@gmail.com
Website: www.incognico.com

Times: 12–3/5.30–11, Closed 10 days Xmas, 4 days Etr, BHs, Su
Directions: Behind Cambridge Circus

226

THE IVY

The Ivy

The Ivy

British, International

Theatreland legend with an accessible menu

1 West Street,
Covent Garden, WC2H 9NQ
Tel: 020 7836 4751

The Ivy's reputation guarantees a following of celebrities and star-gazers, ably supported by agents, West End producers and various media types. The result is surprisingly calm and low key, helped by the clublike atmosphere of oak panelling, wooden floors and stained-glass windows. Dedicated staff make a similar fuss of the famous and the anonymous, and the lengthy menu offers everything from old school comforts (double pork sausages, shepherd's pie, corned beef hash with double fried egg, steamed treacle sponge pudding with custard) to the sophisticated (Sévruga caviar, sautéed foie gras with caramelised apples, and fillet of red deer). Booking is absolutely essential.

Times: 12–3/5.30–12, Closed 25–26 Dec, 1 Jan, Aug BH, L 27 Dec, D 24 Dec
Directions: Telephone for directions

J. Sheekey

Fish, Seafood v

Much loved seafood restaurant in Theatreland

St Martin's Court, WC2N 4AL
Tel: 020 7240 2565
Email:
reservations@j-sheekey.co.uk
Website: www.j-sheekey.co.uk

This London stalwart began life as a seafood stall in the late 19th century, until its owner, J Sheekey, was invited to open a little oyster bar by Lord Salisbury on the condition that he supplied food for his lordship's post-theatre dinner parties. Over time it expanded into the adjoining properties, but today you'll still often see a queue outside the door. Step inside and you'll find a warren of interconnected rooms with closely-set tables, photographs of the celebrities who have dined here and an intimate, buzzy feel. Expect a bistro menu of fish and seafood fare, including the likes of smoked haddock with poached egg and colcannon or lemon sole with shrimps and soft roes. Vegetarian menu also available.

Times: 12–3/5.30–12, Closed 25–26 Dec, 1 Jan, Aug BH, D 24 Dec
Directions: Telephone for directions

JAAN Restaurant

JAAN Restaurant

Modern French, Asian **v**

Impressive cuisine in smart Thames-side hotel

Inside JAAN you'll find a modern, contemporary space with stylish wooden floors and luxurious silks. Service is friendly yet formal. The kitchen's approach is modern French cuisine, enhanced by the delicate flavours of Asia, all delivered via a fixed-price medley, which includes a good-value lunch, tasting options and carte (including a separate vegetarian offering). Top-class ingredients, sparkling technical artistry and presentation, and intensity of flavours all find their place. Expect a stylish opener like wild pigeon and foie gras (served with lentils, chanterelles and a liquorice foam), perhaps a rabbit and lobster roulade to follow (with vanilla bean mash, tomato confit and sauce américaine), while a composite dessert – emphasis on apple – might bring a Bramley crème brûlée, French apple parfait, apple and Calvados confit, meringue shortbread and apple coulis.

Swissôtel The Howard, London, Temple Place, WC2R 2PR
Tel: 020 7836 3555
Email: jan.london@swissotel.com
Website:
www.london.swissotel.com
Chef: Simon Duff
Owners: New Ray Ltd

Times: 12–2.30/5.45–10.30,
Closed 1st wk Jan, BHs, Sun, L Sat
Prices: Fixed D £38 Main £21
Directions: Telephone for directions (Opposite Temple Tube station)
Parking: 30

229

Mon Plaisir

French

A Francophile's delight in central London

21 Monmouth Street, WC2H 9DD
Tel: 020 7836 7243
Email: eatafrog@mail.com
Website: www.monplaisir.co.uk
Chef: Frank Raymond
Owners: Alain Lhermitte

Charles de Gaulle often held meetings here in the 1940s, and this restaurant remains about as French as you can get this side of the Channel; the cosy network of rooms is decked out with modern abstracts and interesting artefacts. The atmosphere buzzes with pre- and post-theatre diners, muffling the conversation from closely packed neighbours. Everything on the classic and modern French menus is freshly cooked, including the very traditional rustic dishes like snails in garlic or pork terrine, French onion soup, coq au vin and ile flottante. All desserts are hand made by the chef pâtissier. Friendly and professional Gallic waiters glide smoothly between the tables.

Times: 12–2.15/5.45–11.15,
Closed Xmas, New Year, BHs, Sun,
L Sat
Prices: 3 Course Fixed D £14.50
Main £14.50–£22.50
Directions: Off Seven Dials

One Aldwych - Axis

Modern European 🍷 NOTABLE WINE LIST

Dramatic, contemporary dining in theatreland

1 Aldwych, WC2B 4RH
Tel: 020 7300 0300
Email: axis@onealdwych.com
Website: www.onealdwych.com
Chef: Jens Folkel
Owners: Gordon Campbell Gray

A double-height ceiling and dramatic abstract cityscape mural – the 'Amber City' by Richard Walker – give this hip and trendy metropolitan basement restaurant its wow-factor. It has amazing muted colours and black leather upholstery, plus a balcony bar with views over the dining room and a sweeping staircase entrance. Staff make dining here far from an impersonal experience, with helpful yet professional table service. Quality ingredients are skilfully prepared with an English and seasonal slant. There are sections on the menu that include catch of the day, grills and roast for two. Take potted crab to begin, followed by poached haddock with clams, baby carrots and spinach, while a lemon meringue tart might catch the eye for dessert. (The Axis, one of two dining options at One Aldwych hotel, has a stand-alone vibe with its own street entrance – see Indigo restaurant right)

Times: 12–2.45/5.45–10.45,
Closed Xmas, New Year, Sun, L Sat
Prices: Main £14.95–£21.95
Directions: At point where Aldwych meets the Strand opposite Waterloo Bridge. On corner of Aldwych & Wellington St, opposite Lyceum Theatre

One Aldwych - Indigo

One Aldwych - Indigo

Modern European v

Trendy mezzanine dining with a buzzy atmosphere

The epitome of modern chic and contemporary styling, this sophisticated restaurant is set on a mezzanine balcony overlooking the buzzy hotel Lobby Bar below, making it the perfect spot for people-watching. Spotlights zoom down on to tables, seats are comfortable, service is focused and the atmosphere fashionable and relaxed. The kitchen follows the theme, with cosmopolitan, flavour-driven, clean-cut dishes delivered on creatively flexible menus that play to the gallery. There's the option to create your own salad dish, others can be taken as a starter or main course, while the more structured fine-dining options might deliver pan-fried monkfish, red mullet and sea bass with a lime and coriander risotto, or perhaps chargrilled Scottish beef fillet and slow-cooked rump steak served with spinach and parsnip purée.

1 Aldwych, WC2B 4RH
Tel: 020 7300 0400
Email: indigo@onealdwych.com
Website: www.onealdwych.com
Chef: Alex Wood
Owners: Gordon Campbell-Gray

Times: 12–3/6–11.15
Prices: Fixed D £29.65–£46.20
Main £15.95–£22.75
Directions: Located where The Aldwych meets The Strand opposite Waterloo Bridge

Orso Restaurant

Modern Italian

Italian food in a buzzing basement

27 Wellington Street, WC2E 7DB
Tel: 020 7240 5269
Email: info@orsorestaurant.co.uk
Website:
www.orsorestaurant.co.uk
Chef: Martin Wilson
Owners: Orso Restaurants Ltd

A discreet, street-level entrance leads downstairs to the cavernous basement dining room (once an orchid warehouse) at this long-established, all-day Covent Garden Italian that reverberates with energy, conversation and the clinking of glasses and cutlery. Smart staff, constantly flitting about, add to the lively, informal atmosphere. The busy bilingual menu showcases regional Italian cooking and offers bags of choice, from pizza and pasta dishes (perhaps tagliatelle with roasted aubergines, tomato, basil and pecorino) to roast saddle of hare with pomegranate and wet polenta. The pre-theatre menu and weekend brunch offer excellent value.

Times: noon/midnight, Closed
24–25 Dec, L Sat–Sun (Jul–Aug)
Prices: 3 Course Fixed D £18
Main £9–£17.50
Directions: Telephone for
directions

The Portrait Restaurant

Modern British

Stylish, contemporary dining with rooftop views

National Portrait Gallery,
St Martins Place, WC2H 0HE
Tel: 020 7312 2490
Email:
portrait.restaurant@searcys.co.uk
Website: www.searcys.co.uk
Chef: Katarina Todosijevic
Owners: Searcys

Offering a stunning London landscape from the rooftop restaurant of Nelson's Column, the Houses of Parliament and the London Eye, this light, sleek and contemporary affair is decked out in grey with a wall of glass windows that lets those views do the talking. Light, colourful, clean-cut, bistro-styled dishes – with the occasional Mediterranean slant – provide a stylish accompaniment to the London skyline. Begin with garden pea and leek tart, glazed asparagus, herb salad and lemon dressing, and follow with pan-fried fillet of sea bass with truffle-crushed baby potatoes, buttered leeks and lobster sauce. A caramelised citrus tart with kumquat syrup and Valrhona chocolate sorbet might round things off. Note that there's a 10 per cent discount for Members of the Gallery.

Times: 11.45–2.45/5.30–8.30,
Closed 24–26 Dec, 1 Jan,
D Sat–Wed
Prices: 3 Course Fixed D
£29.95–£34.95
Main £11.95–£28.95
Directions: Just behind Trafalgar
Square

The Savoy Grill

Modern British **v**

Look forward to flawless cooking when the hotel re-opens

The Savoy Hotel is due to close to facilitate a stunning
refurbishment, but Marcus Wareing will continue to operate this
restaurant of great historical importance when the hotel relaunches
in 2009 after the major face-lift. Thankfully there will be little,
if any, change to Barbara Barry's successful design of this much
loved institution, which brought a successful balance between the
traditional and the more contemporary. The menu retains some
of the restaurant's past tradition but has ushered proceedings
into the present day. The kitchen adopts a modern approach
– underpinned by classical French roots – that is based around
superb-quality ingredients and precise technical skills. Clear, clean
flavours, seasonality and fine balance parade on a repertoire of
fixed-price menus that includes a tasting option. Service fits the bill
too, and is professional and slick without being overbearing.

The Savoy, Strand, WC2R 0EU
Tel: 020 7592 1600
Email:
savoygrill@marcuswareing.com
Website:
www.marcuswareing.com
Chef: Lee Bennett
Owners: Marcus Wareing at the
Savoy Grill Ltd

Directions: Please telephone for
directions

The Savoy

233

Covent Garden

Mapping and Index

The Capital

Restaurant Index

This index shows Rosetted restaurants in London in alphabetical order, followed by their map references, postcodes and page references.

236

AA-Rosetted restaurants in Greater London that can also be found on Plan 1:

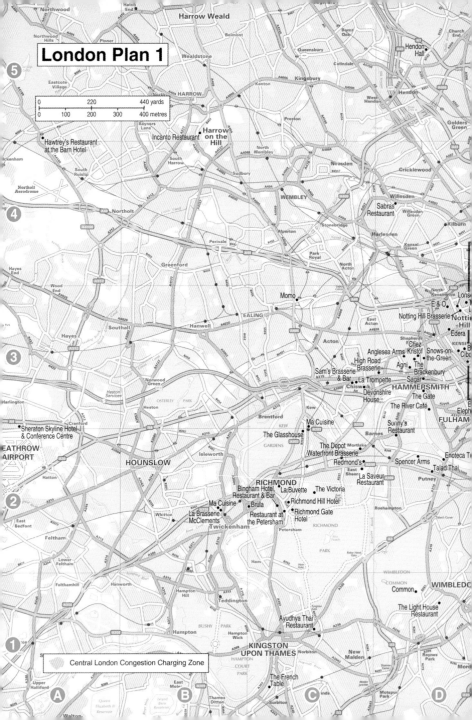

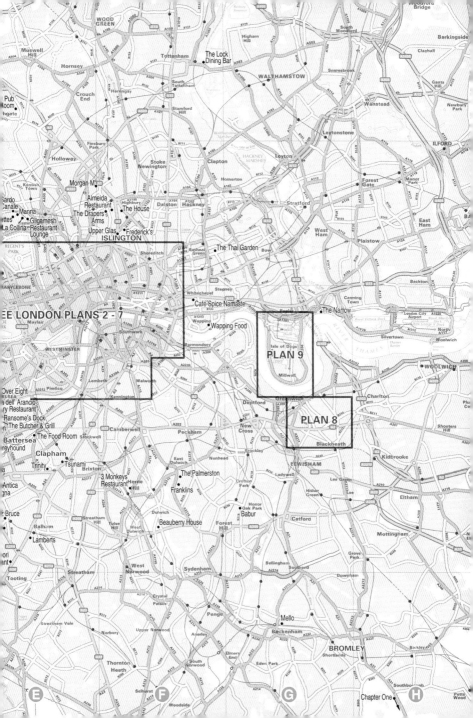

SEE LONDON PLANS 2 – 7

PLAN 9

PLAN 8

E **F** **G** **H**

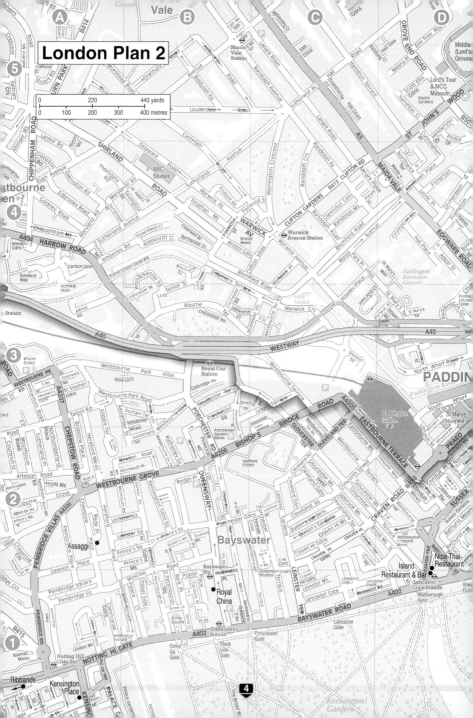

London Plan 2

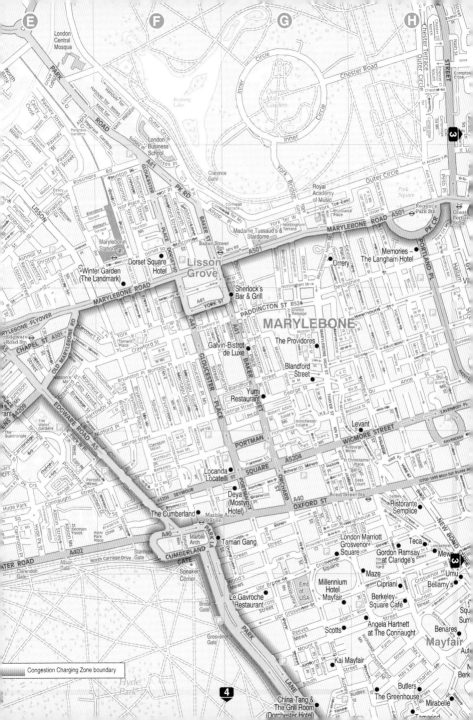

Congestion Charging Zone boundary

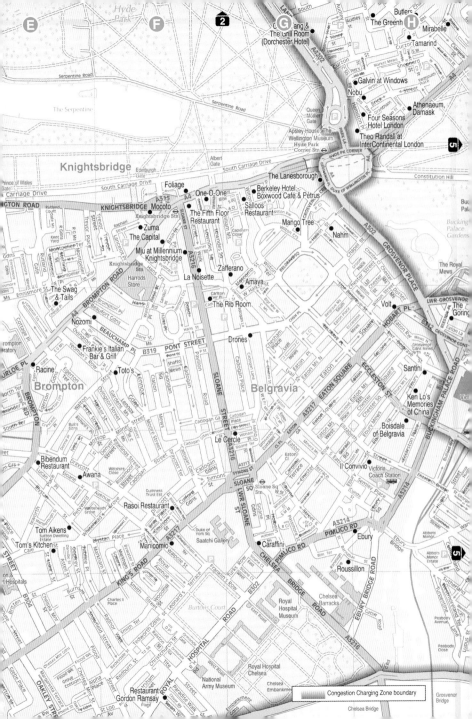

London Plan 6

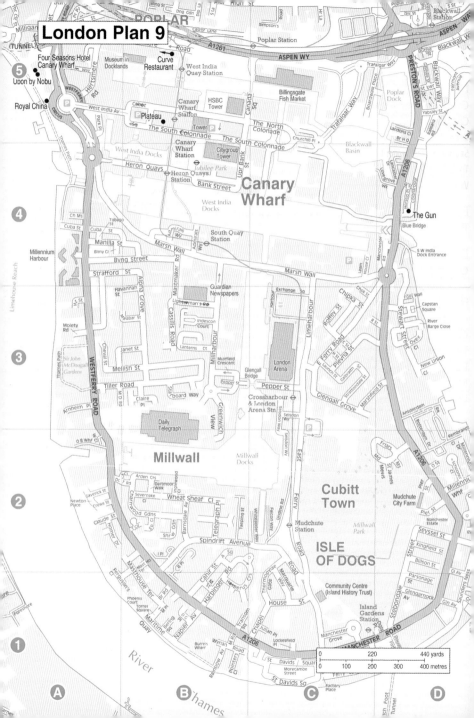

Location Index

The Automobile Association would like to thank the following photographers, companies and picture libraries for their assistance in the preparation of this book.

Abbreviations for the picture credits are as follows: (t) top; (b) bottom; (l) left; (r) right; (AA) AA World Travel Library.

8/9 AA/N Setchfield; 18/9 AA/R Victor; 36/7 AA/R Turpin; 42b AA/J A Tims; 44/5 AA/R Mort; 52/3 AA/C Sawyer; 57b AA/M Jourdan; 66/7 AA/N Setchfield; 89 AA/J A Tims; 105b AA/P Kenward; 113 AA/T Woodcock; 125b AA; 127b AA/G Wrona; 134/5 AA/M Jourdan; 137 AA/J McMillan; 188b AA/R Turpin; 195 AA/N Setchfield; 203b AA/g Wrona; 209b AA/G Wrona; 215b AA/M Jourdan; 218/9 AA/M Jourdan; 227 AA/W Voysey; 233b AA/J A Tims; 234 AA/M Jourdan.

Every effort has been made to trace the copyright holders, and we apologise in advance for any accidental errors. We would be happy to apply the corrections in the following edition of this publication.